CASE STUDIES IN CULTURAL

ANTHROPOLOGY

GENERAL EDITORS

George and Louise Spindler

STANFORD UNIVERSITY

SAMOAN VILLAGE

Then and Now

Second Edition

SAMOAN VILLAGE

Then and Now

Second Edition

LOWELL D. HOLMES

ELLEN RHOADS HOLMES

Wichita State University

Harcourt Brace Jovanovich College Publishers

FORT WORTH PHILADELPHIA SAN DIEGO NEW YORK ORLANDO AUSTIN SAN ANTONIO
TORONTO   MONTREAL   LONDON   SYDNEY   TOKYO

Publisher Ted Buchholz
Acquisitions Editor Chris Klein
Senior Project Editor Steve Welch
Production Manager Thomas Urquhart
Design Supervisor Guy Jacobs/Pat Bracken

On the cover *High Chief and High Talking in Ta'ū village in 1954.*

The map on page 10 is adapted from Paul Templet, 1986.

Library of Congress Cataloging-in-Publication Data

Holmes, Lowell Don, 1925–
    Samoan village : then and now / Lowell D. Holmes, Ellen Rhoads
Holmes. — 2nd ed.
        p.   cm. — (Case studies in cultural anthropology)
    Includes bibliographical references and index.
    ISBN 0-03-031692-8
    1. Ethnology—American Samoa—Fitiuta—Case studies. 2. Fitiuta
(American Samoa) — Social life and customs—Case studies. 3. Culture
diffusion—American Samoa—Fitiuta. I. Holmes, Ellen Rhoads.
II. Title. III. Series.
DU819.F58H65 1992
996.1'3—dc20   91-24633
                                                                                              CIP

Address for Editorial Correspondence: Harcourt Brace Jovanovich, Inc., 301 Commerce
                                                                  Street, Suite 3700, Fort Worth, TX 76102

Address For Orders: Harcourt Brace Jovanovich, Inc., 6277 Sea Harbor
                                          Drive, Orlando, FL 32887. 1-800-782-4479, or
                                          1-800-433-0001 (in Florida)

Printed in the United States of America

2 3 4 5   016   9 8 7 6 5 4 3 2 1

For our children, who have shared our Samoan experience,
and for our grandchildren, who inspire us with their questions.

Foreword

ABOUT THE AUTHORS

Lowell D. Holmes is Distinguished Professor Emeritus of Anthropology at Wichita State University, where he taught for thirty-two years. Born in Sioux City, Iowa, and raised in Minneapolis, he left for service in World War II the night after high-school graduation. His three-year tour of duty in the U.S. Coast Guard took him to all parts of the world and may very well be the reason for his anthropological interests. Holmes, however, entered Northwestern University as an English literature major, and it was not until his junior year that he enrolled by chance in a course in cultural anthropology taught by William R. Bascom, a noted authority on both West Africa and Micronesia. The department's focus on African arts, particularly African-American music, and the cross-cultural perspective of anthropology immediately drew Lowell to the field. Having worked as a jazz musician (alto saxophone) since the age of fourteen, he also was impressed by the fact that he was invited to join the departmental jazz combo, the "Academic Cats."

While originally planning to carry out dissertation research in Africa—among the Kru of Liberia—an unusual turn of events in 1953 sent Lowell into the Pacific, where, on the advice of mentor Melville J. Herskovits, he undertook a methodological restudy of the "coming of age in Samoa" research of Margaret Mead. This interesting theoretical problem, which earned him his Ph.D. from Northwestern in 1957, became particularly meaningful when the Mead/Freeman controversy emerged in 1983. While he has also done research and writing in the areas of gerontology and jazz history, Samoan culture has been Lowell's main concentration for nearly forty years.

Ellen Rhoads Holmes is a native of Waynesboro, Mississippi, and when she entered college initially at Mississippi State College for Women, her goal was to pursue a degree in accounting and to become a C.P.A. Her education was interrupted for ten years by marriage and child-rearing responsibilities, but it was during these years that Ellen discovered anthropology (while living in Boulder, Colorado), when she heard a lecture by Professor Omer Stewart. After the death of her husband in 1964, she decided to complete her undergraduate degree and to take an anthropology course in the process. A year later, she entered Wichita State University, and her first anthropology course was the beginning of a commitment to this discipline as her chosen profession. After completing her B.A. and M.A. degrees at Wichita State, she entered the Ph.D. program in anthropology at the University of Kansas, where she worked with Polynesian specialist F. Allan Hanson, and was granted her degree in 1981.

Having taught both cultural anthropology and gerontology at Wichita State University for over fifteen years, Ellen is presently Associate Professor and Academic Coordinator of the Gerontology program in the Department of Health,

Administration and Gerontology. Her work in cross-cultural gerontology has taken her to Samoa twice to study retirement homes and to research the impact of modernization on elders; she has also done research with Samoan migrants in the San Francisco Bay area.

Lowell and Ellen Holmes have worked together for many years on research and writing projects relating to their common professional interests in Polynesia and gerontology. Since their marriage in 1982, they have also shared interests in jazz, sailing, and travel. They especially enjoy sailing adventures on old, traditional sailing ships. They spend summers at their cottage on Madeline Island in Lake Superior, where they relax, write, and sail their Nor'sea 27 cruising sailboat, *Taupou*.

ABOUT THE SERIES

These case studies in cultural anthropology are designed for students in beginning and intermediate courses in the social sciences, to bring them insights into the richness and complexity of human life as it is lived in different ways, in different places. The authors are men and women who have lived in the societies they write about and who are professionally trained as observers and interpreters of human behavior. Also, the authors are teachers; in their writing, the needs of the student reader remain foremost. It is our belief that when an understanding of ways of life very different from one's own is gained, abstractions and generalizations about the human condition become meaningful.

The scope and character of the series has changed continually since we published the first case studies in 1960. We are concerned with ways in which human groups and communities are coping with the massive changes wrought in their physical and social environments in recent decades. We are also concerned with the ways in which established cultures have met life's problems. And we want to include representation of the various modes of communication and emphasis that are being formed and reformed as anthropology itself changes.

We think of the CSCA as an instructional series, intended for use in the classroom. We have always used case studies in our teaching, whether for neophytes or advanced graduate students. We start with case studies, whether from our own series or from elsewhere, and weave our way into theory, and then turn again to cases. For us, they are the grounding of our discipline.

ABOUT THIS CASE STUDY

The Samoan islands is one of those places where most Americans think they would like to go. The pleasant climate and people are legendary, and the islands have been made famous by the many writings about them, not the least of which is Margaret Mead's well known *Coming of Age in Samoa*. This case study by Lowell Holmes is an informative, straightforward, and interestingly written descriptive analysis of one village in the Manu'a group of American Samoa. The reader who finishes this case study, and once started most will, should still be motivated to go to Samoa, but his or her expectations will be tempered by a cautious appraisal of reality.

European contact with Samoa, insofar as it is recorded, occurred first in 1722, though there is some evidence that contact may have occurred prior to this date, but by only a few years. The first mission was established in 1828 and American involvement began in 1839. The Manu'a group of American Samoa was officially incorporated as a United States territorial holding in 1904. All of Samoa, including American Samoa, has therefore had long-term and rather intensive contact with the West.

This case study will give the reader a working knowledge of the basic elements of traditional Samoan culture, including subsistence; use of traditional materials, structures, and shelters; the principles of rank and the elaboration of roles in the context of different groups; title successon; Talking Chiefs; ceremonies; decision-making; the spiritual world; and the life cycle. The case study is characterized by a happy balance between structural or technical analyses and enlivened descriptions of scenes and events in which the significant features of the more formal and abstract analysis are demonstrated.

Samoan culture, though comparatively stable, is of course changing, and in recent years changing more rapidly than before. The most important changes began when the acceptance of Christianity meant abolishing polygamy, divorce, political marriages, adultery, premarital sex, lavish gift exchanges at marriages, public tests of virginity, prostitution, nudity, liquor, gambling, tattooing, and sorcery. The ways in which the people adapted to what could have been a very disruptive confrontation between native Samoan and Christian belief and practice are described. The description of culture change in the last decade or so, however, raises ominous questions that do not appear to be easily answered. Samoan villages are having difficulties that are being experienced everywhere modernization is taking place. The environment is deteriorating, and sewage and trash disposal is becoming a severe problem. Wage work is displacing a subsistence economy. Many thousands of Samoans have migrated to the United States, particularly to the West Coast. The conclusion of the case study really raises the question that is now becoming universal and applicable to the highly developed industrial societies, such as that of the United States, as well as to those that are in the process of modernization: Is modernization worth the price? For some Samoans, and some of them live in the village of Fitiuta, the answer may well be "no."

Since the above words were written (in 1973) Lowell Holmes and his wife/co-worker have returned to his original field site several times, most recently in 1988. He has observed changes over a thirty-seven year period. This revised edition of *Samoan Village*, as the subtitle *Then and Now* suggests, contrasts the Samoa of 1954 with today's Samoa. The Samoan people are surviving and the conservatism heretofore apparent shows through the heavy overlay of modernization. But sweeping changes have occurred, not all of them positive. Modernization exacts a toll on the environment, on traditions, and on the satisfactions in life available to people who are not rich. Holmes and his wife/co-worker Ellen Rhoads Holmes have developed the contrasts between the traditional and modernizing world most tell-ingly.

This edition of *Samoan Village* is also enriched by a postscript on the "Samoan Character and the Academic World: The Mead-Freeman Controversy." This addi-tion to the case study will be of considerable interest to readers who have heard or read about this controversy. The Holmeses are in a position to make some judg-ments about the issues raised, since their research site is in the immediate vicinity of the village Margaret Mead worked in during the 1920s and upon which *Coming of Age in Samoa* is based. And Lowell Holmes lived in Ta'ū village in 1954 to do a restudy of Mead's research, done twenty-nine years earlier.

George and Louise Spindler
Series Editors

Preface

This account of Samoan culture is based on data collected during field trips to American Samoa in 1954 (eleven months), 1962–1963 (fifteen months), 1974 (four weeks), 1976 (six months), 1988 (six weeks) and to the migrant Samoan community of the San Francisco Bay area in 1977 (eight weeks). The research in Samoa in 1976 and 1988 and in 1977 in California was a collaboration with Ellen Rhoads Holmes, the coauthor of this volume.

On my first trip, I carried out a methodological restudy of the work of Margaret Mead as published in *Coming of Age in Samoa* (1928), *Social Organization of Manu'a* (1930), and many articles in anthropological journals. That research was designed to test the reliability and validity of Mead's pioneer study of Samoan adolescents. The fieldwork was sponsored by the University of Hawaii as part of the Tri-Institutional Pacific Program. Later research—into village leadership and decision-making, the effects of modernization on Samoan elderly, and the nature and extent of cultural change in Samoa—was funded by the National Science Foundation and Wichita State University.

My research in 1954 concentrated exclusively on Manu'an culture. While I resided in Ta'ū village, the site of Mead's 1925–1926 study of coming of age, I also made frequent trips to Fitiuta, the home village of my principal informant, Lauifi. Shortly after my 1954 research in Manu'a, Lauifi was elected to the High Chief position of Iliili, one of the more important titles in Fitiuta. On each of my subsequent field trips, I have returned to Fitiuta to observe and collect data on the dynamics of culture change. Over the years, my major source of information was High Talking Chief La'apui, a man acknowledged throughout Samoa as one of the foremost authorities on *fa'aSāmoa,* the traditional way of life.

During my studies of village decision-making in 1962, my key informant, Va'alele of the Ale family of Fitiuta, convened a council of some of the most knowledgeable titled men in the village (including their principal orator La'apui). We spent many hours debating and reviewing important social and political issues.

While investigating the reliability and validity of Mead's data, I was blessed with the able assistance of several of Mead's former associates: Pepe Haleck, the nurse who served as Mead's language tutor; Napoleone A. Tuiteleapaga, Mead's research assistant; Mrs. Soatoa, the part-Samoan Ta'ū village storekeeper with whom Mead often spent weekends; and Mika, an untitled man who remembered Margaret Mead and who loaned me a copy of *Social Organization of Manu'a* until I could obtain a copy of my own. My main sources of information in 1954 were several untitled men and such important titled men as Manu'a District Governor Lefiti, and chiefs Soatoa, Levao, Solia, Pomele, Galea'i and Tufele.

Because of my village-mapping and census-taking activities, I became acquainted with almost everyone in Ta'ū village. My wife helped in our data collection by interviewing women and observing the domestic and child-rearing activities.

During my fifteen-month period of research in 1962–1963, my family shared a house in Pago Pago with the family of A. P. Lutali (later, governor of American Samoa from 1985 to 1989), and our families interacted daily. My children and his were classmates and playmates.

In 1976–1977, my wife Ellen and I studied the role and status of Samoan elderly in Ta'ū and Fitiuta villages, in the Pago Pago Bay area, and among migrants in San Francisco. This involved observation and extended interviews with members of 120 Samoan households. We also interviewed forty elderly residents of Mapuifa-galele—the Samoan home for the aged—situated just outside Apia in Western Samoa.

Finally, my knowledge of Samoan culture and personality draws on the results of personality testing that I carried out in 1963 and 1974 with 146 high-school students (88 male and 58 female). Not only did I develop a personality profile based on three modified personality tests, but I also obtained additional information concerning classroom behavior and personal background for each of the students from their teachers.

I have managed to maintain contact with several key informants over the nearly thirty-seven-year span of my research on Samoa, and I believe I have achieved much in the way of an insider's perspective. Not only have I come to understand the culture of Samoa from the people's point of view, but I have also gained a special understanding of the life course by observing it at several points in my own aging process. I have personally documented social interactions and attitudes of Manu'a islanders through much of their life cycles; I do not just draw on a single time frame. I have seen my subjects as children, teenagers (coming of age), and young adults, as nuclear family heads, and even as titular heads of extended families attempting to deal with their sometimes unruly offspring—products of Americanization and modernization.

Samoa has changed a great deal since my first field trip in 1954. This monograph documents the traditional culture of Manu'a as I found it—pristine and conservative in 1954—and describes the dynamics of cultural change in Manu'a and in American Samoa as a whole during the thirty-seven years I have studied the culture. I am indebted to literally hundreds of kind and patient Samoans who have shared their lives and knowledge of *fa'aSāmoa* with me. I cherish the longtime friendship of Atimua and of A. P. Lutali and wish them many more years of good health and happiness. I am indebted to Donald Crim of Colorado State University, Joyce D. Hammond of Western Washington University, and Janet E. Benson of Kansas State University for reviewing the manuscript and offering their helpful suggestions. Finally, I would like to extend my thanks to Scott Nicholson for his clerical assistance in getting this manuscript ready for publication.

L.D.H.

Contents

Prologue / Entering the Samoan World

It was 8 A.M. on June 1, 1988, and I was waiting at the airport for my flight from Tutuila, American Samoa, to Ta'ū Island in the Manu'a island group. This would be my fifth visit to Ta'ū, a place I had spent nearly three years of my life studying. The owner of the airline was Tufele Lia, the adopted son of High Chief Tufele Faatuia, now deceased. This was the man who was the paramount chief of the village of Fitiuta and the owner of the guest fale in Ta'ū village, where I lived while doing my initial research in Samoa in 1954.

In 1954, and even up into the early 1970s, the only transportation to the Manu'a group was by boat. Now, several small airlines with somewhat irregular schedules serve the Manu'a islands. On my first flight to Ta'ū, in 1974, we landed on a rough airstrip of grass, cut periodically by villagers wielding machetes. Now, the landing strip is gravel, but landings are still precarious. Planes must land and take off in one direction regardless of the direction of the wind. In recent years, several crashes have resulted in injuries and disrupted service. Tufele's airline, Manu'a Air, was fairly new to the service, but, so far, it had been able to maintain a good safety record which, according to its Manu'a patrons, was due largely to the ability of its Filipino pilot.

When the morning flight was called, I was directed to a small twin-engine Otter aircraft where I found, much to my relief, that the pilot was the much-heralded Filipino. He greeted me and casually suggested that I take the co-pilot's seat. After a short and noisy takeoff, we climbed into the crystal-clear air, cluttered here and there with cotton-candy tufts of cloud floating over the brilliant blue southern sea. To the east, just sixty miles ahead, were the mountainous islands of Manu'a—Ofu, Olosega, and Ta'ū—dark purple in hue, but distinct in outline. In a little over a half hour, we would be there.

How different this trip was from my initial trip to Ta'ū with my family in 1954. Then, the *MV Samoa,* an ancient interisland trading vessel with all sails set and engine throbbing, pitched and rolled its way to Manu'a for more than twelve hours. Our first stop had been Fitiuta, with an arrival in the predawn gloom. As the vessel hove to offshore, surf boats came out through the break in the fringe reef and nestled alongside to take on passengers and cargo bound for the beach.

In the black of the night, our first impressions of Fitiuta were formed only by the shouts of the oarsmen and the crashing of the waves on the reef. Phantom-like forms moved down the ship's ladder, handed down babies, and lowered baskets of housewares and trade goods from Pago Pago stores into the boat below. Then, the

1

oarsmen's voices faded into the sound of the surf as the boat made its way toward the land. The ship's engine again took up its cadence, and we headed for Ta'ū village, six miles down the shoreline.

Now my arrival was a sudden plunge out of the sky toward a tiny gravel landing strip on a mountainside, a bumpy touchdown, and a short taxi to the terminal, a breadfruit tree bearing a sign that read "Ta'ū International Airport." In 1954, we had been rowed in through the reef; had waded ashore when the surfboat grounded on the sand; and then had spent the next half hour dragging our boxes of food, research equipment, and personal belongings up the beach to the Tufele guest house, our home for the next few months.

Settling into that culture and community had been a somewhat depressing experience. While every fledgling fieldworker is warned about culture shock, I don't believe that it is possible for anyone to escape its effects. I have experienced the depression of culture shock on each of my five trips to Samoa, and perhaps I always will. The sudden shift in behavior patterns and norms, the difficulties of communication, and the inability to anticipate behavior (a skill we depend on greatly in our own culture), plus the usual aches and pains and occasional nausea that seem inevitable as one becomes acclimated, make for a temporary—but nonetheless uncomfortable—period of adjustment. One of the more difficult adjustments to make regards the pace of life: Everything seems to move so slowly and inefficiently. Informants don't seem to realize how much information you must acquire in a few short months. They seldom show up on time for appointments and frequently cancel out completely because of "family business." Although you may be willing to pay informants well—by local standards—you seem to shoulder all the responsibility and make all the adjustments. It is as though you are working for them rather than the other way around. Even more frustrating is the case where you cannot establish contact with informants at all, and that was our initial problem after arriving in Ta'ū in the spring of 1954.

While High Chief Tufele had agreed to let us rent his guest house and had told the members of his family to help us in any way they could, we still felt that we were very much on our own. It was sink or swim and, at first, we seemed to be floundering. Tufele told me that I should first contact the two village school teachers, Lauifi Ili and Talanu Moliga, as both were bright young men and could help me greatly with my research project; Lauifi could be particularly helpful, as he was a student of Samoan culture himself.

My meeting with Lauifi was not encouraging. He was polite but noncommital about having the time to work with me. Talanu was friendly (and has remained one of my closest friends for over thirty-seven years), but I realized that he was not the student of his own culture that Lauifi was. Lauifi said he would need some time to decide if he could work with me. He would let me know.

Meanwhile, we just sat—pretty much ignored by our neighbors, who found us interesting (particularly our six-month-old blond baby daughter) but made no effort to establish contact. I was, however, stopped one day by our next-door neighbor who showed me a copy of Mead's *Social Organization of Manu'a,* a volume I did not own, although I had tried desperately to find a copy before leaving for the Pacific.

Tufele's guest house in 1954. Ta'ū, Manu'a.

The guest house in which we were living was huge and ornate and an excellent example of traditional Samoan architecture and craftsmanship. For want of anything better to do, I began carefully sketching the details of its construction. I drew everything to scale and numbered the component parts in the hope that I would later be able to discover terms to match the numbers. My house sketch took several days to complete. Our neighbors were still keeping very much to themselves.

Then I moved my investigations out on the beach and sketched the construction details of a *paopao* (outrigger canoe) and a *va'a alo* (bonito boat). Since I had some boatbuilding experience myself, I was intrigued by how the hulls of the bonito boats were constructed of planks of various lengths that were actually sewn together with coconut-husk twine (sennit) and caulked with breadfruit tree gum.

With these projects completed, and still no prospect of personal contact with Samoan informants, I decided that mapping the village would be a valuable research activity and one that would keep me highly visible. With the aid of a compass, a camera rangefinder, and careful attention to the length of my stride and the number of strides between houses, I set to work measuring and sketching the features of the village as close to scale as I could. I made careful note of the grouping of houses (which I assumed had kinship significance), the nature of the architecture (traditional or European), and the number and kind of houses (guest, sleeping, and out-buildings) which made up each household cluster. Later, I was able to use this map in the taking of a village census and in the construction of genealogical diagrams of village families. The village mapping project was well under way when a teenager arrived at our house one evening with a message from the school teacher, Lauifi, which stated that I should meet him at the school house the next day at 3:30 p.m. I was about to start working with people.

Much to my surprise, I discovered that Lauifi was an anthropologist in his own right. On my first visit, he produced a stack of green, cloth-bound, legal-size ledger books containing his own ethnographic field notes. For years, Lauifi had been interested in family, village, and societal cultural traditions. He spent long hours "picking the brains" of elderly chiefs and talking chiefs for information on Samoan mythology, ceremonials, status hierarchies, supernatural lore, historical traditions about intervillage relations and even about bush medicine. He also managed to acquire considerable data on an esoteric practice that I had not even surmised existed in Samoa—sorcery. I still wonder at the willingness of this man to share his knowledge, but, from the very beginning, I realized that my ethnographic project would be a collaboration. Lauifi believed that Samoan traditions were quickly fading and that was the reason for his green ledger books. In me, Lauifi saw a means of getting his data on traditional Samoan culture—fa' aSāmoa—published for future generations to cherish. He also wanted palagis (Caucasians) as well as future generations of Samoans to have access to accurate descriptions of the traditional culture, not distorted representations. Lauifi believed that by imparting this knowledge to me, he would ensure it would be in safe hands and would not be lost, even if his books were stolen. This belief was prophetic, for Lauifi was killed in a bus accident in 1956. When I returned to Samoa in 1964, I found that neither his wife nor his brother had any knowledge of the whereabouts of the ledgers. The ledgers had completely disappeared.

The first few days working with Lauifi greatly elevated my spirits, and I began to believe that I might have a chance of doing a comprehensive study of Samoan culture. We worked two hours every afternoon; in the evening, by the light of our Coleman lantern, I spent twice that amount of time, at what was probably the only table in the village, organizing and typing my notes. Although I now had a "foot in the door," (figuratively speaking, since Samoan houses had no doors), I was still troubled by my inability to establish myself with the entire community. This was soon taken care of by a dramatic and unexpected event.

One evening as I sat pouring over my notes, I chanced to look outside (an easy thing to do in a house with no walls) and saw, coming along the beach path in single file, a delegation of approximately thirty chiefs—each carrying a kava root, the Samoan welcome symbol. The Tufele family members who worked for us saw them coming as well, and the women immediately began putting mats in place on the coral-pebbled floor so that everyone could be seated at the many houseposts that supported our great beehive-shaped roof. Manino, the young woman who came to Ta'ū with us to help care for our infant daughter, served as interpreter since my Samoan was definitely not adequate for such an auspicious occasion. The delegation was invited to enter our fale and share our evening meal, the preparation of which was frantically taking place that very moment in our umu (cookhouse). The chiefs settled themselves on the floormats—each at a separate housepost—and a round of welcome speeches was given by the talking chiefs. Each speech was accompanied by the presentation of a kava root and required a reply, which I gave through my "talking chief," Manino. Soon, the speeches were over; the pile of kava roots was immense and one of the roots was selected for the preparation of the traditional drink, kava.

Kava, known locally as *'ava,* is a drink prepared by steeping the pulverized roots of the *piper methysticum* plant in a prescribed amount of water until a cloudy, khaki-colored liquid is produced. Kava is in no way alcoholic, but much has been made of its narcotic properties. Early missionaries maintained that the concoction partially paralyzed the lower extremities, making it difficult to walk. More recent partakers of kava have experienced no debilitating effect that could be attributed to the drink. Instead, they have found it to be a refreshing, astringent drink that produces nothing more than a tingling sensation in the mucous membrane of the mouth and a short-lived numbness of the tongue.

I was awarded first kava, the symbol of highest honor, and the kava cup was taken to each of the chiefs in the order of their relative rank. The Samoan members of our household then entered with dishpans filled with a curious kind of goulash made of *pisupo* (New Zealand corned beef), canned tomatoes, and macaroni. This somewhat bizarre "Samoan" meal was devoured with enthusiasm; then it was time for the entertainment. The *aumaga*—society of untitled men—arrived with guitars and with rolled-up mats that would be beaten with "drumsticks" to provide rhythm. This was the musical accompaniment for siva dancing that would go on far into the night—with special command performances by the anthropologist and his wife

Holmes and informant Talanu in Ta'ū village, 1954.

Holmes and Atimua (Talanu's matai *name) in Tutuila in 1988.*

serving as comic relief. We had now met the people. They had signalled their acceptance of us, and we were now part of the village.

In Samoa, it is important first to gain the acceptance of the men of rank. When this has been accomplished, one has relatively free access to all the members of the society. The age and sex of the anthropologist also have a bearing on the ability to establish rapport. Samoa is somewhat of a male-oriented society, and most important ceremonials are attended almost entirely by men. Whatever success I had in studying this society may also be attributed to the fact that I was accompanied in the field by my wife and daughter. Although the chiefs thought me a bit young (twenty-nine), the fact that I was a husband and a father qualified me as an adult and, therefore, worthy of some of their time and information.

My acceptance by Lauifi and by the village council of chiefs seemed to break the ice. Soon, numerous other informants—Telefone, an elderly talking chief with advanced elephantiasis, Talanu, an untitled young man who taught school, and others—agreed to serve as information sources. There was no problem acquiring a representative sample. The village was so small, and there appeared to be so little deviation from traditional norms, that almost any intelligent individual could provide reliable information about its life-style. We did make a special attempt to work with both men and women of all ages and to investigate the specialized knowledge of the master fishermen (*tautai*) and the carpenters (*tufuga*). Nearly everyone, however, knew something about farming and fishing methods, the ceremonial life of the village, and the daily routine. We also tried to share the lives of our neighbors as fully as possible—attending all church services, joining mourning parties at funerals, sharing the joy of wedding celebrations, and going to the plantation lands on the mountainside to work in the copra harvest. I was especially honored with the presentation of an honorary title (*Tuifeai*—terrible cannibal) so that I might be assigned a housepost of my own in the village council of chiefs' meetings (*fono*). Never certain whether the title was presented in humor or in earnest, I accepted the honor with humility and tried to behave as a dignified chief to the best of my ability.

My presence in the society was justified by explaining that I was a teacher whose students wanted to learn how the people of the South Seas lived. Samoans have great respect for education, and teachers have high prestige. These people also have an understanding of what a teacher of anthropology does, and they refer to such a person as *a'oa'o aganu'u* (one who studies the customs of the country). I also explained that I was there to collect information so I could write a history of Samoan life. On my second trip (1962–1963), the Samoans thought this project particularly relevant since there was a growing awareness that traditional Samoan culture was rapidly disappearing. Many people expressed gratitude that someone was interested in recording the particulars of their way of life so future generations could read about how their ancestors lived; therefore, we had to be very careful about the accuracy of the information.

A variety of informants was used, some tradition-oriented and some highly acculturated. One man who worked with me on matters related to village leadership and decision-making held a bachelor's degree in political science from Drake University, while a number of the older chiefs in Fitiuta had little or no education and spoke no English.

Through participant observation in day-to-day events and interviews with chiefs, talking chiefs, untitled men and women, children, and people with special skills, we slowly came to see the culture from the standpoint of the people—always striving, however, to keep that measure of objectivity which must be an underlying condition for any serious study of human culture. Gradually, we began to gain a knowledge that represented a kind of map of the culture, a knowledge that allowed us to find our way through the complexities of a kinship system, a sense of humor, a set of facial expressions, a body language, and a dominant personality set quite different from anything in our own culture. We were soon able to anticipate Samoan behavior and relate to people in ways they would understand and appreciate. Culture shock was no longer a burden to carry day by day. Although the research was exciting, challenging, and rewarding, there were accompanying problems. Life in the beautiful South Sea islands was not without its difficult adjustments, even life-threatening dangers.

As I walked through the village that June day in 1988, I stopped where our house had stood in 1954. It no longer existed, a victim of a 1987 hurricane. I walked to the beach and looked out over the reef, now deserted by the women who often scavenge for eels and small octopi. The surf was down, but I recalled a terrible day thirty-four years earlier, when getting off the island was a matter of life or death, and a savage sea with roaring lines of breakers seemed to be an insurmountable barrier.

In June, 1954, our ten-month-old daughter, Loreen, began having trouble with diarrhea and a low-grade temperature. Paul Godinet, the Samoan medical practitioner at the Ta'ū village dispensary, advised us to take her back to Pago Pago where she could be diagnosed and treated at the government hospital. He also suggested we leave her in the dispensary overnight for observation. There was a Samoan child in the crib next to our daughter's, and, before we left that evening to go home, we gave the child some toys and tried to play with her. The child appeared to be somewhat malnourished and did not respond much to our efforts, but did not seem to be much sicker than our own child. When we returned in the morning, we learned that our daughter was somewhat improved, but that the Samoan child had died during the night. We attended the funeral of the dead child that morning, and, when we returned home, we put Loreen down for a nap. When she awoke, she was burning up—her temperature had soared nearly to 105 degrees, and the diarrhea had worsened.

An interisland vessel had arrived that day at noon—a real miracle since none was scheduled—and we were determined to be on it when it left, seeking the security of modern medicine in Pago Pago. The crew of the Ta'ū village surfboat looked at the turbulence on the reef (the worst in many weeks), however, and shook their heads. They doubted that a passage through the crashing surf could be made safely. The crew felt that they might be able to make it if they had Upega, the village's best coxswain, at the sweep oar. Unfortunately, Upega was ill with some strange weakness of the lower limbs and could not even walk. There was not much hope of getting through the reef that day, and the interisland boat would leave that night.

Upega, who lived in the house next to ours, heard of our plight and asked the surfboat crew to carry him to the boat and place him at the stern, next to the sweep oar. He told us to get aboard and then sat for a time studying the line of breakers as they approached the shore. He then gave the order to row, and we headed toward the maelstrom that spilled through the channel aperture of the fringe reef. We plunged through combers that threw us about, but we shipped no water. The worst was still ahead of us, however. Suddenly, we found ourselves staring up at a huge wave that was beginning to break at the crest. I grasped the gunwale with one hand and clutched our baby closer to my body, but a crewman quickly shipped his oar and prepared to take Loreen from me if we should turn over in the surf. The boat shot up at a 60-degree angle, and, after what seemed an eternity, we plunged down the other side of the wave. In a few seconds, we were outside the breaking point of the waves. Upega had taken us through.

Our boat crew let out a whoop of triumph and pulled for the interisland vessel with all their strength. When I looked back at Ta'ū village, I saw that scores of people had lined the shore to watch our passage through the reef—and they were also cheering! I was deeply touched by their concern for the *palagi* anthropologist and his family. I still feel a special warmth for these gentle, loving people who let us share their lives and who cared so much about our safety. It is one of the reasons I have reacted so strongly against Derek Freeman's 1983 book wherein he character-izes Samoans as naturally aggressive, violent, and authoritarian.

The trip to Pago Pago was a nightmare. Loreen was burning up with fever, vomiting, and experiencing diarrhea off and on for over ten hours. Somehow, we made it through the night, and, as we caught sight of the Pago Pago harbor range lights, we dared to believe that everything would soon be all right. On the dock, we found a friend who drove us to the hospital. The nurses summoned the doctor on call and, even before he arrived, inserted needles in Loreen's legs so that intravenous fluid could begin counteracting her extreme dehydration. When the doctor arrived, a massive dose of penicillin was administered, and we were told to go home and get some rest. Everything would now be all right.

It was almost dawn when we arrived at a Samoan friend's house where we would stay. As I lay down on the bed, the emotional dam broke—I cried like a baby. We had been so close to tragedy, but now we were safe. Several hours later, we went back to the hospital, and there was our daughter, laughing and running around the crib. Loreen did have a black eye from falling out of the crib when someone left the side down, but that seemed only a minor problem compared to what she had been through earlier. That was the end of Loreen's Manu'a residence—mother and child would stay in Pago Pago from that time on—but I returned to the island of Ta'ū for another six weeks to finish the work that had been interrupted.

FORMAT OF THE VOLUME

Chapter 1, "The Samoan World," introduces the reader to this Polynesian microcosm, its location, racial identity, cultural history, and language, and prepares us for a closer look at the social and political organizations, ways of getting a living, the religious belief system, and the life cycle in the chapters that follow. Chapters 2 through 5 represent a baseline account of the Samoan way of life as it was observed and recorded in 1954. It was a life-style little affected by the outside world and only slightly by the American-controlled government of American Samoa.

Chapter 6, "The Changing Samoan World," documents the acculturative effects of the last three-and-a-half decades in the villages of Ta'ū island and describes the contemporary scene. Chapter 6 also presents a wide-angle view of change encompassing all of American Samoa (and, in some cases, Western Samoa as well) and deals with territorial modernization, social disorganization, emigration, economics, and politics—in short, the changing face and personality of these islands that, rightly or wrongly, have long been reputed to be "paradise." Since the publication in 1983 of *Margaret Mead and Samoa, The Making and Unmaking of an Anthropological Myth* by Derek Freeman, there has been controversy concerning the validity of Margaret Mead's 1925–1926 research on coming of age in Samoa. The Postscript examines a variety of opinions about Mead's work, including Lowell Holmes's exhaustive critical analysis conducted in Samoa in 1954. This should provide some perspective on what many have referred to as the most important anthropological controversy in 100 years.

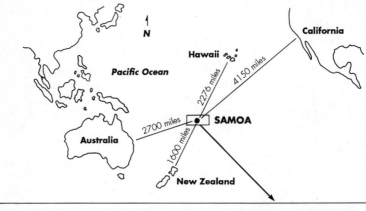

N

Pacific Ocean

California

Hawaii

2276 miles

4150 miles

SAMOA

2700 miles

Australia

1600 miles

New Zealand

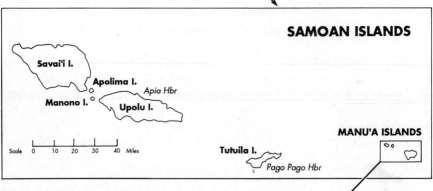

SAMOAN ISLANDS

Savai'i I.

Apolima I.

Apia Hbr

Manono I.

Upolu I.

Scale 0 10 20 30 40 Miles

MANU'A ISLANDS

Tutuila I.

Pago Pago Hbr

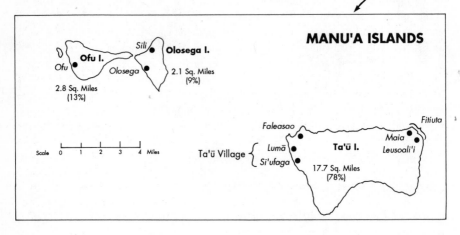

MANU'A ISLANDS

Sili

Olosega I.

Ofu I.

Ofu

Olosega

2.1 Sq. Miles
(9%)

2.8 Sq. Miles
(13%)

Scale 0 1 2 3 4 Miles

Faleasao

Fitiuta

Maia

Ta'ū Village

Lumā

Ta'ū I.

Leusoali'i

Si'ufaga

17.7 Sq. Miles
(78%)

1 / The Samoan World

The Samoan archipelago lies in a general east-west direction at 14 degrees south latitude and between 168 and 173 degrees west longitude. The islands lie approximately halfway between Hawaii and New Zealand. The chain is divided politically: On the west is the independent nation of Western Samoa, consisting of the large islands of Savai'i and Upolu, and two islets, Manono and Apolima. Prior to Western Samoa's independence in 1961, New Zealand governed these islands under a trusteeship charter of the United Nations. Today the nation's population numbers 160,000, occupying 1,097 square miles of land. Its capital and principal seaport is Apia, with a population of 45,000 (O'Meara 1990).

Forty miles east of Upolo is the island of Tutuila. It is the largest of the six inhabited islands making up the territory of American Samoa—a possession acquired by the United States at the turn of the century. Tutuila, with its famous port Pago Pago, is roughly eighteen miles long and six miles wide. It has a population of approximately 44,600 people in fifty-seven villages. The land is mountainous and most of its villages are located along its irregular coastline. One ridge of mountains (the remains of an ancient volcanic crater), partially encloses Pago Pago Bay, one of the largest and best protected harbors in the South Pacific.

Sixty miles east of Tutuila, one encounters the Manu'a group consisting of the islands of Ta'ū, Ofu, and Olosega. These islands, which have always been the most culturally conservative in Samoa, were ceded to the United States in 1904—four years later than Tutuila—when the Tuimanu'a (king of Manu'a), exchanged his crown for a district governorship. There are six villages in Manu'a: Ta'ū, Faleasao, and Fitiuta on the island of Ta'ū; Olosega and Sili on the island of Olosega; and the village of Ofu on the island of the same name. The largest villages are Fitiuta, with a population of about 450, and Ta'ū, with 436 inhabitants.

Western Samoa is agriculturally more productive than American Samoa. Its great expanses of farmland yield substantial quantities of cash crops such as taro, bananas, breadfruit, cocoa, and copra. Their chief market is American Samoa, which has little or no agriculture of its own because most of the labor force works for either the government or one of the two large tuna canneries. Western Samoa's harbor at Apia is relatively poor compared to Pago Pago, but manages to carry on a significant volume of international trade in agricultural products. Apia gives the impression of being a more naturally evolved South Sea community than Pago Pago, since the latter began as a naval base and still retains that flavor despite being under the control of the United States Department of the Interior today.

TOPOGRAPHY, FLORA, AND FAUNA

The Samoan archipelago is volcanic in origin and was created relatively recently (late Pliocene to mid-Pleistocene era). All the islands in the chain have a similar topography. There are low coastal areas with sand beaches (where the majority of villages are located), beyond which the land rises abruptly to highland ridges. Coral reefs fringe nearly all the coastline. On the island of Savai'i, mountain summits reach an altitude of 6,000 feet, but on the island of Tutuila, the highest peak is Matafao with an altitude of 2,141 feet.

Because this region is tropical (warm temperatures and rainfall averaging 150 inches per year), vegetation is dense and green. Bushes, ferns, grasses, and vines carpet the mountain slopes beneath stands of high-quality timber such as *ifi lele* (*Intsis bijuga*), *tavai* (*Rhustaitenis*), and *asi* (*Syzygium inophylloides*). Mosses, lichens, and ferns clothe the mountaintops, where there is a general absence of trees.

The animal population of the archipelago, aside from domesticated varieties such as chickens, pigs, dogs, and a handful of horses and cattle, is meager. There are a few wild bush pigs, two species of nonpoisonous snakes, a dozen varieties of lizards (including the gecko), and land crabs. Fruit bats (*Pteropus ruficollis*), sometimes referred to as "flying foxes," are common as is the small Polynesian rat (*Rattus exulans Peale*). While this rodent probably arrived in Samoa with the original settlers, the large wharf rat (*Rattus norvegicus*) found around port towns is of recent introduction, having arrived on European vessels. There are thirty-four species of land birds including such game fowl as the golden plover, wild duck, and three varieties of pigeon. The most important bird culturally is a small green parakeet with red markings, the *sega,* referred to as the "chief's bird." Its colorful feathers are used to decorate the Samoan's most prized possession, the finemat.

Insects are numerous in this tropical climate, but only two cause serious problems. The mosquito (*Stegomzia pseudoscatellaris*) is a carrier of filariasis, the disease which in its advanced stages develops into elephantiasis. There is no malaria in Samoa. The rhinoceros beetle (*Oryctes rhinoseros*), on the other hand, is a costly pest in that it destroys the coconut palm. Two varieties of centipede and a single variety of scorpion are present in the archipelago. Their bites, while painful, are seldom fatal. Cockroaches, which often attain a length of two inches, are annoying creatures that persist in destroying clothing and finemats. Flies are present in abundance and represent a potential health hazard.

PHYSICAL TYPE

Culturally (and geographically), the Samoan people are identified as Western Polynesians, a category they share with inhabitants of Tonga, Niue, the Tokelaus, and, to a certain extent, with the people of the Fiji Islands. Although there are cultural similarities and several historical traditions concerning political interaction between Samoans and Fiji Islanders, the two are markedly different in physical type. While Fijians are usually classified as Oceanic Negroes and related to

Melanesians to the west of them, Samoans are Polynesian in physical type and thus constitute a racially hybrid group exhibiting a blend of physical characteristics. W. W. Howells described the Polynesian physical type as follows:

> The Polynesians are tall and rather like the Whites in body form, though a little more solid. In this, but mainly in the head and face, they strongly suggest a mixture of Mongoloid and White, with possibly a little Negroid causing occasional frizzy hair. This is going by appearances; we do not know what actually went into the recipe, but it is hard to mistake the force of the White elements (1967:329).

Some claim that Samoans resemble Europeans more closely than does any other group of Polynesians. The color of their skin is a medium yellowish brown, and their hair is black or dark brown and wavy or straight in form. Samoan men average five feet seven-and-one-half inches in height and women five feet three inches. Faces are broad with straight noses of medium breadth, dark brown eyes, and full, but not protruding, lips.

LANGUAGE

The language of Samoa is a dialect of the linguistic family known as Austronesian (formerly called Malayo-Polynesian). This language stock, which began to spread throughout the Pacific islands as early as five thousand to six thousand years ago, involves more than four hundred languages in Melanesia and approximately forty in Micronesia and Polynesia (Pawley 1981). The Micronesian and Polynesian languages belong to the Samoic subgroup, a category which also includes languages spoken by inhabitants of Tokelau, Tuvalu, eastern Futuna, and Tikopia. It is a pleasant-sounding language because of its liberal use of vowels and has often been referred to as the "Italian of the Pacific." Roger Green (1966:34) maintains that Samoan was one of the earlier established languages of Polynesia, although not as old as Fijian or Tongan.

Samoan has only nine consonants: p, t, f, v, s, m, n, g (pronounced ng), and l. The five basic vowels used in English—a, e, i, o, u—are augmented in Samoan speech by the use of long vowel sounds. For example, *tama* (boy) ends in a short a and is pronounced tahm-uh, but the word for "father" is *tamā* (long vowel indicated by the accent mark above the "a") and is pronounced tahm-ah. As is true of most Polynesian languages, one or more vowels separates every consonant in Samoan as seen in the following sentence: *O le ā o fafine a tata lavalava i levaitafo.* (The women will go to wash clothes in the river.) Furthermore, there is the feature of the glottal stop (indicated by '), which is a choking-off of sound as in words like Savai'i, Ta'ū, Manu'a, or *va'a* (boat). This interruption of sound is phonemically very important because a similarly spelled word without the glottal stop has a very different meaning. For example, *fai* means "do," and *"fa'i"* means "banana"; *sao* means "to escape," and *sa'o* means "straight."

Samoan has a smaller vocabulary than English, but then Samoan culture is somewhat less complex—at least technologically. Its basic stock of morphemes is often called upon to do yeoman service in satisfying the society's communication needs. The word *lau*, for example, has nine meanings: "leaf," "lip," "brim of a cup," "thatch," "breadth," "hundred," "your," "fish drive," and "to sing a song verse by verse."

A characteristic feature of the Samoan language is its use of compound nouns formed by the root noun plus another part of speech that qualifies its meaning. The Samoan word meaning "store" (*faleoloa*), for example, is compounded from the noun *fale* meaning "building" and the noun *oloa* meaning "goods." The word for "orator" (*failauga*) combines the verb *fai* (to make) with the noun *lauga* (speech). The Samoan word for "wickedness" (*agaleaga*) is compounded by pairing the noun *aga* (conduct) with the adjective *leaga* (bad).

Verbs also differ markedly from those found in English. The tense of the verb, for example, is never indicated by the form of the verb itself. Verb spellings remain the same for past, present, or future. To indicate tense, Samoan speakers add what might be called verb particles. For example, *O lo'o* expresses continuous action in the present, as in *O lo'o galue Ioane* (John is working.); *Sa* or *Na,* express the past, as in *Sa e alu i Fituita masīna talu ai?* (Did you go to Fituita last month?); and *O le ā*, expresses the definite future, as in *O le ā timu.* (It will rain.).

The most unusual feature of the Samoan language is the special set of honorific terms known as the "Chief's language." This is a class of polite or respectful words that are substituted for ordinary words when one is speaking to someone of chiefly rank. For example, an untitled man has an *'aiga* (meal), but a chief has a *taumafataga;* an untitled person puts a hat on his *ulu* (head), but a chief places it on his *ao;* an untitled person may become *ma'i* (ill), but a chief becomes *gasegase;* and a chief may *maliu* (die), but a commoner will merely *oti.*

ORIGINS—THE ANTHROPOLOGICAL VIEW

The origin of the Samoan people is a matter of some debate in anthropological circles. As we have pointed out, their language is a branch of the Austronesian family, a language stock spoken by Pacific peoples from Easter Island to the Southeast Asia mainland, and their physical type is strongly Asiatic. While most anthropologists reject the Thor Heyerdahl "Kon Tiki" theory—that Samoans as well as other Polynesians are of New World origin—the exact chronology, routes, and methods of migration of all Polynesian peoples out of the Old World are only now becoming clear. At one time, anthropologists postulated mass migrations of maritime-oriented people out of southern China or Southeast Asia with cultural systems already of the Polynesian type. These migrations were assumed to have been through the islands of Micronesia or past New Guinea and other eastern Melanesian islands, with the first long-term settlement taking place in Samoa or the Tonga Islands.

Today, as a result of substantial linguistic evidence and an ever-increasing fund of archaeological data, most Pacific specialists believe that the peopling of the Pacific was a gradual and complex process spanning many millennia. For example, parts of Australia and Papua, New Guinea, may have been settled by migrants from

Southeast Asia (hunting-gathering people labeled Sundanoids) as long as forty thousand to fifty thousand years ago (Oliver 1989:3). It was not until about nine thousand years ago that a new migrant population with horticulture and better watercraft arrived from the west. Then, about five thousand years ago, Austronesians arrived on the scene and, with outriggers or possibly even double-hulled catamarans, moved along the northern coast of Papua New Guinea, through the Solomons and Vanuatu, and into the Fiji island group, which they occupied about 1500 B.C. Settlements were also established in the Tonga islands in approximately 1300 B.C. and in Samoa about 1000 B.C.

These ancient voyagers are identified by the pottery they produced (called Lapita) and are believed to have subsisted mainly on fishing, shell fishing, fowling, and horticulture. They had domesticated animals—pig and fowl bones are present at most archaeological sites. Lapita pottery was slab or coil built, tempered with sand and shell, and fired at low temperatures. Most of the pots were undecorated cooking utensils, either globe shaped or shouldered with narrow necks or outward-flaring rims. A few pots—mostly open bowls or beakers—were decorated with incised designs made by a tool very much like the small rake-like implements used in Polynesian tattooing for hundreds of years. Lapita sites in Tonga and Samoa have produced shell and stone adzes, coral and sea urchin files, shell bracelets, pendants and beads, bone needles and tattooing chisels, shell octopus lures, fishhooks and net sinkers, and obsidian flake tools.

ORIGINS—THE SAMOAN MYTHOLOGICAL VIEW

The Samoans explain their migrations differently from anthropologists. The Samoan myth of creation, still passed on from generation to generation, is as follows:

In the beginning, there were only the heavens and the waters covering the earth. The god Tagaloa looked down from his place in the sky and considered creating a place on the earth where he could stand. So he made a resting place by creating the rock called Manu'atele [Greater Manu'a]. Tagaloa was pleased with his work and said, "It would be well to have still another resting place." He divided the rock Manu'atele so he would have other places in the sea that would serve as stepping stones. From these pieces of rock, he created Savai'i, Upolu, Tonga, Fiji, and the other islands that lie scattered about the wide ocean.

When Tagaloa had finished fashioning all of these islands, he returned to Samoa. He measured the distance between the islands of Savai'i and Manu'a and found it to be too great. So he placed a rock halfway between and designated it as a place of repose for the chiefs. He called this last island Tutuila.

Tagaloa then sent a sacred vine to spread over the rocks. The leaves of the sacred creeper fell off and decayed and things like worms grew from them. Tagaloa saw that the creeper had given birth to worms that had neither heads, nor legs, nor breath of life. So the god came down and provided these worms with heads, legs, arms, and a beating heart. Thus the worms became men. Tagaloa took a male and a female and placed them on each of the islands that he had created. The man, Sa, and the woman, Vai'i, were placed on one island and the place was called Savai'i. U and Polu were placed on another and it became known as Upolu. The couple Tutu and Ila were the first inhabitants of Tutuila. To and Ga went to a place that Tagaloa named Toga [*Tonga*], and Fi and Ti were taken to the place to be called Fiti [*Fiji*].

Then, Tagaloa decided that men should be appointed to rule the different islands and so he created the title of Tui [*king*]. He created the titles Tuiaga'e, Tuita'ū, Tuiofu, Tuiolosega, Tuiatua, Tuia'ana, Tuitoga, and Tuifiti, and thus established lords of the islands.

Then, Tagaloa looked upon all he had created and decided that there should be a king greater than all the others and that he should reside in Manu'atele, his first creation. He selected the son of Po [*night*] and Ao [*day*] to be the king of kings. When this boy was to be born it was found that his abdomen was firmly attached to his mother's womb. Because of this, he was given the name Satia i le Moaatoa [*attached by the abdomen*], and the whole island group that would be his domain received the name Samoa [*sacred abdomen*]. When the child was born, he sustained a great wound as he was ripped from his mother's body. From this came the name of the place of his birth, Manu'atele [*the great wound*]. When this boy grew to manhood, he became king of all the Tui [*kings*] and carried the title Tuimanu'a Moaatoa.

THE COMING OF THE EUROPEANS

The first documented contact between Europeans and Samoan islanders took place on June 14, 1722. Admiral Jacob Roggeveen, commanding two ships in an exploratory voyage for the Dutch West India Company, sighted the Manu'a Island group and dropped anchor off the village of Ta'ū. Whether the villagers had ever seen such vessels before is debatable, but if they felt fear at seeing these tall ships, it was easily eclipsed by their curiosity. They launched an outrigger, brought it alongside Roggeveen's ship, and climbed aboard. Once on board, they produced coconuts that they traded to the ship's company for six rusty nails. After a two-hour visit, the Samoans departed, leaving the impression in Roggeveen's mind that they were "good people, . . . gentle in their deportment towards each other," and in his judgment, "the most civilized and honest of any that we had seen among the islands of the South Sea" (Burney 1816:576).

From Ta'ū, Roggeveen and company sailed some seven miles to the twin islands of Ofu and Olosega. There, an outrigger canoe containing "the High Chief of Ofu village" and his *taupou* (ceremonial village virgin) came out to meet the ship's longboat, which had been rowed to a point just beyond the fringe reef. During his parley with ship's officers, the chief pointed to a blue necklace worn by the *taupou* and indicated that he would like another like it. When the boat crew made it clear that they did not have one to trade, the negotiations were terminated, but not with hostility. Since Roggeveen seems to indicate that Manu'a islanders were familiar with iron nails and since the *taupou* was wearing a common trade item of the day, there is reason to believe that Captain Roggeveen and his crew were not the Samoan islanders' first European visitors.

Manu'a islanders did not see European ships or men again for forty-six years. On May 3, 1768, French navigator Louis Antoine DeBougainville, commanding the ships *La Boudeuse* and *L'Etoile*, sighted the Manu'a group and established contact with the inhabitants of Ofu and Olosega. Here, he traded bits of red cloth for coconuts, barkcloths, lances, and "bad" fishhooks. According to his account, these Samoans were not interested in nails, knives, or earrings—trade items he had found very much in demand in Tahiti. While DeBougainville was impressed with Samoans as sailors and boat builders—naming their archipelago the "Navigator's Islands"—his opinion of them as people was less favorable than that of Roggeveen. DeBougainville stated that they were not as gentle as Tahitians and that "we were always obliged to be upon our guard against their cunning tricks to cheat us by their barter."

After leaving Manu'a, DeBougainville sailed past Tutuila and probably Upolu. While none of DeBougainville's men landed on any of the islands, trading with natives in outrigger canoes occurred at several places.

The first Europeans to set foot on Samoan soil were members of the Comte J. F. de G. La Perouse expedition. For this, they paid dearly with thirteen lives. On December 6, 1787, the frigates *Boussole* and *Astrolabe* sighted the Manu'a group, where they traded with people of Olosega Island (again at sea) before continuing on to Tutuila. Since the ships needed fresh water, and the people of Manu'a had proved to be friendly, La Perouse decided to land at the village of Fagasā, on the north coast of Tutuila. Captain M. DeLangle, commanding *Astrolabe,* proceeded to the village of A'asu, several miles to the west. Meanwhile, La Perouse went to the village of Fagasā, where he was welcomed and permitted to fill his water casks from two streams that ran through the village. He strolled about the village, visited several Samoan *fales,* and was impressed by the wealth of the society as represented by foodstuffs and game fowl. The only things that detracted from his visit to what he characterized as a South Sea paradise were evidence of battle wounds on his Samoan hosts and a scuffle that developed between a native and a sailor engaged in filling the water casks. The native had struck the sailor with a mallet, and, in retaliation, the boat crew threw the native into the water. Another account stated that the Samoan was hung by his thumbs from the top of the longboat mast (Rowe 1930).

DeLangle did not take his men ashore for water until the next day. The passage through the reef at A'asu appeared to be a dangerous one to negotiate. Therefore, the crew anchored two deep-draft barges outside the reef and took two shallow-draft longboats ashore. On the beach, the crew began filling their water casks from a freshwater stream while two hundred Samoan spectators watched their progress. When the crowd suddenly grew in number to more than a thousand, the French sailors became alarmed. DeLangle noticed that several men, whom he perceived to be chiefs, were attempting to maintain order over a crowd that was showing signs of becoming unruly. These men were given a few blue trade beads, but this only angered the others. At this point, the mob began to stone the French sailors. DeLangle was among the first hit and, when he fell, was clubbed to death. The survivors of this first volley of stones attempted to launch the longboats, but could not because of the low tide. The French sailors abandoned the boats and waded to the edge of the reef where they had moored the two barges.

DeLangle and twelve of his crew lay dead on the beach and reef flat, victims of what some believe to have been retaliation for the punishment of the Samoan involved in the scuffle with one of La Perouse's men at Fagasā on the preceding day. The Samoan villagers claim that those who precipitated the massacre were not local people at all, but a visiting party from the island of Upolu. A monument to the dead sailors still stands in the village of A'asu, and, on modern charts, their cove is labelled "Massacre Bay."

Strangely enough, the next day, the Samoans paddled their outrigger canoes out to the French ship and attempted to trade, as though the previous day's incident had never happened. This action, and the fact that the French dead were buried with honors and their graves preserved, may indeed substantiate the claim that those responsible for the deaths were foreign visitors and not A'asu inhabitants at all.

Captain Edward Edwards visited Samoa in 1790 while engaged in his search for the Bounty mutineers. His ship, HMS *Pandora,* dropped anchor off the island of Tutuila for a short time for purposes of trading. The Samoans, who traded food-stuffs for iron tools, proved to be so friendly that Edwards had great difficulty getting them to leave his ship as he prepared to depart.

MISSIONARY ACTIVITY

The first missionaries to arrive in Samoa were the Wesleyans in 1828. The mission's commitment to the area, however, was token, consisting of two native teachers from Tonga. Seven years later, more teachers arrived under the leadership of Reverend Peter Turner, and a permanent mission settlement was established on the tiny island of Manono. Although the Wesleyans were the first to arrive, they were soon challenged in their race for converts by proselytizers of the London Missionary Society (LMS).

The first LMS station in Polynesia had been established in Tahiti in 1797 with the sanction of King Pomare. From there, the LMS extended its operations west-ward, arriving in Samoa in 1830. In that year, the head of the LMS mission effort in the Pacific, John Williams, called at Upolu in the brigantine *Messenger of Peace* and left two native teachers to begin organizing a local church. The first European missionaries arrived in 1836, setting up formal mission stations on Tutuila and in the Manu'a group under the leadership of Archibald Murray and George Lundie.

Although missions were established by the Roman Catholics in 1845, by the Mormons in 1888, and in recent years by the Seventh Day Adventists, Nazarenes, and a variety of Pentecostal churches, the major religious influence in Samoa over the years has come from the London Missionary Society, now known as the Congregational Christian Church of Samoa. Beginning with their project of reducing the Samoan language into writing in 1834, the London Missionary Society workers have had a profound impact both religiously and educationally upon Samoan lives. Although most Samoans are still familiar with ancient mythology and retain some aspects of traditional spirit lore, nearly all modern Samoans would identify themselves as both Christian and literate.

The church today plays the most vital role in Samoan society of any institution other than the family, enjoying a central position in all aspects of Samoan life— social, economic, or political. It remains a pervasive influence in Samoan lives. It stands as a symbol of *fa'aSāmoa* and undoubtedly provides psychological comfort for a people presently undergoing radical cultural change.

THE WILKES EXPEDITION

The first American explorer to call at the Samoan islands was Commodore Charles Wilkes, commanding six ships on a survey mission known as the United States Exploring Expedition. Wilkes has been recognized by American scholars as a competent man of science. Although there is evidence that he was something less than an ideal naval commander, Wilkes produced an excellent six-volume report of his enterprise, documenting local customs, languages, and physical characteristics of native peoples on scores of South Pacific islands. The orders for what has become known as the "Wilkes Expedition" directed the commodore to explore and survey the South Pacific Ocean in the interests of American commerce and whaling and "to extend the bounds of science, and promote the acquisition of knowledge." His expedition was specifically directed to visit the Society, Samoan, Fiji, and Hawaiian Islands.

The Wilkes Expedition arrived in the Samoan archipelago in October 1839, and spent five weeks surveying the entire group. Wilkes' first introduction to Samoan islanders came on the island of Ta'ū (which he erroneously called Manu'a), where he arrived just in time to discourage a war between Christian converts and the "devil's men." He anchored off the northeast coast of Ta'ū and went ashore at a village that his account suggests was Faleasao. Here, he and his party were immediately surrounded by Samoans wanting to trade for fishhooks and tobacco. Wilkes found the Manu'an people to be "a finely-formed race, . . . lively and well-disposed, though in a wilder state than those of the Society Islands." He pronounced them "not altogether honest," for, in their trading transactions, they were inclined toward "selling their articles twice over; for after he made a purchase from one, another would claim the articles as belonging to himself, and insist on also receiving a price for it."[1]

In a tour of what we may assume was Faleasao village, Wilkes observed thick stone walls that he presumed to be fortifications (although they could have been enclosures for pigs), chief's houses on raised stone terraces, and large outrigger canoes "capable of containing twenty or twenty-five men, and . . . very swift."

There is no evidence that Wilkes visited the village of Fitiuta, although his survey boats took soundings around the entire island of Ta'ū. The expedition stopped at Ofu and Olosega; Wilkes states that at the latter of these islands he met the Tuimanu'a (king of Manu'a), who was temporarily living in Olosega instead of his usual residence in Ta'ū out of fear for his life. The king claimed that two warring factions—the Christians and the devil's men—had made his self-imposed exile

---

[1]It is very likely his accusations of dishonesty resulted from a lack of understanding of the communal nature of family property.

necessary. After eating with the king and participating in a kava ceremony (where Wilkes refused kava in favor of the liquid of a fresh coconut), the commodore experienced difficulty in leaving the island: The king and several other chiefs climbed into the ship s longboat and refused to leave until they were given gifts of fishhooks.

After surveying the Manu'a Group, the Wilkes Expedition moved on to Tutuila, Upolu, and Savai'i. While at Upolu, Wilkes appointed John C. Williams as consul to represent American interests in Samoa and to work with local chiefs in guaranteeing protection for the American whaling fleet. Williams was the son of the London Missionary Society worker responsible for the establishment of the Samoan mission in 1830. His appointment as consul was never actually confirmed by the American government, although he was officially named to the post of commercial agent for the United States five years later.

COLONIAL POWER STRUGGLE

America had commercial interests in all of the Samoan islands during the mid-nineteenth century, but so did Germany and Britain. A lively trade in coconut oil began about 1842. While the United States participated in this commercial venture, its main interests centered around the harbor at Pago Pago because of its potential as both a commercial depot and as a coaling station for commercial steamships and United States naval vessels.

In 1872, the USS *Narragansett,* under the command of Commander Richard W. Meade, anchored in Pago Pago harbor. Meade had orders to negotiate a treaty giving the United States the exclusive right to build and maintain a naval base on the shores of Pago Pago Bay. In return, the people of Tutuila would receive "the friendship and protection of the great government of the United States."

The chiefs of Tutuila, headed by High Chief Mauga, convened and negotiated a treaty with Commander Meade on February 14, 1872. It established a set of commercial regulations for the port of Pago Pago and named a port authority board consisting of High Chief Mauga, the agent of the California and Australian Steamship Company, and the consuls of the major powers with interests in Samoa. The treaty was never given official congressional sanction, but the document did represent the first formal working agreement between the Samoans and the United States.

As far as the major powers—the United States, Germany, and Great Britain—were concerned, the real struggle for control of Samoa was going on in Apia. There, each of these Western giants maintained consuls and commercial agents, and these officials constantly involved themselves and their countries in political intrigues. Each supported one or another of the warring native factions competing for dominance of the Samoan chain. The struggle between two of these factions—the Malietoa line and the Tamasese line—became so intense that by 1889 the United States and Great Britain (both backing King Malietoa) were on the brink of war with Germany, which had thrown its support behind King Tamasese.

On March 16, 1889, seven warships—three German, three American, and one

British—rode at anchor in Apia, ready to provide military support for the actions of their respective consuls. However, none of these warships ever fired a shot in their nations' struggle for control of Samoa: Before the day was over, all but one—HMS *Calliope*—lay wrecked on the Apia reef, victims of a great hurricane that suddenly swept down upon them, taking the lives of 146 sailors. Believing the tragedy to be providential punishment, the three Western powers sent representatives to a meeting in Berlin on April 29, 1889, where they negotiated a treaty recognizing Samoa's independence under King Malietoa and restricting Western control solely to the town of Apia. This treaty maintained a shaky peace until December, 1899, when the Western powers again came together and signed a convention decreeing that the Samoan islands be divided between Germany and the United States, with 171 degrees west longitude as the dividing line. Thus, the islands of Savai'i, Upolu, Apolima, and Manono became a German colony, while Tutuila, Aunu'u, and the Manu'a Group became an American territory. Britain withdrew all claims to Samoa, but gained political rights in other South Sea areas such as Tonga and the Solomons.

Even before the final three-power settlement, the United States had moved ahead with its plans for a naval base on the island of Tutuila. However, no construction had yet begun—the Pago Pago Bay coaling station consisted of a huge pile of coal laying out in the open, and, every time it rained, the run-off from the pile discolored the bay. Refueling ships taking on fuel were tied up to buoys in the bay, and the coal was ferried out by lighter.

In April, 1899, Commander B. F. Tilley, commanding the USS *Aberenda,* delivered a cargo of coal and structural steel to Pago Pago. He then sailed for Auckland, New Zealand, to obtain more materials, but returned in four months to become the first commanding officer of the naval station under construction. When completed, the new installation would include a steel dock, a corrugated iron shed for coal, a storehouse, a residence for the man in charge of the coal depot, and a freshwater reservoir.

THE AMERICAN NAVY IN SAMOA

The three-power convention of December 1899, imposed more responsibility on the United States Navy than was originally envisioned. The Americans hoped for an independent Samoa, but found themselves charged with the protection and development of five inhabited Samoan islands. In February 1900, President William McKinley turned over to the Navy control of the islands ceded to the United States. It became the duty of Commander B. F. Tilley to negotiate a deed of cession with the ruling chiefs of both Tutuila and Manu'a. The Tutuila chiefs, under the leadership of High Chief Mauga of the village of Pago Pago, were exceedingly cooperative and a deed was signed with them April 2, 1900. Negotiations with the people of Manu'a, however, were not as successful.

In March 1900, Commander Tilley went to the island of Ta'ū, the seat of King Tuimanu'a Eliasara. He landed at Ta'ū village and was taken to the ceremonial guest house of the king, a middle-aged man who was a graduate of the London

Missionary Society college, Malua, in Upolu. Tuimanu'a Eliasara was quick to inform the commander that the Manu'a Group was politically independent of Tutuila, had never played any part in the power struggle between European powers, and did not want to align themselves with any faction. The king stated that the Manu'ans would acknowledge the United States' sovereignty and would accept its protection, but he vehemently refused to cede his islands to the United States as the chiefs of Tutuila had done.

This stalemate continued until 1903, when Commander E. B. Underwood, the newly appointed commandant of Pago Pago naval base, visited Manu'a and was confronted with a complaint by the Manu'an king concerning the poor quality of education in the Manu'a islands. The Tuimanu'a informed Underwood that the London Missionary Society school was no longer operative and that there were four hundred or five hundred children who needed formal education. The king thereupon presented Underwood with a letter, addressed to the president of the United States, requesting a school, a teacher, and the necessary educational materials. Seeing a chance to use this issue as a bargaining point in extracting a deed of cession, Underwood promised that the United States would provide one hundred dollars a year for a new school, that Eliasara would be named district governor of the Manu'a District, and that the Manu'a chiefs who would sign a deed of cession would receive recognition and gifts equal to those given to the chiefs who had signed the Tutuila deed. The king and the paramount chiefs of Manu'a accepted these terms, and on June 14, 1904, Manu'a was officially incorporated into the territorial holdings of the United States.

AMERICAN INFLUENCE IN MANU'A

Government control over the Manu'a Group has never been oppressive. Generally, the Navy has kept well within its initial agreement that:

> The customs of the Samoans not in conflict with the laws of the United States concerning American Samoa shall be preserved. The village, county, and district councils consisting of the hereditary chiefs and their talking chiefs shall retain their own form or forms of meeting together to discuss affairs of the village, county or district according to their own Samoan custom.

When the United States Department of the Interior took over the governance of the Samoan islands in 1951, this policy was continued and is honored today.

No other portion of the Samoan archipelago is more isolated than the islands of the Manu'a Group. Prior to the early 1970s, transport to and from Pago Pago was by way of an interisland motor vessel that was forced to anchor outside the fringe reef and have passengers and cargo ferried ashore in whaleboats known as *fautasi*. For many years, the interisland vessel—known as the *M.V. Samoa*—visited Manu'a approximately once a month. Then, in the 1960s, the District of Manu'a purchased a surplus minesweeper and turned it over to the government of American Samoa, which provided weekly transportation to Manu'a.

Air service to Ofu and Ta'ū began in the early 1970s when airstrips were established, and a private operator with small single-engine aircraft began offering irregular "daily" service to the islands. From the beginning, Ofu had better landing facilities—the airstrip there was paved—but there was no official communication system between Tutuila and Manu'a to assess weather conditions. Safety of air travel to Manu'a has been questionable for some time.

Harbor facilities were built at Ofu in 1976 and Ta'ū village in 1979 at a cost of $2 million each. While the Ofu harbor is satisfactory because it is sheltered, the harbor at Ta'ū experiences a heavy surge of swells and is only nine feet deep. Not only is it difficult to enter the harbor, but unloading cargo can also be problematic.

Until 1967, when Americans were first employed to teach at the high school in Ta'ū village, there were no permanent white residents in Manu'a. Two Navy pharmacist's mates were assigned to the Manu'a area during the Navy's administration, and there have been occasional Mormon missionaries living in Fitiuta, but generally, white visitors have been transient—government doctors, school supervisors, or economic experts—on short trips of inspection for the government of American Samoa.

Western medicine is represented in the Manu'a Group by Samoan nurses who maintain small dispensaries on each island. For anything other than minor problems, Manu'a residents must travel to the hospital in Pago Pago for treatment.

Manu'a has relatively little economic development; foreign goods and foodstuffs are sold in small, family-operated stores, most of which have limited inventories and remain in business for only short periods of time because of poor management, lack of sufficient capital, and limited access to an adequate flow of goods.

Because of its relative isolation and its strong, conservative local government—dominated by middle-aged and elderly *matai*—Fitiuta has remained one of the least acculturated villages in the Samoan archipelago. Young people in search of greater opportunities, more independence, and adventure tend to leave their villages and take up residence on Tutuila or in the United States, which has led to declining population as well as change in structure of the population in Manu'a.

2 / The World of the *Fale* and the *Fono*—Fitiuta, 1954

The sky offshore was a brilliant blue, but on the island of Ta'ū, near the summit of the mountain known as Lata, great pillows of clouds were building up as the moisture-laden trade winds climbed higher and higher up its slopes. As they neared the top of the 3,056-foot peak, the wetness of the winds was turned to white. Buoyed by these gentle drafts, a gull wheeled and soared, a thousand feet or more above the white line of surf that marked the reef. From this altitude, the houses of the village of Fitiuta, sheltered as they were in a long valley extending inland from the beach, resembled little more than irregular strings of somber beads. Those shaped round or oval were the thatched domes of traditional Samoan *fales,* while the rectangular ones were the rusting galvanized roofs of *palagi* (European) styled structures. Mostly the shapes were round.

The village stretched more than a mile and a quarter into its cradling valley, the exact length of a concrete sidewalk that served as the village's central thoroughfare. The walkway, scarcely wide enough for two people to pass, was flanked at irregular intervals by Samoan dwellings with grounds landscaped with hibiscus bushes, *pua* gardenia trees, and decorative green-and-yellow *lautalotalo* plants. A carpet of well-kept grass covered the valley floor, giving the entire village the appearance of a well-planned park—perhaps even Hollywood's idea of an idyllic South Sea settlement.

The village of Fitiuta is actually made up of two hamlets—Maiā and Leusoali'i. While the residents of each are quick to claim their separate affiliation, and while each hamlet has its own group of chiefs that rules on local issues, there is also a "Great Council," known as the *fono faleula tau aitu,* where chiefs of the many families of both Maiā and Leusoali'i meet together and cooperate in matters of government business and local affairs that concern them all. The visitor to this community would hardly be aware of the division of Fitiuta, for the two hamlets share a dispensary building, a school house, and a church. There is community-owned land—planted with coconuts—which all community members work cooperatively, and both hamlets use the same boat house, copra shed, and surfboats.

The people of Fitiuta are very proud of their community, for legends and myths—repeated throughout the whole of the Samoan archipelago—relate that it was here, in a place called Saua, that the god Tagaloa chose to create the first

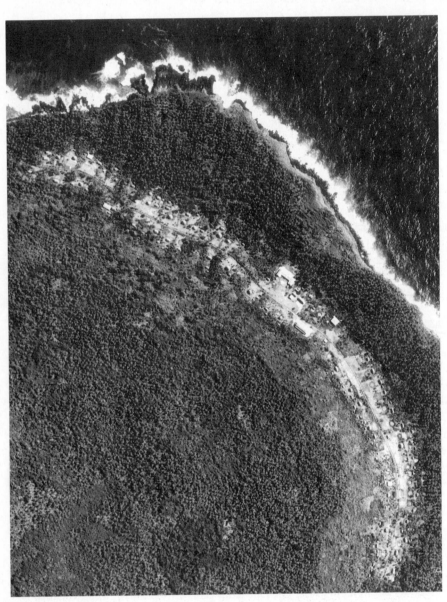

Air view of Fitiuta as it existed in 1954.

human being and crown the first human king, the Tuimanu'a. It was also near Fitiuta, so the myths say, that the first kava ceremony was performed, and it was from here that the first couples were sent forth by Tagaloa to settle the many islands of Polynesia that the god had created as stepping stones across the Pacific. This pride in living on the site of such important ancient events is reflected in the fact that Fitiuta today remains more traditionally Samoan in its village organization, cere- monial commitment, and even in its language than most villages of American Samoa. The people of Fitiuta retain the traditional *t* sound in their speech, while most other inhabitants of Samoa have replaced the *t* sound with a *k* sound. Thus, to most outsiders, the name of this ancient village is Fikiuka. Village pride is also reflected in its immaculate appearance and stable social and political structure. For many, Fitiuta is the epitome of *fa'aSāmoa* (the Samoan way).

Entree to the village is by way of a beach on the north side of the island of Ta'ū. Here, a boat passage has been blasted through the coral reef. Here, too, is where the boathouse for the village *fautasi* (surf or longboat) stands. Near the boathouse is the village copra shed, where bags of coconut kernel are stored awaiting the monthly visit of the interisland motor vessel.

The concrete walkway begins just past the narrow strip of white sand beach. It seems strangely incongruous in this indigenous South Sea setting. For the citizens of Fitiuta, however, it is another source of pride, a product of local financing and labor. The walkway negotiates a gentle slope leading up into the hamlet of Maiā. It leads past the village lands and houses of chiefs[1] La'apui, Paopao, Nunu, and Sega,

Fitiuta fales *in 1954.*

[1] Titled men (*matai*) in Samoa are generally called "chiefs" (lower case), but chiefs may be of two types—"Chiefs" and "Talking Chiefs" (using capitals with these titles). If referring to a titled man in general, lower case is used, but if reference is made to a particular kind of chief, capitals are used.

past the London Missionary Society (now Congregational Church of Samoa) chapel, the village school, and the home of the *faifeau* (pastor), then enters the hamlet of Leusoali'i and transverses the household lands of chiefs Ale, Ili, Pomele, and Moa. The sidewalk then ends, and a well-used dirt path continues on through plantation lands, eventually winding its way down to the sea in a place known as Saua, the mythical Samoan Garden of Eden.

At midday, Fitiuta is a sleepy village. The humid, sultry air hangs heavy—even the smoke from the cooking fires seems to ascend slowly and with difficulty. Most of the villagers have sought the shade of their *fales,* and there is little movement on the village path. Now and then, a teenager emerges from a house to fetch water or to retrieve a toddler, and there is activity in the school building near the heart of the village, but most of the people of Fitiuta, particularly the men, are resting, for they have already put in the better part of a day's work. The men have risen well before dawn and travelled several miles to clear agricultural lands, to plant, to weed, or to harvest, and they have earned their rest. In some houses, small groups of women sit cross-legged on the mat-covered floors and converse softly as they weave pandanus mats or embroider floral designs on pillow cases. Behind many main household buildings, a handful of young men and women tend the cooking fires where taro, bananas, breadfruit, and, occasionally, bundles of leaves containing fish are prepared for the evening meal. After an hour's cooking, the food is removed from the beds of heated rocks with bamboo tongs and placed in woven baskets to cool. In the *fales* near the school, it is more difficult for the men to rest, for education in Samoa is a noisy business requiring unison recitation of English words and sentences and answers to arithmetic problems.

Rising on either side of the village are steep slopes that, at their summits, flatten out to plateaus containing agricultural lands owned by Fitiuta families and uncleared sections owned communally by the village. On these plateaus are found the major stands of coconut trees, as well as quantities of banana and breadfruit trees. Some taro may be found in this area, but the main beds are found farther from the village and higher on the mountain sides, where the land is more fertile.

SOCIAL STRUCTURE

In Fitiuta, as in all parts of the Samoan archipelago, the important units of social organization are the household *(fua'ifale)*, the extended family *('āiga)*, and the village *(nu'u)*. There are approximately sixty-five households, with an average size of nine to ten people. A titled male, known as a *matai,* is in charge of each household. This individual (sometimes referred to as "father") is responsible for the behavior and welfare of all who live under his authority. Each household maintains a village plot of land on which are located several sleeping houses *(fale o'o)* with elliptical floor plans and a large, round guest house *(fale tele)*. To the rear of these buildings is usually a simply constructed cook house *(fale umu)* and frequently a privy *(fale'ese* or *falevao)*.

Those who live with the *matai* usually include his immediate family (spouse and offspring) plus an assortment of collateral relatives such as elderly parents, grand-children, aunts and uncles, brothers and sisters of the *matai*, and their families. The group also may include people who have been formally or informally adopted by the household head. The largest household in Fitiuta numbers twenty-two persons. Household composition is, however, somewhat impermanent because Samoans have a wide choice of households in which they may live, and mobility from one household to another is a common feature of Samoan family life. People are normally welcome in any household with which they have blood or affinal ties.

The head of each household holds the title of chief of a given extended family ('*āiga*) or branch thereof, and, depending upon the traditional nature of that title, will be either a Chief (*ali'i*) or a Talking Chief (*tulāfale*). The nature and status of a given title largely depends on mythological or legendary traditions. A Chief may be recognized as being of paramount rank, for example, because it is commonly recognized that the initial holder of the title was a direct descendant of the Tagaloa family of gods. A very high Talking Chief title may derive its status from the acknowledgement of legends that the original title-holder rendered exceptional service as an orator for a king or represented his village well in some historic negotiation with other villages or island kingdoms. Lesser titles have been created by the village council of chiefs as rewards to men who have served their community well. Sometimes, powerful families have prevailed upon the village elders to allow them to create secondary family titles for men who were exceptionally capable, but who would not ordinarily have a chance to attain chiefly rank until the family title-holder died.

Titles are conferred upon men for life, through election by the members of the extended family, and the title is considered to be as much the property of the family as are the lands and other forms of material property associated with it. Every Samoan '*āiga* has, in effect, a home village where its elected *matai* resides and where its village and agricultural land is located. Only a portion of the '*āiga* lives with the *matai* on these lands, but they are responsible to the larger group for the general maintenance of the status of the title and the welfare of the property.

Since Samoans claim membership in a given '*āiga* by virtue of blood, marriage, or adoption ties to the original or subsequent title-holders, all Samoan '*āiga* are large. Any given Samoan can always trace a relationship to, and, therefore, membership in, a dozen or more '*āiga*. Because personal status can be derived from being related to important families, Samoans pay a great deal of attention to genealogical matters. It is a poor Samoan indeed who cannot claim at least one king or paramount chief as a relative. Needless to say, '*āiga* with important titles tend to be large, and '*āiga* with recently established or lower-ranking titles contain few individuals.

Normally, the '*āiga* tends to be invisible. That is, it becomes a visible entity only when the *matai* dies and the '*āiga* must select a successor; when it is called upon to contribute goods to the *matai* when he must represent the family in a gift exchange at the time of a funeral or wedding; or when a large church donation is required for the construction of a new village house of worship.

Some insight into the approximate size of an '*āiga* with a high-status title may be gained from court records of succession disputes that required adjudication because the family could not settle the issue themselves. In one case, a panel of one American and two Samoan judges attempted to settle the dispute by having members of the various factions submit petitions with the signatures of those supporting the faction's candidate for the *matai* post. The total number of people claiming *'āiga* membership, and therefore eligibility to vote for one candidate or another, amounted to 961, or approximately one-thirtieth of the total population of American Samoa, although some names appearing on the petitions were actually residents of Western Samoa. The factions in this court case were branches of the family and were what Samoans refer to as the *faletama* (houses of the children).

The phenomenon of *faletama* may be explained as follows: Let us say that the original title-holder in a particular family had two sons and a daughter. This would mean that, for all time to come, the family would be recognized as composed of two male branches and one female. Theoretically, the male branches are more eligible for title succession; therefore, special privileges are provided the members of the female branch, known collectively as the *tamasā* (sacred child) or *ilāmutu* (sister's children). The relationship existing between the male and the female branches of a family is called *feagaiga*. As Milner (1966:83) defines it, *feagaiga* involves the male branches pledging "to pay respect, to render services, and to observe certain obligations towards those descendants" in the female branch or branches.

It has been said that the female branch has the power of veto over decisions of the family. In reality, however, any family difference would rarely go that far, since Samoans believe that ignoring the wishes of the *tamasā* faction would result in family misfortune—even sickness or death of family members.

This general pattern of deference to the female side of the family is also reflected in the patterns of daily face-to-face interaction between siblings and other relatives of the same generation who are of the opposite sex. Samoans have a classificatory system of kinship terminology; therefore, cousins as well as siblings must abide by a set of norms which is commonly labeled "brother-sister avoidance." Relatives who stand in this real or fictive relationship must not use language that is salacious, or even suggestive, in each other's presence; they must not remain alone together in a house, dance on the same dance floor, or give any impression of affection for each other that could in any way be suspected of any degree of intimacy. Such rigid restrictions, while related to incest prohibitions, no doubt also serve as constant reminders of the more general obligations of deference owed the female side of the family.

When a family title is vacated because of the death of its holder, members of the various branches of the *'āiga* come together to deliberate the selection of a successor. Often, each of the faletama has its own candidate for the post, and deliberations are frequently long and painful. Some students of Samoan culture maintain that the selection of a successor tends toward primogeniture while others have suggested there is a special "right of the brother" to the position. Examination of several dozen genealogies through several generations revealed, however, that, while it is common for a son to succeed to his father's title, there was no evidence of a "right of the brother" to the vacant title.

Men are elected to hold titles on the basis of their service to the family, individual intelligence and initiative, knowledge of ceremonial protocol, age (a *matai* younger than forty is an oddity), and, in recent years, amount of formal education, wealth, and ability to deal effectively with Europeans in economic or political affairs. If the son of a deceased *matai* meets the criteria for family leadership, he has a strong chance of acquiring his father's title, but this acquisition of title is more a matter of family service than direct kinship tie. A young man living in the household of the *matai* and taking an active part in day-to-day operations has a decided advantage over someone with close blood ties residing in another household. Qualification for title succession can involve a good deal of gamesmanship. For example, a young man wishing to become a *matai* may very well see it to his advantage to take up residence with an uncle who has no male children. Potential for title succession may also be a factor in marital residence. It is often a better investment for the future if a young man moves in with his wife's family, where there is no viable successor for the family title, than to live in his own household, where he may be a second or third son and therefore have formidable competitors in his efforts to make notable contributions to the family welfare. In recent years, some faithful and hardworking young men have been greatly disappointed when they were bypassed as title successors in favor of someone who has been working or studying in the United States—thus absent from the household, in some cases, for many years—but who returned when the *matai* title became vacant. Families are often unduly impressed by stateside experience and feel that people with such a background can enhance the status of the family.

Family deliberations in the choice of a new *matai* may go on for several days, even weeks. A *matai* who is related to the family usually presides over the meetings, and everyone over the age of sixteen has his or her chance to comment on the qualities of the men under consideration. It may be pointed out that one's favorite candidate is "familiar with the legends and myths of Samoa," that he is "a man well respected by the other *matai* of the village," or that he is "a man of wisdom who can help the village in matters of agriculture and livestock raising."

Candidates do not speak in their own behalf, but are well represented by their supporting relatives. When a family comes to an agreement on a given individual, a kava ceremony involving only the family will be held to honor the new *matai*. He will drink first kava (the premier position) and later will be the honored guest at a family feast. In addition to the preparation of food and kava, it is also the family's responsibility to send a representative to the village council of chiefs to inform them officially of its choice. The village council will then set a date for the *fono tau a'a ti*, the official ceremony of title installation. On the appointed day, the new *matai* will enter the council meeting, sit at the housepost reserved for his title, and drink kava in the order of his new rank. He will then be expected to deliver a speech, known traditionally as the *a'a ti*. This is, so to speak, the *matai's* first test within the village council. In the speech, he is expected to show his wisdom, his grasp of oratorical protocol, and his expertise in turning a phrase or alluding to mythological or legendary events appropriate to the occasion. It is said that, in old Samoa, if the chiefs found this speech lacking in quality, they would refuse to recognize his right to sit in council, but this practice is no longer followed. After the new *matai* speaks, his fellow chiefs will give speeches in the order of their rank, each imparting a bit of advice to the novice.

The newly elected family head faces a second test by the village—his ability and willingness to provide food in generous quantities for village feasting. Not only must the new *matai* and his family provide food for all families, but each of the *matai* in the council expects to receive substantial gifts such as finemats or money. These gifts are presented to the chiefs by a titled relative of the newly installed chief. This distribution of property, called *mālō toga,* will be accompanied by pronouncements such as, "This is the time we give you finemats for the new *matai*." The council is then dismissed, and the newly installed chief returns to his family to begin his new lifetime role as family head and "father" to his household.

While *matai* are theoretically selected to serve for life, there are exceptions. Occasionally, an irresponsible, lazy, or cruel chief may have his title removed by his family through an action somewhat akin to impeachment, or an elderly chief may find the responsibilities of his role beyond his abilities and voluntarily remove himself as *matai* allowing a younger, more energetic, man to take over.

ROLE OF THE *MATAI*

Once elected to head the family, the *matai's* responsibilities are manifold. He serves as the family patriarch, promoting family unity and prestige; administering all family lands; settling disputes among family members; promoting religious participation; and representing the family as its political spokesman in the village council of chiefs (*fono*). The *matai* must even strive to take on a new personality, for once he is a chief, he becomes a man of increased importance, a man of responsibility. Something of the nature of the role may be gleaned from the following statement of a young chief recorded by Margaret Mead:

> I have been a chief only four years and look, my hair is grey, although in Samoa grey hair comes slowly. . . . But always, I must act as if I were old. I must walk gravely and with measured step. I may not dance except upon most solemn occasions, neither may I play games with the young men. Old men of sixty are my companions and watch my every word, lest I make a mistake. Thirty-one people live in my household. For them I must plan, I must find them food and clothing, settle their disputes, arrange their marriages. There is no one in my whole family who dares to scold me or even to address me familiarly by my first name. It is hard to be so young and yet to be a chief (1928:36–37).

All land in and around Fitiuta that is not designated as "village land" belongs to one or another of the extended families who have *matai* in the village. Private ownership of land is almost nonexistent. The *matai* is said to have *pule* over the land of his family. This means that he has the power to determine the uses to which the family land is to be put, that is, what portions are to be cultivated and for what crops. While a *matai* may lend land to be used in growing certain short-term cultigens by friends or relatives who do not live within the household unit, he does not have the authority to alienate family lands through sale or gift. Any transaction which would result in permanent loss of *'āiga* property must be entered into by all members of the extended family, and a unanimous decision must be reached. Such an agreement is difficult to obtain, for Samoans are extremely reticent to be separated from landholdings. The government of American Samoa supports this sentiment by stipulating that no one with less than 75 percent Samoan ancestry may purchase land.

Most Fitiuta families work their lands as a family unit, moving section to section as a single workforce. Village members often combine their efforts in working for community projects that will benefit the whole; however, in normal subsistence agriculture or in cash cropping, there is little cooperative labor outside the family circle.

The fruits of family labor are theoretically shared equally among all the members of the household, regardless of how much labor each individual member has actually contributed. The *matai* is responsible for making an equitable distribution, but he is also expected to accumulate wealth which can be used by the family in times of economic crisis or to meet social obligations such as gift presentations at a kinsman's wedding or funeral or as a special church donation.

The communal nature of family property and labor is beginning to break down. More and more, young men demand opportunities to earn money of their own. In a place like Pago Pago, this is not a problem because young men can obtain jobs with the government, in some aspect of the tourist trade, or in one of the commercial establishments such as the fish cannery. In Fitiuta, however, private enterprise requires the cooperation of the *matai*, since agriculture on family lands is the only available source of cash income. There has always been an opportunity for young men to go high on the mountain slope, clear bush land, harvest a crop, and sell it for personal gain. Now, however, there is increasing pressure on *matai* to divide family lands and allow heads of nuclear families within the household to work the lands as private enterprises. Such changes in the economic operations of the family have not, however, impaired the position of the *matai* in the family and village structure. Young men now have the opportunity to manage their own money, but the obligations due their family and their *matai* remain the same.

Even though individual family members often cultivate "private" plots, much of the family agricultural work is still a joint family enterprise under the direction of the *matai*. In most cases, the *matai* works beside the members of his family, expecting no special privileges. There are times when the *matai* must attend the village council meetings, but generally, he contributes as much physical labor as any member of his group.

The *matai* will select an assistant, commonly referred to as the *matai taule'ale'a*, to assist in the planning and execution of family labor activities. This assistant is an untitled man, often the chief's son, who serves as labor foreman and takes over the *matai's* duties when the latter is away from the village or involved in council deliberations. Every morning, the *matai taule'ale'a* is expected to go to the family head and discuss work plans for the day. Together, they may decide, for example, that half-a-dozen young men and women should spend the morning weeding the taro patch on the upper slope, while two young men should remain behind to repair the thatch on the sleeping houses or perhaps cook for the family. Still other family members may be assigned to fish or search for small octopi or shellfish on the reef flat.

There has been a lack of understanding among foreign observers concerning the power and authority of the *matai* and the *taule'ale'a* to make demands on the labor of the household members. Some observers believe that the *matai* has almost a life-and-death control over his family and that these poor individuals have little choice but to obey the dictates of their autocratic leader. But Fay Ala'ilima writes in her book *A Samoan Family:*

> The *matai* might give his *taulele'a*[2] orders but he was also obliged to train and to see they were happy. The village *fono* made him pay the fine when his *taulele'a* got into trouble. His *taulele'a* came to him with their personal needs and *fa'alavelaves* (troubles). The whole village would laugh at him if his *taulele'a* became dissatisfied and left. A *taule'ale'a* might not talk back directly to his *matai* but he had other ways of expressing himself. Pai had yet to see a Samoan feel or act like a slave. The very thought made him smile (1961:29).

Actually, the Samoan household group is run very democratically. With the freedom that Samoans have concerning choice of residence—for example, they are always welcome for any period of time in the home of any relative—no *matai* can really force anyone to work for him unless that person wants to. One informant confided that, when he was a child, he would always change households just prior to the time when he knew he was about to be assigned a particularly disagreeable task. Young people and adults, however, usually take the bitter with the sweet, and, unless their *matai* is particularly authoritarian and unreasonable, they are quite willing to abide by his decisions for the sake of an efficient and prosperous household. *Matai* of high traditional rank tend to be more demanding of their people, because they realize that being associated with a household of a high-ranking chief is prestigious and there is less chance that people will seek residence elsewhere, even though they may find certain demands oppressive.

Much of the agricultural work demands strength. Land may require clearing with axes and bush knives, and very heavy loads of produce must frequently be carried long distances over rough terrain. However, hours spent in agricultural work normally are not long. The average family can provide itself with ample food for a week with only six to eight hours total labor in a seven-day period. Additional time may be spent keeping houses or pig fences in repair or fishing on the reef, but, in 1954, few Samoans had experienced the oppressive situation of the American or European eight-hour day. Normally, Samoans farm in the cool of the morning, nap in the heat of the day, fish when the tide is right, and care for their buildings when they require attention. They work with speed and enormous energy to complete difficult tasks; when they are finished, they feel no guilt in sitting around idle and unproductive. The Westerner's concept of "keeping busy," whether or not there is a worthwhile or necessary task to be completed, is foreign to the Samoan's value system. In tasks which Samoans and Europeans would find equally important, the latter would be hard put to compete either in terms of expenditure of energy or in dedication.

---

[2]*taulele'a* is the plural form of *taule'ale'a*.

CHIEFS AND TALKING CHIEFS

All *matai* titles may be categorized as Chief (*ali'i*) or Talking Chief (*tulāfale*—one who sits in the front of the house). Within the Chief category, the uppermost station is that of the *ali'i sili*, or High Chief. Such individuals often hold the paramount rank in a village or may share top honors by being part of a group of "brother chiefs" who have great influence over village affairs. *Ali'i sili* titles are always very old and usually have a great deal of traditional lore associated with them. A holder of such a title is usually quick to relate that his title, for example, was originally awarded to an ancestor for extraordinary bravery in battle or for wise and faithful counsel to a Manu'an king. One Fitiuta *ali'i sili*, Galea'i, documents the high status of his family title with myths (recorded by Williamson and Churchill) that the Tagaloa family came down from heaven and bestowed the *ao* (crown) title upon a newly born Manu'an boy named Galea'i who thereupon became the first chief of all Manu'a. *Ali'i sili* titles were awarded to families as dowry or as gifts by important personages in elaborate gift exchanges with distinguished and deserving subjects. When High Chiefs take their reserved seats (identified in terms of house posts) in the village council house for meetings of the *fono*, they are located at the ends of the elliptical floor plan.

Next in order of importance within the Chief category are the *ali'i* (Chiefs) who are also heads of extended families or of branches of families, but who do not have titles of sufficient traditional status or authority to warrant special attention in the power structure of the village. In village council meetings (*fono*), they sit on the flanks of the *ali'i sili*, at the ends of the house.

The lowest rung within the Chief category is the *ali'i fa'avaipou* (between-the-posts Chiefs). These men are also *matai*, but usually of branches of large families. Their titles are often recently created, and they are usually younger men who will perhaps later be selected for more prestigious titles. They often sit near the Chief who holds the paramount title in their family and usually side with him in village decisions. As the term for these Chiefs indicates, they frequently do not have assigned posts where they may regularly sit in council meetings, but must often resort to sitting cross-legged on the mat near the senior Chief of their family. It is quite likely that most of these titles were especially created long after the original village hierarchy was established and the accompanying seating plan for the village council was formalized.

Talking Chiefs also may be described as occupying three levels of importance. Of highest rank is the *to'oto o*, or *tulāfale sili*. These men are often orator chiefs for High Chiefs and usually serve as spokesmen for the entire village in intervillage ceremonies or negotiations. Their posts in the *fono* seating arrangement are at the front and the back of the council house. They are flanked by Talking Chiefs of secondary rank known in Fituita as *vae o to'oto'o* (feet or legs of the Talking Chief). Next to them, and sometimes without permanent post assignments, are the lowest rank of Talking Chiefs, the *lauti laulelei*, or *tulāfale fa'avaipou* (common, or between-the-posts Talking Chiefs).

It is difficult to generalize the functions of the various grades of Talking Chiefs when we consider Samoa as a whole, for each village tends to have its own structural peculiarities. Buck states, however, that

> there are grades of prestige among the Talking Chiefs depending, no doubt on the political influence held by the family from which they derive their titles. The higher grades of Talking Chiefs are naturally those historically associated with ruling high titles. Where the lesser *tulāfale* represented their family groups, the higher ranks represent the village which is a combination of families (1931:72).

Some observers of the Samoan political scene give the impression that Chiefs and Talking Chiefs come in pairs, that is, every Chief has a Talking Chief who does his speaking. This is generally true in the *fono,* but not necessarily in individual families. There are cases where the senior title in a family is a High Chief title, and a lesser title is a Talking Chief title. In such cases, the orator chief will speak for his Chief, making his wishes known much as a lawyer speaks for his client. Chiefs can, and often do, speak for themselves in village council meetings. The paramount title in some families is of the Talking Chief variety, and its holder is therefore obligated to express his family's wishes himself. In the *fono,* he may speak not only for himself, but he may be historically linked to another family headed by a High Chief; this, of course, increases his oratorical responsibilities since he may have to speak for both families.

Roles of Chiefs and Talking Chiefs   The role of Chief varies with his rank within the village hierarchy. In some villages, there is but one individual known as *ali'i sili* (High Chief), while in others, there may be a group of "brother chiefs" who hold *ali'i sili* rank. High Chiefs preside over the village council, help settle disputes that arise there, and serve as advisors to the Talking Chiefs. Such an individual is a village leader and maintains a great guest house for the entertainment of important visitors to the village. In many cases, the High Chief traditionally has had the right to appoint his daughter or a close relative to the position of village ceremonial maiden (*taupou*), and his son was qualified to serve as the leader or *manaia* of the village society of untitled men, the *aumaga*.

A High Chief's rank permits him to drink first at kava ceremonies and he is entitled to the first portion (*sua*) of food when chiefs eat together. When large amounts of food are distributed at feasts or at gift exchanges, his portion always consists of the most desirable portion of the pig, fish, or fowl. A High Chief's share of a pig, for example, is the loin. Some *ali'i sili* have the right to impose tapu, which amounts to declaring the reef off limits for fishing for a period of time prior to a community fishing drive (*lau*) or forbidding anyone to harvest taro before a great feast. Some insight into the traditional role and status of the High Chief may be gained from the fact that they are collectively known as *fa'atui* (second to the king).

The roles of the second- or third-rank Chiefs differ very little from one another. Being of lesser rank, they do not have the responsibility of giving their opinions in village council deliberations. They may, however, contribute to decision-making discussions; some of these men exhibit great wisdom and analytical ability on such occasions. If the High Chief is absent from the council meeting, a Chief of secondary rank will occupy his post and preside over the meeting after the fashion of a vice-president in an American club or business meeting. While High Chiefs are permitted to carry a large and bulky fly whisk as a symbol of office, Chiefs of secondary rank carry only a small whisk, which is more appropriate for shooing flies than signifying rank. Secondary Chiefs must be very careful that their symbols of office do not compete with those of higher-ranked Chiefs, or they may be accused of "assuming above their rank." In times of high ceremony, High Chiefs are expected to wear tapa cloth wrap-arounds, but lesser Chiefs are not expected to appear so formally or ceremonially garbed.

The *tulāfale* are undoubtedly the most colorful of titled men, particularly the High Talking Chiefs, who occasionally are identified as "the difficult people" because of their ability to persuade, cajole, or intimidate through their artistry with words and protocol.

Samoan tradition explains the division of titles into Chief and Talking Chief categories by citing the *māvaega* (last will and testament) of the culture hero Pili, who divided the islands of Upolu and Manono among three of his four sons, but gave the fourth son the fly whisk and the right to speak for the Chiefs of the family. Regardless of whether such an event ever occurred, the fact remains that Talking Chiefs have special advantages over Chiefs, as well as special opportunities for gaining wealth and public acclaim. Buck comments that specialization of chiefly functions

> reached its highest in Samoa where a class of hereditary talking chiefs termed *tulāfale* created such a mass of observances in etiquette, precedence, and a special chiefs' language, that the high chiefs were unable to do without them. No high chief could travel to other villages without his official *tulāfale*. Not only did the talking chiefs create increased ceremonial around the high chiefs, but they became administrative chiefs with regard to the distribution of food and presents and thus acquired a great deal of power previously exercised by their superiors (1965:166).

As with Chiefs, there are various levels of Talking Chiefs. The High Talking Chief, who has the traditional right to carry an enormous *fue* (fly whisk) serves as principal village orator, settling disputes between villages, welcoming important persons or delegations (*malaga*) upon their arrival in the village, directing and announcing important kava ceremonies, and overseeing distributions of food and other property when events involving the entire village take place. The High Talking Chief's skill at persuasion is often so great that few individuals except High Chiefs dare oppose him. In village council meetings, it can be said that he sets the agenda and is often responsible for placing motions before the assembly.

In addition to his key role in the village council, the High Talking Chief is closely associated with the phenomenon of the *malaga*. A *malaga* is an official party of titled individuals who journey to another village or island for the purpose of carrying out some practical or ceremonial function. There is, for example, the *malaga tapa fala* (the visit to ask for mat-making materials), the *malaga ta'aloga* (the visit to engage in competitive sports), the *malaga si'i* (the visit to exchange property associated with a marriage), and many others. In every case, the visiting party must be accompanied by a High Talking Chief and must be welcomed, feted, entertained, and ceremonially bid good-bye by the High Talking Chief of the host village. Each of these aspects of a ceremonial call presents a major occasion at which orator chiefs may demonstrate their rhetorical ability—flattering the guests and bringing honor to themselves and the village as masters of protocol and perfect hosts.

Oratory is a fine art among these men. There are highly prescribed procedures that must be followed and elaborate structures for speeches, which must be committed to memory. Most important is the knowledge they must have of *fa'alupega,* the official list of names and relative ranks of a village s Chiefs and Talking Chiefs and the appropriate esoteric and symbolic references that relate to the social and political structure of the village. Since 1946, *tulāfale* have had some help in acquiring this information: The London Missionary Society Press published a book containing the *fa'alupega* of all the villages in the Samoan archipelago. The Talking Chief of a *malaga* arriving in Fitiuta, for example, would have to include in his remarks to the host village the following recitation of Fitiuta village organizational characteristics:

> *Tulou na Fitiuta*
> (Hail to all the Chiefs and Talking Chiefs of Fitiuta.)
> *Tulou na le faleula tau aitu.*
> (Hail to the red house of the spirits—the *fono* of Fitiuta.)
> *Tulou na le Tamaa'ita'i o le Ao.*
> (Hail to the Lady of the Dawn—symbolic reference to the title of High Chief Galea'i.)
> *Tulou na le Vaimagalo. O le susu mai le Pulefano.*
> (Hail to Galea'i and Soatoa, ambassadors to the court of the King of Manu'a.)
> *Tulou na lau afioga Tufele.*
> (Hail to High Chief Tufele.)
> *Tulou na Faleifā ma Ma'opū o le Alofiamoa.*
> (Hail to the four houses of Chiefs and the *Ma'opū* division of Chiefs.)
> *Mamalu maia fetalaiga ia te outou To'oto'o.*
> (Hail to the Speakers, the High Talking Chiefs.)
> *Tulou na le Suafa o Nu'u.*
> (Hail to the rulers of the village)
> *Tulou na le So'oso'o Ali'i ma le Taua'ese'ese.*
> (Hail to all Chiefs and Talking Chiefs of secondary rank.)
> *Tulou na le aumaga paia le i fafō.*
> (Hail to the sacred society of untitled men seated outside the council house.)
> *Tulou na le alofi e magalo ai mea uma.*
> (Hail to the kava ceremony which cleanses everything.)

Once past the elaborate courtesy phrases, the orator is free to use his imagination and creative skill. The bodies of speeches are always ornate—filled with obscure references to mythology and amply supplied with Biblical phrases and allusions. In its ceremonial context, oratory functions less as communication than as art. Great orators have a multitude of devices for holding attention or highlighting important statements and ideas. Generally, the voice volume rises from a whisper to nearly a shout as the speech proceeds. Now and again, a special point will be emphasized with a gesture of the fly whisk or a sudden clipped phrase. A momentary pause or a sudden reduction of voice volume highlights a thought of which the orator wants his audience to make special note. When interest appears to lag, a bit of sarcasm, humor, or a proverbial cliché may be used to renew flagging attention spans. As in all Samoan social interaction, reciprocity is evident in oratory. It is a gracious institution which honors and flatters others, but also brings great satisfaction, prestige, and community admiration to the artful practitioner.

The Talking Chiefs are also the poets of this society. At the time of kava preparation or as a part of a speech, they are responsible for a recitation or even the composition of verse known as *solo*. *Solo* often feature rhyming couplets and predictable meter patterns and usually deal with mythological or legendary subject matter. They undoubtedly owe much of their form to the age-old chants of Polynesia. While *solo* lose a great deal in translation (particularly rhyme and meter) and often deal with mythological events which have little meaning for those outside the culture, these poems hold a measure of appeal, even for the foreign reader.

Solo ia Afoafouvale

Sleep, I sleep deeply;
I awaken.
Did I dream, did I call out in my sleep?
Did I anoint myself in oil?
Did I dye my hair with the juice of the puni leaf?
Did I sleep in the company of noble women?
What is the confusion of men's and women's voices?
Is there a distribution of finemats?
Is there feasting?
Has the sacred fish of the sea arrived for the feasting?

While the greater share of ceremonial glory goes to the High Talking Chiefs, second- and third-rank Talking Chiefs also play important roles. Their fly whisks do not match those of first-rank orators in size nor do their occasions for speech-making match those of the High Talking Chiefs in importance, but there is still an ample portion of prestige to be enjoyed. They have adequate opportunities to speak in the decision-making deliberations in village council, and it is here that they develop their skills to be used in other ceremonial contexts. Many *malaga* arrive with only an orator of secondary rank, and this gives the host village orators of equivalent rank an opportunity to perform. The Samoan sense of fair play eliminates the possibility of their matching the skills of a High Talking Chief with those of a lesser-ranked orator in the exchange of speeches that mark the initial stages of intervillage interactions.

Talking Chiefs of secondary rank also serve as messengers to other villages and often represent the interests of their extended families in disputes and deliberations with other *'āiga* within the village or in other villages. The Talking Chiefs are generally thought of as the masters of ceremony on any occasion. It is the importance of the occasion that determines the appropriate rank of the one who will officiate.

THE *AUMAGA*

The untitled men of the village are known as *taulele'a* and represent the main labor force in both the household and the village units. At the village level, the untitled men (often referred to as "young men" regardless of age) are organized into a cooperative work group called the *aumaga*. This unit has both labor and ceremonial functions and serves the village council and the village as a whole. Sometimes referred to as "the strength of the village," this associational group assists the chiefs in ceremonial activities and carries the bulk of responsibility and effort in all village cooperative enterprises. They plan and provide the bulk of the labor force in such activities as cutting copra for church money-raising projects, repairing village paths, housebuilding, ferrying passengers and cargo in longboats to vessels anchored outside the reef, planting and harvesting the village taro patch, and group fishing (*lau*) on the reef flat.

For the village council, the *aumaga* cooks and serves food at all *fono* meetings and on all ceremonial occasions. They have the prime responsibility in the wringing and serving of kava. They also serve as a kind of police force, enforcing all village council legal pronouncements.

The *aumaga* is an entirely voluntary association made up of the untitled men of all the households in the village. The leader of the group is called the *manaia,* which literally translated means "a fine-looking man." In his ceremonial and leadership roles, he serves as a kind of village "prince" since he is the "son" of the paramount Chief. While this young man may not be an offspring of the paramount Chief, he is always a relative whom the chief refers to as *atali'i* (son), and this may also include grandsons, brothers' and sisters' sons, and even adopted sons.

When the *manaia* convenes his group, the result is a junior version of the village council. The *manaia* presides as his father does in the village council, and the sons of Talking Chiefs carry out oratorical functions similar to that of their fathers. *Aumaga* decision-making procedures are much the same as those followed in the *fono,* and, in the actual carrying out of work projects, the chain of authority mirrors that of the hierarchy of chiefs. One significant difference between this group and the senior elite group is that the *aumaga* serves its members' recreational needs. The *aumaga* members often come together to play cricket or to play cards far into the night. They aid one another in courtship activities and they often rehearse and perform group dances (*sasa siva*) to entertain visiting *malaga* or in dance competitions at church dedications or Flag Day[3] celebrations. Occasionally, the group will get together for a beer party—much to the disapproval of the village chiefs.

THE *AUALUMA*

The female counterpart of the *aumaga* is the *aualuma*. It is an organization of unmarried women, with representatives from the several household family groups which make up the village. Their function, like the *aumaga,* is to contribute to the general welfare of the village through a variety of social, economic, and ceremonial activities. However, while the *aumaga* has remained relatively unchanged in its structure and function over the years, the *aualuma* has changed drastically. Originally, the *aualuma* was a group of handpicked unmarried women who served the village ceremonial virgin princess, the *taupou,* as handmaidens and chaperones. They were constantly in attendance, sleeping with the young woman and caring for

---

[3]April 17, the day the American flag was first flown over American Samoa.

Village aumaga *competing in group dancing at a Flag Day celebration in 1954.*

all of her needs. The *taupou,* who stood in the same relationship to the paramount Chief as the *manaia,* that is, a real or fictive daughter, was the center of ceremonial attention and, in most villages, was the principal kava preparer and dance leader. She represented the "cream" of the village young women, and her virtue was carefully protected in anticipation of a "noble" marriage with an important chief or *manaia* from another village. At the time of her marriage, the *taupou* had to submit to a public defloration ceremony in which the village High Talking Chief inserted his finger into her vagina (wrapped with snow-white bark cloth) and, hopefully, obtained the scarlet evidence of her purity.

There is still a group of young women in every village who are known as the *aualuma,* but the traditional *taupou* institution has passed. There are no permanent ceremonial virgins today and, therefore, no need for the *aualuma* as originally constituted. *Taupous* are appointed by paramount Chiefs from the ranks of female relatives for specific occasions, such as the entertainment of a group of official visitors (*malaga*), but these young women are often married women with children— obviously not virgins.

Even in the 1950s, the *aualuma* serves a very different function. Composed exclusively of unmarried girls and widows, it is part of a larger village organization known as the Women's Committee, which also includes wives of untitled men, Chiefs, and Talking Chiefs. While still a recognizable entity, the *aualuma* works closely with other committee women in public health and infant welfare activities, raising money for the village church, and entertaining *malaga.* It is characteristic of the group to come together and weave mats or house blinds for the pastor's residence or the dispensary, even to produce them for sale to raise money for village enterprises. The Samoan medical practitioner has come to depend on these women for promotion of the weekly baby clinic and for the extra dispensary equipment and supplies that the government does not provide.

The *aualuma* serves much like the *aumaga* in that it undertakes much of the heavier work that middle-aged and elderly chiefs' wives are incapable of doing. They are particularly singled out for such activities as group dancing, an indispensable feature of every Flag Day celebration. Because the age range of the *aualuma* is between thirteen and twenty-one, these young women are the logical candidates for the strenuous and exacting demands of this art form. On ceremonial occasions, the *aualuma* appears with their appointed *taupou* in specially prepared costumes and go through a painstakingly learned series of unison body movements which comprise the *sasa siva.* The *aualuma* also occasionally carries out special work projects apart from the Women's Committee. Under the direction of an elderly widow, they often plan and undertake collective shellfish forages on the reef flat or meet together to make tapa cloth, which will serve as valuable exchange property for future *malaga* encounters or as a village gift at some future church dedication celebration in a distant village.

The principal leadership of the Women's Committee comes from the High Chiefs' and High Talking Chiefs' wives, who rule the organization by virtue of their husbands' positions in the village hierarchy. Their official meetings are similar to those of the *fono* in form and function, as the pattern of decision making is almost identical in this group as in that of their spouses.

A DAY OF DECISION

The first hints of midday heat were appearing as the *matai* of Fitiuta began to assemble in the village council house. The sun was high, and the low overhang of the thatched roof provided ample shade for most of the posts where the chiefs settled themselves, ready for a prolonged period of discussion and debate in the *fono faleula tau aitu*. Many of the older chiefs had already laid out their bundles of coconut fiber and had begun braiding the fibers into stout sennit. The men talked softly and lit their large "cigarettes" of locally grown tobacco rolled in dry banana leaves. There was some discussion of the topics that would be debated during what promised to be a long day. The most important decision that would have to be made concerned what would be done about reconstruction of the village guest house which was destroyed by a recent storm. The roof had been blown off, and there was damage to the center posts and to the posts that support the superstructure around its oval floor plan. The house clearly had to be rebuilt from top to bottom. Unfortunately, such an undertaking was beyond the abilities of anyone currently in the village. While there was a group of excellent carpenters residing in Fitiuta, they were presently engaged in a project in another village and would not be available for several months. Today, the *fono* must decide what to do. Should they wait until their own carpenters returned—and possibly suffer the loss of prestige for being unable to quarter guests in a house of great quality and size—or should they summon carpenters from another village and have the work done immediately? If carpenters from another village were summoned, they would have to decide where the village would get the money for a down payment, for the carpenters' food throughout the time of construction, and for the final payment upon completion of the job.

La'apui and other high-ranking village orators had already discussed the problem in a meeting known as a *taupulega*, which is an informal caucus seeking a consensus position prior to the formal *fono* discussion. This particular *taupulega* had explored the issues, but not settled them. It had assessed support for, or opposition to, the matters to be debated. Such meetings are considered important because Samoan chiefs are wary of putting their full support behind projects in which they cannot count on some aid from their fellow chiefs. Finally, the Talking Chiefs set a date to bring the matter before the *fono,* and today was the day. They had taken the responsibility of announcing the *fono* well in advance, so that each *matai* would have ample time to discuss the issues with his family and form his opinion.

When the Chiefs and Talking Chiefs arrived in the council house—and the *aumaga* had taken its position in two tight rows outside—the *to'oto'o,* La'apui, the orator who would preside over today's gathering, welcomed and thanked the council members for attending. Although the chiefs and their untitled aides were all present, and all in attendance were anxious to get to the issues, there were formalities that must take place before any debate could begin. In Fitiuta, and in every village in the Samoan chain, the kava ceremony is invariably the first act of any meeting of the village council. After the kava has been mixed and served to each *matai* in order of rank, it would be time to begin the business at hand. The kava

would, in a way, ensure that success would be achieved in the subsequent deliberation.

The kava ceremony began with La'apui selecting a kava root from the many that
had been laid out before him on the mat. The appropriate root was then handed to a
member of the *aumaga,* who cut it into pieces ceremonially referred to as "scales of
the sacred fish." The "sacred fish" alludes to the fact that kava, like many *tapu*
foods, is the exclusive property of the elite ranks. The pieces of kava were then
pounded into pulp, the consistency required for proper steeping. While the kava was
being pounded on the concave surface of a rock, other *aumaga* members washed the
multilegged wooden kava bowl and brought clusters of coconut-shell containers
filled with cool, fresh water.

While these preparations were being made, an air of reverence prevailed within
the council house. Chiefs spoke only in whispers, and no one smoked. At a location
near the back of the house, three members of the *aumaga,* positioned the great
wooden kava bowl and sat cross-legged behind it, with the *manaia* seated directly
behind the bowl. A fourth man stationed himself outside the house, ready to carry
out his function as strainer cleanser. The *manaia* would prepare the potion. The man
to the right of the *manaia* emptied a leaf full of pulverized kava root into the bowl
and filled the bowl half full of water. The man to the left of the *manaia* sat patiently,
with dignity. In time, he would serve the finished product to the assembled chiefs.
The youth about to prepare the drink wore nothing above the waist, and his *lavalava*
was turned up so that it would not extend below the knees.

The role of the *manaia* in this ceremony is a highly prescribed one, permitting
little innovation or departure from established procedure. Almost without thinking,

Kava ceremony in Manu'a in 1954.

he went through the traditional motions of steeping the kava. First, using a fibrous strainer made of hibiscus bark, he covered the kava in the bottom of the bowl. Then, with the heels of his hands, he pressed down on the strainer. Pulling his hands toward him, he collected the kava pulp and lifted the strainer high above the bowl. Then, with a motion similar to that used to grip the handle of a baseball bat, he wrung the strainer three times. He bent his hands forward so the kava would not run down his arms and waited for the last of the golden liquid to cascade into the bowl. He repeated the entire process two more times and, with a sweeping motion of the arm, threw the pulp-filled strainer backward out of the house, where the strainer cleanser skillfully snared it and removed the kava pulp with several snaps of the fibrous bark strainer. It was then thrown back into the house, and the *manaia* repeated his earlier steeping procedures. Each time the kava fell into the bowl from the wringing, the *manaia* observed its color and listened to the sound of its splashing, which would tell him when the potion was ready for drinking. When he judged that it was, the *manaia* wiped the rim of the bowl, cleansed the strainer by snapping it, dipped the strainer into the bowl one final time, and raised it so that a generous stream of kava showered down into the bowl. This gesture, known as the *sila alofi*, permits the chiefs to judge if the kava requires more water. On this occasion, observing that the kava did not need more water, La'apui began the ceremony by singing out in a high-pitched voice: *"Ua usi le alofi"* (The kava is already cleansed). In response to this announcement, the assembled chiefs clapped their hands, not as applause, but for protocol.

La'apui announced who should be served, in many cases using cup titles rather than *matai* names. Cup titles are poetic or honorific phrases that draw upon mythological allusions and occasionally mention sacred events, persons, or places. The cup title of one of Fitiuta's High Chiefs is "The Dawn of Saua which is the supreme authority." This title refers to the creation morning in the Samoan Garden of Eden. Only Chiefs of considerable status have cup titles. Talking Chiefs receive their cup after only the words *"Lau' ava"* (Your kava), and the Chiefs of secondary rank with the invitation *"Taumafa"* (Drink).

The order in which the *matai* receive their kava is of vital social importance. The Chief of highest traditional rank drinks first; then the highest ranking Talking Chief. The cup is then passed to the second ranking Chief, the second ranking Talking Chief, and so on down the elite hierarchy. In some villages, groups of chiefs drink before other groups, thereby placing somewhat less emphasis on the individual's unique social position. Regardless of the procedure, the greatest prestige is associated with being first to drink and, strangely enough, the last to drink. In Samoa, the cliché "last but not least" has been made an institution.

When the bowl was empty, La'apui announced *"Ua moto le alofi."* (The kava is finished). *"Ale le fau ma le ipu e tautau"* (The bowl will hang with the strainer and the cup). Having concluded the necessary ceremonial commitments, the council turned to the business at hand—the question of construction of the guest *fale*.

The opening speech was made by a High Chief of the Ma'opū division of the Fitiuta council. The speech was noncommittal and expository in nature and represented an attempt to clarify the issue without taking a definite stand. The other members of the council recognized the speech as a deliberate attempt to feel out public opinion on the matter.

The second speech came from a Talking Chief of low rank speaking for his High Chief, a member of the Faleifā branch of the council. The speech resembled the one preceding it, although it further clarified the issue at hand and set forth alternatives. While the speech contributed little, it represented an opportunity for a young chief to display his wisdom and oratorical skills.

Next to speak was a low ranking Talking Chief from the family of Ve'e, a High Talking Chief of the Suafanu'u group of orators. He was not speaking for the senior chief of his family, but merely expressing his own opinion. He felt that the village should wait for its own carpenters to return and not go to the expense of importing builders who would be, after all, strangers. This opinion was seconded in a speech by another lesser ranking Talking Chief of the family of the presiding officer of the *fono*.

High Chief Ale offered a contrary opinion: They must soon have a guest house or be embarrassed when *malaga* arrived and had no place to be entertained. If it meant they had to bring in carpenters, so be it. High Talking Chief Ve'e agreed with Ale, thus expressing an opinion contrary to that of the junior Talking Chief of his family. High Chief Nunu spoke in favor of importing carpenters as soon as possible, and High Chief Paopao stated his agreement. Thus, the position of the village elite was known: They wanted to build a guest house as soon as possible. Opposing them had been only two lesser ranking Talking Chiefs. La'apui, the presiding officer of the *fono*, sensed a majority opinion had been established. Hearing no further arguments in opposition, he stated that the village would contact a head carpenter from another village (probably on Tutuila) so that work could start as soon as possible. Ways of financing the enterprise would be discussed at a future meeting.

The decision was considered by the chiefs to be unanimous. If there had been further opposition to the position of Ale, Ve'e, Nunu, and Paopao, there would have been an attempt to reach a compromise resolution. In this case, however, the opposition disappeared when the majority opinion became apparent. A Samoan majority is not calculated in numerical terms, for the opinions of the higher titles carry more weight then those of the lower-ranking *matai*. Even if half-a-dozen lower-ranking chiefs opposed the opinion of the four high-ranking members, the verdict would have been the same. Every *matai*, regardless of rank, has the right to speak. If his arguments are convincing, he may very well influence how the men of high rank vote. There are no raised hands, no "aye" or "nay" responses, and no ballots. Speeches represent votes, and the presiding chief must assess the mood of the council from their oral pronouncements. Samoans believe that decisions should be reached only after a period of spirited discussion, but if that discussion is going their way, chiefs will refrain from speaking, since silence is interpreted as approval of the general point of view dominating the debate. *Fono* meetings are often long because council members believe that the more important the issue, the longer it should be deliberated.

Many decisions are reversed at a later date, providing the dissenters can marshal sufficient support, for Samoans believe decisions should never be inexorable.

Although the opinions of men of high rank carry great weight, there is a genuine attempt in all discussions to arrive at a solution that will be agreeable to all council members regardless of rank. Samoan decision makers realize that only those decisions seen as group products are effective in promoting council and village harmony and solidarity.

3 / The World of Work—1954

In Fitiuta, every man can build his own house, fashion a canoe *(paopao)* out of a breadfruit log, plant and harvest a field, and bring home an adequate meal for his household after an afternoon of reef fishing with a hook and line or a throwing net. While a great deal of knowledge of the world of work is shared among the members of Fitiuta village, there is also an easily recognizable division of labor between men and women, the young and old, and the ordinary worker and the specialist.

Tufuga in Samoa means "specialist" or "expert" and should not be confused with the use of the term in eastern or central Polynesia, where it essentially refers to a religious specialist, a priest, but also may be used for experts in other fields. In Samoa, a *tufuga* may be an expert tattooer, boat builder, house builder, or surgeon (in the case of circumcision), but the term is *not* used to designate a religious specialist or an expert fisherman.

Most work is a cooperative affair, and people toil together in family groups, in special association units such as the *aualuma,* the *aumaga,* or the Women's Committee, or in a group involving the total village. The fruits of labor are shared freely without regard to the relative input of individuals. The industrious and lazy alike enjoy adequate food, clothing, and shelter, but there is pride and prestige for those who do their share and more. For the young, untitled male, efficient and conscientious labor is a way of distinguishing himself as a promising candidate for a future family *matai* title.

Samoans are mainly subsistence agriculturalists, devoting only a fraction of their time to exploiting the resources of the sea. Most cultivable land is associated with one *matai* title or another, but there is some bush land—technically the property of the village—that is available to individuals with enough motivation and energy to clear it and keep it under cultivation.

The *matai* is said to have *pule,* or administrative control, over the family lands. He has the power to determine the uses to which family lands are put, but this control does not allow him to negotiate any transaction that will permanently alienate the land—this can only be done with the unanimous consent of the extended family. The *matai* does, however, have the authority to lend—to neighbors or family members living outside the household—fallow lands for growing short-term crops. While modern practice permits the *matai* to allocate portions of family land for personal use and profit, all family lands remain the property of the extended family. When the *matai* dies, the *pule* passes to his successor. It is not possible for a *matai* to bequeath sections of land to his offspring, even though they may have been farming the lands on an individual basis for an extended period of time. The only case in which the rights to a given section of family land may be acquired by an individual is a *tofi,* which is a gift of land made, with total family consent, to a member who has made an outstanding contribution to the group's welfare.

The pattern of land ownership and utilization has been much the same for centuries and involves the following categories: (1) village house lots, (2) plantation plots, (3) family reserve sections, and (4) village land.

Village house lots are grassy sections of village land on which the household dwellings stand. This cluster usually consists of a guest house, sleeping houses, and assorted outbuildings. Graves of deceased relatives are found here, and, in some cases, a section has been set aside for a small taro patch. There may be a few breadfruit, papaya, or coconut trees on the lot, but generally, village sites are not considered appropriate for agriculture.

Plantation plots are found along coastal areas outside the village limits and on the lower slopes of hills rising over the community site. Coastal plots are considered best for coconut groves, and slopes are favored for breadfruit trees and banana plants. Every family has a number of "plantation" plots (usually not contiguous) in various locations outside the village. Rights to plantation lands are clearly defined, and everyone is aware of the natural features (rocks, particular trees, streams) used in determining exact boundaries. Most plantation land is grown up with underbrush, and agriculturally important trees and plants are not planted in orderly rows. It is possible that one who is not familiar with South Sea island flora could walk through a plantation without realizing it is under cultivation. Some taro is found in this area, but, more frequently, the main taro patches are located higher on the slopes, in what could be called family reserve sections.

Family reserve sections are also the property of village families and have well-recognized boundaries, but they are used less intensively than the plantation plots. These sections are normally planted with more quickly maturing crops such as taro, yams, and bananas. This land is more frequently loaned to friends or neighbors for the growing of a single crop or two, but is rarely loaned on a long-term basis. Samoans find no difficulty in differentiating between land owner-ship and crop ownership. In many cases, land will belong to one family, and the crop growing on it will belong to another. In such cases, the landowners have no claim to any of the produce unless they have been specifically given that right by the cultivator. The fact that one's family owns the land does not alter the fact that to take food planted by someone using the land on loan is still theft.

Village land lies even farther up the mountain slopes than family reserve lands and is used only occasionally by villagers—and then only with express permission of the village council. An individual with energy enough to clear this densely covered bush land has claim to the land as long as he continues to cultivate it, but once his plot is taken over by underbrush, he loses claim. These lands also may be used by any of the villagers for wild pig or pigeon hunting.

Village land includes not only high bush land on the mountains, but also includes reef and sea frontages which may be used any time by individuals for angling or net fishing (unless the area has been temporarily declared to be *tapu* by the village council) by the village as a whole or by a component organization, such as the *aualuma* or *aumaga,* for large-scale fish drives *(lau).*

AGRICULTURE

Both men and women engage in agricultural work, although generally it can be said that men do the strenuous work, such as land clearing and planting, while women weed and help in harvest activities. Both men and women can be seen carrying unbelievably heavy loads of produce home from the plantations in woven coconut-leaf baskets placed on the ends of a wooden carrying pole that serves as a yoke.

Land is cleared using axes to cut down the large trees and bushes and bush knives to remove high grass, ferns, and other scrub vegetation. The plot is then left for a week or more so the leaves will drop from the trees, and the trunks and branches can more easily be cut up for burning. These sections of trees, as well as brush, are disposed of in controlled bonfires, but the land itself is never burned over.

The principal tool used in planting is the pointed hardwood digging stick, *oso,* which is two to four inches in diameter and between three and four feet long. This implement is used both to pry out rocks from the fields and to break ground by forcing the stick into the soil and pulling it backward in the direction of the planter. Bits of tuber (in the case of taro, sweet potatoes, and yams) or young plants or suckers (in the case of bananas) are placed in the hollow made by the digging stick. The earth is then packed down with bare feet or hands. Once a banana grove is flourishing, there is little need for fresh planting. When harvested, the stalk of the old plant is merely cut off close to the ground, and the young suckers growing around its base are allowed to mature into another plant. In the case of breadfruit, new trees are started from saplings found growing wild in the bush and transplanted. Papaya trees are rarely planted, but merely spring up from seeds discarded when the fruit is eaten by people working on plantation lands. Oranges and mangoes are collected from trees growing wild, but some families purposely propagate them from seeds. Coconut trees, which supply Samoans with the major share of their cash income, are planted from whole nuts that are allowed to sprout and buried approximately two feet deep.

No terracing is done and no irrigation is practiced. Ditches may be dug to retain rainwater for wet taro beds, but for most crops, the tropical rains—which occur almost daily—provide sufficient moisture. No special fertilizer is used, although *gatae* trees *(Erythrina)* are planted on agricultural land so that their fallen leaves may decay and improve the quality of the soil.

Of all the products of Samoan agriculture, the coconut is unquestionably the most useful. Besides being about the only product from which the Fitiutans derive cash income (from copra), this tree provides a host of useful products. The strong, heavy wood is used for some house components, headrests, rollers for canoes, cricket bats, and fuel. The leaves are woven into baskets, house blinds, food trays, fans, hats, floor mats, sandals, toys, and units of thatch, although sugarcane thatch is preferred. Sennit, the cord used in all house and outrigger lashings, is made from the fibers found in the outer husk. The meat, besides being dried and sold for copra, has numerous uses as a foodstuff. The raw kernel of the mature nut is often eaten as a snack by people working on the plantation or is taken along on bonito fishing expeditions as a nutriment. The meat of the green nut is especially prized when eaten raw or grated and used as a basic ingredient in a number of dishes. Grated coconut, when compressed in a strainer, produces a whitish liquid known as "coconut cream," which is also a vital part of many Samoan recipes. Coconut shells provide Samoan cooks with many of their culinary utensils. They serve as water bottles, dishes, and food scrapers. Discs of coconut shells also provide the game pieces in a competition known as *lafoga*, which is a game similar to shuffleboard. Coconut shell also is used in the manufacture of hooks for bonito fishing.

The kernel of the mature nut, when compressed in a strainer woven of hibiscus bark, produces oil *(lolo)* that Samoans use for a variety of cosmetic and medical purposes. It is used to groom the hair, oil the skin (on ceremonial occasions), and, since it is often scented with fragrant blossoms, it is used as a perfume or cologne. Swimmers oil their bodies for warmth, and *lolo* is used as a dressing for cuts and sores. It is rubbed on the chest as a remedy for coughs and taken internally to relieve stomach aches or constipation. *Lolo* is, however, *never* used in foods or as an oil in pan or deep frying.

The cool, slightly sweet tasting water found in the immature nut is a refreshing drink, and to offer a guest a freshly opened drinking nut is often an initial gesture of welcome. When the coconut matures, the liquid is replaced by a spongy white substance that serves as a basic food for pigs as well as an occasional snack for humans.

While the coconut is a more valuable all-around agricultural product, the Samoans' favorite foodstuff is taro. The starchy green tuber of this plant is prepared by boiling or baking, but it is usually eaten cold and never mashed into *poi* as is the practice in eastern Polynesia. Bananas, prepared by boiling or baking and also eaten cold, are also a preferred foodstuff. In most cases, the fruit is used while still green; it is rare when Samoans allow the fruit to ripen. While people do occasionally just peel and eat a yellow banana, fruit in this state of ripeness is usually pulverized and mixed with other ingredients in dishes such as puddings and fruit drinks.

Although less preferred than others, the food that seems to find its way to the Samoan food tray more frequently than any other is breadfruit. During the three breadfruit bearing seasons, the trees produce fruit in such abundance that much of it falls to the ground, rots, and produces a terrible stench. Breadfruit is often buried in the ground in what the people refer to as *masi* pits as insurance against possible future crop failure or other natural disaster. When these storage pits are uncovered, often many years later, the breadfruit will have decomposed into a foul-smelling mass not unlike very old cheese. It will be cut out in chunks, wrapped in leaves, and baked. It is considered a great delicacy. When prepared fresh, breadfruit is usually baked, but there are a number of recipes that use pulverized breadfruit in the form of dumplings.

Everyone in Samoan society is first and foremost an agriculturalist. Even traditional specialists, like tattooers, house builders, canoe builders, and master fishermen spend part of their time on the agricultural lands. There are no agricultural experts, although some people are recognized as being more successful than others. Agriculture is everybody's job, child and adult, male and female; the assigned tasks are merely different for those in different age and sex categories.

Many Manu'a villages attempt to establish a weekly work schedule so that there will be some coordination of effort within the community. These are formulations resulting from village council deliberation. Fitiuta has such a plan and it involves the following schedule:

> *Monday*—All untitled men and their *matai,* along with the younger and stronger women, work their own land—clearing, planting, and harvesting. Only fuel and subsistence foods may be brought back to the village. One product which must not be harvested is bananas. That is done on Tuesday. No cash crops (copra in particular) are to be harvested.
>
> *Tuesday*—Family work groups cut bananas for household use for Tuesday, Wednesday, and Thursday, and other subsistence food may be harvested. Copra can be cut with the permission of the village council.
>
> *Wednesday*—Rhinoceros beetle searching is carried on between six a.m. and noon. Plantation work, or repair work on houses, pig fences, or village paths is appropriate for the afternoon. Wednesday is often a copra-cutting day.
>
> *Thursday*—Necessary chores are carried out as designated by family *matai.* Village regulations do not specify appropriate nature of work.
>
> *Friday*—Bananas are harvested for family use for Friday, Saturday, Sunday, and Monday. Cooking for weekend needs is begun in the evening.
>
> *Saturday*—A cooking and fishing day. Little or no agriculture is carried on. Since meals are more elaborate on Sunday, fish are obtained in order to add variety to the normally vegetable diet. Because Sunday is a day of rest, food preparation is carried out on this day.

Work plans are formulated with a definite rationale in mind. They are not merely arbitrary creations of chiefs who want to wield power. Since some people have more coconut trees than others, village council regulation is a means of making sure there is some control over theft. If all families work their groves on a given day, there is less opportunity for thieves to go unobserved. On other days, thieves bringing copra back from the bush can easily be spotted, because this is not appropriate product for the day. Limiting the harvest of bananas to Tuesday and Friday is also done to control theft. Although Sunday is designated as a day of rest, and families are forbidden even to prepare food, the day does not officially start until daybreak, and many cooks rise early and carry out their food preparation activities before dawn.

FISHING

There is a commonly held fallacy that Polynesians spend a lot of time fishing or gathering shellfish. This is not true, as the work schedule above will testify. While Samoans are extremely fond of fish and prefer it to other forms of protein, they spend very little time angling, spear or net fishing, or scavenging on the reef. Undoubtedly, more time was spent in these activities in the past, but it is often easier to send someone to the bush store for a tin of sardines, tuna, or salmon than to spend hours trying to catch fresh fish.

While fishing activities consume perhaps one-tenth of the time and energy devoted to agriculture, Samoans have devised an impressive array of methods for exploiting their sea resources. Fitiutans fish singly or in groups for a variety of creatures ranging from reef worms to giant turtles and sharks. Individual methods include the use of three kinds of throwing nets for capturing a host of brilliantly colored reef fish; wooden traps for taking eel, lobsters, crayfish, and crabs; bamboo rods with lines outfitted with metal hooks and lures of stone, shell, or live bait for catching sea bass and red snapper; nooses for snaring small eels that have been lured out of their lairs in the coral by sticks with small fish secured to the end; tridents for impaling and bush knives for slashing a variety of fish and sea creatures; poisons and dynamite for killing whole schools of fish within the fringe reef; and spear guns resembling slingshots, made of wood and strips of innertubing which launch long missiles made of heavy fence wire. The latter device is used on the reef flat or by swimmers operating well offshore who tread water for hours collecting whole strings of fish, which they wear like a belt.

Three-man crews in twenty-seven-foot outrigger canoes—often well out of sight of land—fish for bonito, and danger-loving shark fishermen in rowing boats stalk their prey with heavy rope nooses that they slip over the heads of the sharks lured to the side of the boat with chunks of meat. Turtles are captured by men in boats who place large banana leaves on the water as shade for the animals. The men return later and pick up the leaves. If they are lucky, they will find at least one turtle under the leaves and be able to wrestle it into the boat. Community fish drives (lau) are carried out on the reef flat by large numbers of men and women who drag long streamers (made of coconut fronds twisted about vines) through the water and drive schools of fish toward men who wait with gill nets and spears. In some cases, a rock cairn is prepared beforehand so that the frightened fish—seeking shelter—are concentrated in one small area. Gill nets are placed around the cairn; as one man unpiles the rocks, others spear or shoot the fish with missiles launched from spear guns.

Reef scavenging is carried out almost entirely by the women. They probe the holes in the coral reef with sticks and are occasionally successful in locating small octopi, which they drag from the shelters and kill by biting or by beating the creature on a rock. Crabs, lobsters, crayfish, and squids are also objects of their search.

The Fishing Specialist   An expert fisherman in Samoa is not referred to as a *tufuga,* as are other experts, but as a *tautai.* The term is peculiar to bonito fishing, and this is the only variety of angling that recognizes specialists. Bonito fishing is done from a twenty-seven-foot outrigger canoe known as a *va'a alo.* Men sitting in the bow and the waist of the canoe are paddlers (and occasionally bailers), while the *tautai* sits in the stern. He is not only the fisherman, but also the captain of the craft. While many families in the village have bonito boats, not all families have *tautai* to command them and must contract with a specialist to operate their boat and fish for them. December is considered the best month for bonito, but the boats go out in all months except March, April, August, and September. Samoans actually recognize three bonito seasons. Bonito feed in schools, and lookouts watch for the telltale disturbances on the surface or for flocks of birds that prey upon the small fish attempting to escape the bonito. Once a school is located, the bonito boats attempt to position themselves in the center and stay there. While the paddlers maintain their position relative to the school, the *tautai* gives his full attention to his rod and line. A heavy fourteen-foot bamboo pole is put in place in a special set of blocks so that it points directly astern and forms a forty-five degree angle with the surface of the water. This pole streams a heavy section of line just long enough to allow a white clamshell lure with an unbarbed tortoise shell hook to skip along on the water. When a fish bites, the *tautai* gives a sudden jerk on the pole, pulling the bonito out of the water. Expert *tautai* can jerk the pole in such a way that the fish flies free of the hook and lands in the canoe. Since the boat may lose its position within the school at any moment, removing the hook from the mouth of each fish consumes valuable time. A very successful *tautai* may land as many as seventy or eighty fish, and it is often necessary for some of the crew to swim alongside the boat so there is room for the catch.

Bonito fishermen usually fish in fleets, and there is a great deal of ceremony connected with this activity. When the day's fishing is over, all the boats are expected to meet just outside the reef by order of a special chief who rules the fleet. At this meeting, the chief of the fleet offers up thanks to God for the success of the enterprise and then asks the *tautai* how many fish each has caught. Those who have caught many must share with those who have caught few, so that every boat arriving home will have an equal number. Then, the chief selects enough fish to feed all the crews; these fish are divided and eaten raw. The first share in each boat goes to the *tautai*. After this ceremonial meal, known as the *aleaga,* the boats come ashore individually. The families owning the boats meet the crews, divide the catch, pay the men (with fish), and return home with their newly acquired wealth. Families of crews, as well as families of boat owners, are forbidden to work while the fleet is out. They are expected to remain idle and "pray for the fishing." *Tautai* say they know when families do not observe this tradition, for the bonito constantly slip off the hook before they can be landed. Those who remain idle are collectively referred to as the "family of Tuiatua," Tuiatua being a patron spirit of fishermen.

HOUSEHOLD TASKS

Cooking The culinary arts are the special preserve of the men. Since the members of *aumaga* have always been designated as the special servants of the chiefs, ceremonial cooking has, over the years, been their responsibility and has probably established men as the proper cooks of traditional foods. While it has been claimed by some that women may not touch ceremonial foods because they menstruate and are therefore unclean, it should be pointed out that the most sacred ceremonial element, kava, is, in most villages (although not in Fitiuta), prepared almost exclusively by the *taupou,* the village ceremonial virgin.

While the older, more traditional, ideas concerning strict divisions of labor are fading away, there still seems to be a pattern of men serving as the chief preparers of food, even in the household. In Fitiuta, there is a tendency for men to cook the more traditional foods and for women to take over the preparation of the newer, foreign foods. Things that come out of a can or a box (such as cake mixes) have become the special concern of women; they are the ones who have taken to pan and deep frying and to such modern devices as kerosene or white gas pressure stoves. Women have also added to the list of feast foods, which now include dishes such as chop suey, goulash, potato salad, pie, and cake.

The most traditional method of cooking, therefore the one used almost exclusively by males, involves the earth oven, the *umu*, in which a fire is built over a pile of cooking stones placed on a level or slightly hollowed-out floor of a *fale umu* (cook house). The pit cooking methods found in places such as Tahiti or Hawaii are not practiced in Samoa. The first step in preparing the oven is stacking and igniting kindling on top of a layer of fist-sized black rocks. When the fire is burning well, other stones are placed on top, and within thirty to forty minutes, using wooden tongs, the fiery embers and bits of charcoal are removed from around the glowing stones. The stones are then spread out in a circle some three feet across, and the food (green bananas, taro, breadfruit, and, often, fish in leaf wrappings) is placed toward the center of the circle of heated stones. Wooden tongs are again used to lift stones from the outside of the ring and place them on top of the first layer of food. Then, another layer of food is added, followed by another layer of stones. Leaves are often placed between the stones and the food so that the food will not become charred. Finally, a blanketing cover of large breadfruit and banana leaves is added to hold in the heat and complete the oven preparation.

The food is left to cook in the completed oven for approximately an hour; the oven is then dismantled with the wooden tongs used to build it. The steaming food is placed in a basket woven from coconut fronds and taken into the guest or sleeping house and allowed to become cold before it will be served.

Another traditional method of food preparation uses a large, carved, wooden

Samoan umu *cooking.*

food bowl and the heated stones from the *umu*. In the preparation of the much desired *tafolo sami*, for example, sea water and coconut cream (a liquid pressed from grated young coconut meat) is placed in the bowl and brought to a boil by dropping in hot stones. Then, golf-ball sized spheres of mashed breadfruit are added to the mixture and allowed to cook until they acquire the consistency of dumplings. Arrowroot and papaya puddings are also prepared using this general cooking method.

Of all the foods cooked in the Samoan ovens, pigs have the most ceremonial importance. No feast or celebration would be complete without pork as part of the menu, and the calculation of the number of pigs cooked is a way of documenting the degree of importance of a ceremonial occasion. However, very little pork is eaten at the feast itself (partly because most of it is undercooked), but large slabs are taken home by each of the guests to be enjoyed by their families on the following day.

Pigs are strangled by laying them on their back and standing on a stick placed across their throat. The carcass is then dragged across the heated stones of the earth oven in order to singe off the hair and bristles. The abdomen is then cut open, and the internal organs are removed and wrapped in leaves to be cooked separately. The hollow abdominal cavity is filled with papaya leaves, which supposedly flavor the meat and act as a tenderizer. The whole pig is then placed on the circle of heated cooking stones, with the feet tucked under the carcass. After receiving a cover of leaves, and sometimes a layer of damp burlap bags, the pig is allowed to cook for approximately one hour. In this period of time, the animal will only partially cook—only the outside portions are done enough to eat at the feast—but the important thing is that the meat can be easily divided without falling apart. It is important that these divisions be accurately made, for there is a standardized system of distribution according to relative rank. In any ceremonial distribution, a Talking Chief representing the host family or village will make the official presentation of the pig's head to the *aumaga* (the cooks); the neck and foreleg to the Talking Chiefs; the shoulder to the Chiefs of secondary rank; the loin to the High Chief; the rump to the wives of the Chiefs and Talking Chiefs; and the wall of the abdomen to the village ceremonial maiden, the *taupou*. Similarly precise divisions are made of chicken, turtle, shark, bonito, and various other large fish.

Barkcloth   While barkcloth making is not an art that requires highly specialized talents, it is a skill that is reserved for women, and tapa cloths, called *siapo* in Samoa, figure significantly in *toga*, which, according to long-standing tradition, is the property associated with the female side of the family. It is exchanged ceremonially for *oloa*, the property of the male side.

Aside from their value merely as property to be exchanged, barkcloths have a number of practical uses. *Siapo* is often given to Talking Chiefs as a token of appreciation for duties rendered to a Chief or a village council. The cloths, which usually measure approximately four feet by six feet, are valued as ceremonial clothing and are worn by titled persons as wrap-around kilts. A more commonplace use of the cloths is made by women, who use them as wrappers when they go out of the house at night. Larger cloths are used to partition off a section of the house or to grace a chief's European-style bed as a bedspread.

Barkcloths are only one class of items in the general category of *toga,* which also includes finemats, floor mats, and, in modern times, lengths of trade cloth. Finemats are produced by plaiting strips of hibiscus bast less than one-eighth inch wide. The finished mat measures six to eight feet square and has a texture similar to that of a Panama hat. Red feathers from the Fiji parakeet *(sega)* are often used for decoration. Finemats continue to retain their position as the most valuable of the *toga* items; old finemats are carefully protected in family storage chests and passed from family to family as occasions for property exchange arise. Most owners know the history of ownership of the finemats, their age and the occasions of importance when they were exchanged. In the mid-1950s, new finemats had a monetary value of about twenty dollars, but a very old and venerable one was worth several hundred dollars. Few finemats are made these days, except by those elderly women who have the time to devote to the activity and who have sufficiently good eyesight to cope with the hundreds of slender strips of hibiscus bast that form its warp and woof.

Barkcloth, on the other hand, is produced in moderate quantities by the women of nearly every household. Village women are always careful to make sure there is a sufficient number of paper mulberry bushes under cultivation so that a ready availability of materials exists for their periodic manufacturing sessions.

While women are responsible for nearly all stages of barkcloth production, it is the men who carve the boards used in printing geometrical designs on the snow-white mulberry bast. These boards are made of hardwood, but, in earlier times, *siapo* tablets were made of pandanus leaves placed in such a manner that their midribs formed designs. Modern boards measure about one by three feet and perpetuate the same kind of geometrical designs as were found on the old leaf tablets. Thus, design motifs tend toward diagonals, squares, diamonds, and, occasionally, circles, or petal figures. While Samoans find rich floral designs appealing in trade cloth, the boards rarely follow suit. Thus, early limitations imposed by materials have produced a design tradition from which Samoans do not readily depart, although the use of carved boards offers no design restrictions.

Each household usually has only one board; this means that all cloths produced by that household will have the same printed design and, therefore, can be easily associated with its producer. Variety is introduced by way of secondary painting with darker pigments over select elements of the design; however, the uniqueness of design does not really determine barkcloth value.

The process of *siapo* manufacturing begins with the stripping of bark from a section of mulberry branch about an inch in diameter. The outer bark is separated from the inner bast, which is then soaked in water. Clam shells with carefully sharpened edges are used to remove the green coloring matter and coarser particles clinging to the bast. Next, the back of the shell is applied to the bast, making the bast smoother and wider. Several strips are bundled and beaten with a hardwood beater on a *toi*-wood log to fuse the fibers and extend the cloth to the proper width. This process can be compared to felting. When the individual sheets attain a width of about twelve inches, they are stretched on the mat to dry, with stones weighting the edges.

When dry, sections of the bast are placed on the printing board *(upeti),* and a wad of barkcloth dipped in a dye extracted from the bark of the *o'a* tree is rubbed over the fiber, the pressure bringing out the design of the tablet underneath. As sections of the mulberry fiber are imprinted, they are folded over, and another section is glued in place using a glutinous adhesive (arrowroot). The printing process is then repeated.

Weaving   The making of pandanus floor and sleeping mats is a lifelong chore for Samoan women. Girls twelve years old and sometimes younger are introduced to the various stages of mat production. They learn to collect leaves of proper width and length, process them, and plait them into mats, which form the main items of household furnishings.

The pandanus leaves *(laufala)* used for floor mats are approximately six to eight feet long and about five inches wide. The midribs are removed, and the leaves are laid in the sun four to five days to dry and bleach. Since the leaves often develop longitudinal wrinkles during this process, they are wrapped around the hand to flatten them and then wound into a large coil that the women refer to as a *māsina* (moon). The two-inch-wide leaves are then split in half, thus producing the strips that are used in the actual plaiting. Mats are woven diagonally in a simple checkerboard pattern and, in finished form, measure six feet by two feet. Floor mats are not dyed or decorated in any way.

Sleeping mats differ from floor mats in that sleeping mats have narrower wefts and, because the lead strips are steamed before plaiting, are softer. Sleeping mats are often decorated on the edges with yarn fringe, and, occasionally, a portion of the pandanus wefts is dyed and worked into designs over the whole or part of the mat.

Weaving sessions occur with some regularity in each household, but special mat-weaving bees are also organized by the Women's Committee, or just by neighbors, to produce a stockpile of mats for special purposes such as outfitting the dispensary or the pastor's *fale*. The weaving bee may, on the other hand, be organized for social purposes—women enjoy getting together for work projects, believing that the work does not seem as difficult if they can share each other's company.

THE CARPENTER'S CRAFT

Myths relate that the first Samoan house was built by Tagaloa-Lagi in his heaven on top of the highest mountain on Ta'ū island. The family of Tagaloa felt the need for such a shelter, for up to that time, people lived only in caves or in the trees. Initially, the family could not decide whether they wanted to build a house first or a boat. They decided to build the boat, but then realized the trees overhead would provide insufficient protection from the sun and rain. They finally solved this problem by deciding to build a house first, then build the boat inside the house. To this day, bonito boats are built inside houses.

First, Tagaloa-Lagi had to decide what materials would be used to build his house. He resolved that he would build it out of people; so a group of people were instructed to form a circle, thus providing posts. Others were directed to climb on the shoulders of the human posts in order to form the parts of the roof. Tagaloa-Lagi

Elderly woman weaving a floor mat.

saw that the shape was good, but that the house needed more support. The god then brought three fish from the sea, the *Falala* (filefish), the *Fe'e* (octopus), and the *Lupota* (crevalle), to serve as center posts. There was still a problem of support. A wise man of the village suggested that a shelf *(fata)* be added, as well as a ridgepole, arched gable beams, and a cross beam above the center posts. Other people climbed up and formed these parts of the house. Tagaloa-Lagi saw that the house was now strong and well shaped, but decided that the house should be made of wood rather than people. He called to all the people to come down and go out to find a kind of wood from which to make the house. Of all the varieties of wood they brought in, only the breadfruit was judged suitable—and so the first house was built of breadfruit wood, the material still preferred by carpenters. When the house was completed, Tagaloa-Lagi said he was too old to build any more houses. He chose various members of his family to carry on the housebuilding tradition, and selected Sao to be the chief carpenter of Manu'a. To this day, the *tufuga* (specialists) who are builders are known ceremonially as Sao, and, although carpenters do not have any sort of guild organization, all men in this trade are generically referred to as belonging to "the family of Sao."

The term *Sao* includes not only house builders but also boat builders. Some carpenters specialize in houses and some in boats, but there are craftsmen capable of constructing houses, canoes, bonito boats, and rowing boats *(fautasi)*. Many builders of rowing boats are young, having learned the techniques of European boat construction in school. Rowing boats are made from stock lumber, using screws and nails as fasteners. Bonito boats, on the other hand, use hand-hewn planks sewn together with sennit and caulked with breadfruit gum. Their construction usually requires the talents of older, more tradition-oriented craftsmen.

To become a carpenter, a young man will approach an established artisan and request an apprenticeship. He need not be a relative of the carpenter, although most crews are made up of kinsmen. The young man will work with the carpenter and his crew of laborers until he feels competent to branch out on his own. If he can negotiate a building project with someone, the young man will collect a group of workers, and he is in business. He has, it might be said, acquired the status of Sao.

THE SAMOAN *FALE*

Samoan houses consist of a floor of coral pebbles, a series of outer posts set in a circular or elliptical pattern, and a beehive-shaped roof supported primarily by three center posts. Houses often rest on elevated platforms, called *tia,* their height corresponding to the relative rank of the elite occupant. While *fales* are normally open on all sides, blinds *(pola)* woven from coconut fronds may be let down from under the eaves, in the manner of venetian blinds, in times of inclement weather or to provide for protection from the sun.

The roof of the house is composed of three parts—two gables *(tala)* and a center section *(itu)*. This superstructure is a maze of beams, rafters, purlins, and ribs—all held together with hundreds of sennit lashings, many of which are decorative in nature. No nails or other modern fasteners are used.

The thatch, which is put in place by the owner and his family rather than carpenters, is made up in units composed of sugarcane leaves twisted about a three-foot-long wooden rod. Like other parts of the house, the thatch units are held in place with sennit lashings.

The traditional mainstay of the carpenter's kit is the adze, armed today with a steel blade instead of the stone head of former times. Other modern elements in the housebuilding complex include Western tools such as the plane, the hand saw, and the brace and bit, but the product produced by these differs little from those built a century ago with cruder tools. Carpenters build without blueprints or plans, and measurements are made in terms of standards somewhat less than acceptable to Western carpenters. The units of measurement are the *gafa* (the span of the outstretched arms—roughly a fathom), the *vae fatafata* (the distance from the tip of the outstretched arm to the middle of the chest—half a *gafa*), the *vae luaga o le lima* (the distance from the tip of the fingers to the bend of the elbow—one-fourth of a *gafa*), and, finally, the unit most frequently used, the *aga* (the distance from the tip of the thumb to the tip of the index finger in maximum spread). A typical order from a carpenter to one of his helpers would be to bring a post twenty-six *aga* in length.

THE COMMISSION

When a *matai* wishes to have a new house constructed, he will call the members of his extended family together and request a contribution of food and sometimes money for an initial, or contract, payment to a carpenter. This food gift is known as the *fa'amoe* and is presented to a head builder *(latu)* in order to reserve his time and services as well as those of his group of workers who are collectively known as his *au tufuga*. The request may be for the construction of a *faletele* (round guest house), a *faletofā* (long sleeping house), or a variety of out-buildings, although these require less skill and are often built by the members of the family themselves.

It takes from one to three months to build a Samoan house, depending on the size and type of the dwelling, the speed of the carpenters, and whether wood from an old house can be used in the construction of the new one. Breadfruit—the wood largely used in *fale* construction—is extremely durable, and the same wood is often used in as many as three houses. Round houses are easier to build and take less time than long houses. It is easier to find the shorter lengths of wood used in round houses, and construction does not require the many splices characteristic of long-house construction. All in all, the long house is a more expensive dwelling, requiring more wood, more sennit for lashings, and more labor.

The man who contracts for the building by presenting the *fa'amoe* payment to a head carpenter is referred to as the *taufale*. When the carpenter receives the contract gift, he distributes the food and money among his workers and sets a day for the commencement of construction.

With this date in mind, the members of the *taufale's* family begin to search for suitable timber. Breadfruit is the preferred wood, but if the family lands do not contain enough of this wood of the proper size, other woods are substituted. *Asi (Syzygium inophylloides)* may be cut for houseposts and *Poumuli (Securinega* species) for house beams. If insufficient woods are available on family lands, uncultivated brush lands may be tapped, but these are often great distances away from the village. The family is not only responsible for supplying a large share of the wood, but also is responsible for providing a *tāpuaiga* to ensure the success of the work. A *tāpuaiga*—"one who prays for the work"—is a member of the family for whom the house is being built. The *tāpauiga* does not actually pray, but merely sits and serves as a conversationalist for the workers. He is not permitted to be critical of the quality of workmanship, but, by his very presence, he probably does help to eliminate inferior performance. The *tāpuaiga* is usually an old male, and the tales he tells of traditional customs and the legends he relates are often of deep interest, particularly to young carpenters.

The day the carpenters arrive to erect the main house posts is one marked by ceremony. This ceremony, known as the *fa'atuga o le fale* (the causing of the house to stand upright), is attended by the carpenters, the owner's extended family, and other chiefs who are special friends of the family. All bring food for the owner to distribute among the carpenters, as well as thirty fathoms of sennit apiece to present to the owner, since the owner's family is required to provide all the sennit used in the house lashings, which amounts to thousands of fathoms. The ceremony honors the carpenters, and there are speeches by Talking Chiefs, a presentation of kava roots to the head builder, a kava ceremony in which the chief carpenter drinks first and receives his cup in the name of Sao, and, finally, a feast in which the owner's family, the carpenters, and the village chiefs each eat in their own separate groups. When the meal is finished, the carpenters go to work. Augmenting the carpenter's crew on this first day are several other chief carpenters, who volunteer their labor to get the project well underway. Collectively, this opening-day workforce is referred to as the "family of Sao."

After the initial ceremony, all guests are given food gifts to take home, and baskets of prized morsels are taken to the village pastor, village school teachers, the village nurse, and other important personages who were unable to attend.

The building of a house is not taken lightly in Fitiuta. The owner *(taufale)* must constantly strive to keep the builders happy and well supplied with food and tobacco, and he usually has a member of the family prepare a bowl of kava for the workmen to drink at their leisure. Younger household members are assigned to keep a good supply of drinking nuts available to quench the workers' thirst and, of course, the owner must keep up his payments for the work.

Before the work begins, there is general agreement on the price and what will constitute payment. They may agree to payment in full in cash, or part of the payment may be in finemats, tapa cloths, or other traditional articles of value. In addition to this payment, the *taufale* provides all the food for the workers while on the job. The price of a house varies according to the rank and status of the chief contracting its construction. A lower-ranking chief pays the equivalent of about $500, while a chief of high status may pay twice that amount for the same size house. If the original agreement specified that payment take place over a specific period of time, and the owner fails to make the proper payments on time, the carpenters may very well abandon the project. This represents a crisis for the owner because, under these circumstances, it would be impossible to get another group of workers to finish the house. The house, therefore, would stand unfinished—a testimony to all in the village that the owner does not meet his obligations. The only way the problem can be resolved is for the owner to go to the carpenter with the promised payment plus large amounts of food, tapa cloth, finemats, and kava roots, all of which serve as a penalty for his indiscretion.

The day the building is completed is another occasion for ceremony, as well as the time final payment must be made to the artisans. The *taufale* once again summons his extended family to come with money and goods. The chief carpenters of the village, and often from other villages, are invited to once again make up the "family of Sao"; their only obligation is to bring kava roots and their tools for doing part of a day's work, which is more ceremonial than helpful. There is a kava ceremony in the morning, a period of work, and a good noon meal. In the afternoon, chiefs arrive with goods to help their friend in his final payment and to participate in one of the more prestigious ceremonies of traditional Samoan life.

The central feature of the final day's ceremony is the payment of the *uma sā*, the final portion of the carpenter's fee. The family of the owner first presents the carpenter with a selection of mats and other household articles, which are earmarked for the carpenter's wife. Theoretically, she has played an important function in the construction of the house because, in addition to her "praying" daily for the success of the work, she has helped weave units of thatch for the house, she has kept the carpenter's sleeping house clean, and she has washed the clothing of her husband's workers during the entire period of their work project. The second portion of the final payment is for the services of the head carpenter and his artisans, and it is divided among all the workers. If the payment is large, gifts will also be presented to the guest head carpenters who have gathered to celebrate the completion of the house; if the payment is modest, the guest craftsmen will carry home only baskets of food.

4 / The World of the Spirit

Christianity came to Samoa on the ship *Messenger of Peace* in the year 1830. Its apostle was an English ironmonger, John Williams, who, after establishing London Missionary Society stations in Tahiti and Rarotonga, undertook the building of a sixty-foot sailing vessel in order to expand mission operations into western Polynesia and eastern Melanesia. Sailing with Williams were Charles Barff and several Rarotongan and Tahitian missionary teachers who would pioneer the establishment of a Samoan mission. This enterprise was destined to be successful beyond expectations because of two unforeseen factors.

The first of these factors had to do with the party's accidental meeting with a Samoan chief by the name of Fauea, when their ship called at the Wesleyan mission station in Tonga. Fauea had been converted to Christianity and wanted passage to Samoa. Williams was happy to accommodate the new convert and was more than rewarded when they reached Samoa, for Fauea turned out to be a highly respected chief and an excellent ambassador in helping the missionaries gain rapport with the island people. The second factor that would work in Williams's favor became apparent upon the ship's arrival at the island of Upolu. This had to do with the recent death of the *Tamafaiga*. Williams writes that the *Tamafaiga* was a kind of prophet who was reputed to have such great *mana* that he could inflict disease, even death, upon those that did not comply with his wishes. Even chiefs of very high rank brought him tributes in the form of property or women. Feeling free to confiscate anything that struck his fancy, the *Tamafaiga* had very recently singled out the wife of a powerful chief as a sleeping companion. This chief, perhaps less awed by *Tamafaiga's mana* than other men of rank, collected a group of fellow chiefs, and, together, they slew the *Tamafaiga* as he lay with the woman. His body was dismembered, and the skull was returned to his family as evidence of the deed. This action precipitated a war of revenge that was raging when Williams arrived at Upolu.

When the Christian chief Fauea heard of the death of *Tamafaiga,* he told Williams, "The devil is dead. Our land will now embrace the new religion." He explained that if the *Tamafaiga* was still alive, he would have objected strongly to Christianity. Now, however, the people would accept the new religion and would never again select another *Tamafaiga*.

In 1830, the Samoan archipelago presented a different religious picture from the other areas where London Missionary Society enterprises had been started in the South Pacific. The inhabitants of the Samoan chain were referred to as the "godless Samoans" by Polynesian peoples in other parts of the Pacific. One early observer of the Samoan cultural scene maintained that, while other Polynesian societies worshipped deities, the Samoans worshipped their own social and political structure.

Actually, the Samoans did have one important god, Tagaloa, and they mentioned others in their mythology, but it cannot be said they worshipped a deity at all. The *marae* (religious centers with temples and altars) of eastern Polynesia were strangely absent in Samoa, and the priesthood, if it can be called that, consisted of chiefs (with the exception of the rather extraordinary *Tamafaiga*) who derived power more from their social and political status than from any supernatural sanction. These people were chiefs first and religious practitioners second. While there was an elaborate creation mythology, a weak concept of *mana,* and hints of totemic food observances, no one really worshipped any deity in special ceremonies. Villages or families had tutelary gods or goddesses who may have been called upon for aid in times of war and natural crisis, but there was no religious philosophy *per se* that provided moral direction or demanded ritual observance.

The focal point of village life was not a temple, but the *malae,* which did not serve as a holy place, but as a village square where the village council met to decide issues of morality and to determine civil and military courses of action. It was the arena of the Chief and Talking Chief rather than of the village priest.

To a large extent, therefore, when Williams landed his group of native missionaries from eastern Polynesia, there was little in the way of vested religious interests to deter them in their goal of spreading Christianity throughout the Navigator Islands. The Samoans had a concept of spirits, or ghosts, which they called *aitu,* but they did not see this concept as being incompatible with a religious philosophy that stressed a spiritual life after death. Many of their minor gods became "devils" *(tiapolo)* in the new theology. The Samoans also had little in the way of "idols" or other religious paraphernalia, so they were hard pressed to demonstrate their new-found faith, as other Polynesian peoples had, by destroying temples, altars, or pushing over tiki statues. Williams reports that the only direct action taken by the people upon conversion was the deliberate eating of totem animals or fish and one incident of deliberately "drowning" an old piece of matting that was purported to be the symbolic representation of a deity.

The London Mission experienced great success throughout the islands, but their religious teachings were not accepted without a great deal of deliberation and debate. Before a community decided to join the *lotu* (church), a village meeting was called by the chiefs in order to explore the issue. Williams reports lengthy deliberations revealing remarkable insight. Some chiefs urged embracing the foreign religion since it would provide them with an avenue through which they could acquire valuable possessions such as the ones that belonged to the white man. Williams (1832) quotes a native chief as follows:

> Only look at the English people, they have strong beautiful clothes of various colours while we have only leaves, they have noble ships while we have only canoes, they have sharp knives while we have only bamboo to cut with, they have iron axes while we have only stones, they have scissors while we use the shark's teeth, what beautiful beads they have, looking glasses and all that is valuable. I therefore think that the God who gave them all these things must be good, and that his religion must be superior to ours. If we receive this God and worship Him, He will in time give us these things as well as them.

There is even some evidence of the development of a kind of cargo cult among these native people who seemed to be so impressed with the material wealth of

Christians. Wilkes' record of his 1839 visit to Samoa carries a picture of a facsimile of a European ship being built deep in the forest. Wilkes describes the phenomenon as follows:

> An odd amusement of the natives was seen in the forest, in one of the clearings near one of the heathen villages, and at a short distance from Apia. A fine large tree had been lopt of its branches (except at the very top), for a mast; around this a framework of timber, after the model of a vessel, was constructed; all the timbers were carefully fastened together with sennit, and with the requisite curvature; from the bow a large and long piece of timber projected, and at the stern a rudder was contrived, with its tiller; but instead of its ordinary movements as with us, it was intended to act vertically, in the way to which they were accustomed in managing or steering their large canoes with an oar; vines and creepers were used for the rigging; ballast had likewise been placed in the hold.
>
> This afforded them great amusement, and showed an ingenuity in the construction of this Papalangi ship, as they called it, which had cost them much time and labour (1845:137).

It is tempting to interpret this unusual mock shipbuilding behavior as the kind of phenomenon that has been reported again and again in Melanesia, where Christian ideas have been combined with ideas concerning the affluence and technological capabilities of the West to produce strange religious ideas about the arrival of supernatural ships and planes that will discharge vast amounts of material wealth for distribution among the faithful. Worsley (1957) and others report incidents of cargo warehouses being built to resemble airplanes or facsimiles of aircraft being constructed to serve as decoys to lure the elusive cargo carriers.

Some chiefs claimed that, if all villages accepted the new religion, wars would be prevented. For some, the ceremonialism of the worship services was appealing. The Samoan love and appreciation of oratory brought a favorable response from many who enjoyed listening to the almost interminable sermons delivered by mission pastors. Even today, the role of substitute pastor is one eagerly sought by village Talking Chiefs anxious to exhibit their versatility and eloquence in the area of ceremonial and formal rhetoric. Many chiefs took a characteristic Samoan position in relation to the new religion—that acceptance or rejection be delayed until they knew more about it.

When Williams's ship *Messenger of Peace* called at Upolu, there were several cases of influenza among the passengers and crew. Immediately after its departure, an epidemic of the disease swept the Samoan island chain. Gray believes that the reaction to this crisis tells us something about the state of the indigenous religion. He writes:

> The Samoans' . . . acceptance of this plague, coinciding with the arrival of the Messenger of Peace, is evidence of the weakness of their religion, for no authoritative voice was raised to argue it was punishment for too ready acceptance of strange gods (1960:36).

Not all Samoans accepted the new religion, and, in the beginning, many villages were split over this issue. Whole communities held out and were described locally as being the "property of the devil." Antagonism between the saved and the unsaved often erupted into armed conflicts and had to be quelled by the missionaries, working in cooperation with village chiefs.

The first formal mission station was established on the island of Ta'ū in 1837 under the supervision of a Rarotongan and a Tahitian mission teacher. By 1840, the London Missionary Society characterized the Manu'a Group as one of its principal strongholds.

In order to understand many of the attitudes and activities of the modern church in Samoa, it is necessary to know something of the values held by the early missionaries who first brought Christianity to the area. All of the early English missionaries seemed to be unable to separate their religious beliefs from their cultural values. John Williams, for example, believed that sloth was the deadliest of sins and saw it as a paramount responsibility to keep the people busy, partly to keep idle hands from devil's purposes and partly to ensure sizable donations to the church. In 1825, the native London Missionary Society congregation at Raiatea, in the Society Islands, was commanded by missionaries to build a larger church, although the one they had built five years earlier was more than adequate for their needs. Such demands were communicated to the Samoans as well, and a church-building mania—still evident today—began.

Education was always tied to proselytizing. During the middle and late 1830s, missionaries devised a written form of the Samoan language, printed religious tracts—usually portions of the Bible—and began forming classes to teach the people to read and study the truths of the Christian theology. In 1839, Charles Wilkes estimated that there were approximately 10,000 literate Samoans. The reason for this was that the ability to read was a prerequisite for church membership.

The Samoans were quick to appreciate the new mythology taught by the mission teachers, the sermons, and the ceremonialism of the liturgy. Bible stories were added to the oral literature, and Talking Chiefs found new avenues for achievement—delivering sermons on Sunday mornings or serving as elders or deacons in the village church organization. In a culture where speechmaking had traditionally accompanied any formal gathering, long sermons involving even a new set of gods and heroes found compatibility with existing cultural forms. In addition to the ritual of the kava ceremony, the people now had Communion, and they immediately took to the new symbols and trappings that adorned the church interiors. Generosity in gift exchange had always been an admired quality, and Christianity provided the opportunity of acquiring additional respect from one's fellows by lavish giving to the church.

The prophets of the new religion—sometimes Europeans and sometimes native mission teachers from Tahiti or Rarotonga—quickly impressed upon their converts the "Thou shalt nots" of the religion. These prohibitions were not novel, either, for although *tapu* was not as strong a concept in Samoa as in eastern Polynesia, it was recognized. Christian *tapu* priorities seemed to rest in the area of sex and family relations, and Samoans were directed to abolish such practices as polygamy, divorce, political marriages, marriages between Christians and non-Christians, adultery, premarital sexual relations, lavish gift exchanges at marriages, the public test of virginity, and prostitution. Violation of any of the tenets of the church meant expulsion from membership. Somewhat less serious, but of great enough import to warrant special attention from missionaries, was the matter of nudity. New standards designated "full coverage" for women, and for men, who normally covered what the missionaries considered the necessary areas in their everyday dress, special church dress of shirts, ties, and, often, coats was prescribed in addition to ankle-length wrap-arounds (*lavalava*) of cotton trade cloth.

Beyond the sphere of family life, there was yet a greater list of *tapu* behavior. War and violence were forbidden except in defense of life or property. Consumption of liquor and kava and the use of tobacco was prohibited. There was to be no gambling, tattooing, bush medicine, or sorcery, and funeral feasts, which missionaries considered wasteful, were discouraged as much as possible.

In exchange for all these prohibitions, the Samoans received literacy; the idea of the dignity of work; new ceremonialism in the form of christenings, weddings, funerals, and Communion; new songs to sing with strange new harmony; and the promise of salvation in a hereafter that resembled, in some ways, the Pulotu in which they had believed for centuries. What Samoans probably expected, although the European missionaries were not aware of it, was that, ultimately, they would also acquire some of the white man's magic for getting material wealth.

In 1845, a seminary known as Malua College was established on the island of Upolu, and the London Missionary Society began training its own Samoan teachers and village pastors (*faifeau*). The graduates of this school were supposed to be paid a salary of ten pounds a year, but good intentions soon outstripped the London Missionary Society coffers, and individual villages were made responsible for the support of the local pastor. This system still prevails. Village pastors receive their salary from church donations, and, in many villages, the pastor and his family are provided with all of their food—each family taking a turn supplying, even cooking, daily sustenance.

In order to understand the nature of the Samoan religious system today, it is important to know something of the indigenous beliefs, as many of those beliefs survive in contemporary Samoan religion. Traditional understandings have also led to reinterpretations of Christian doctrines.

As has been pointed out earlier, John Williams found Samoa without idols, altars, or priests and without formal worship of the gods. Williams's (1832) journal alludes only to "mouth worship," that is, prayers offered in low muttering terms in times of crisis such as the serious illness of a relative. Other observers tell of prayers to village or household gods being said prior to family meals. Since this practice was apparently traditional, we are somewhat less impressed by missionary claims of "great success" in teaching Samoans to offer prayers of thanksgiving for their daily bread.

While the names of a large number of Polynesian gods are included in Samoan myths, their supreme god or creator was Tagaloa. Elsewhere in Polynesia, this deity had a restricted sphere of influence, being primarily the god of the sea and fishermen. The Samoans believed in a Tagaloa family who lived on ten mountains, which they referred to as *lagi* (heavens). The most important of the Tagaloas was Tagaloa Lefuli (unchangeable) who was also known by the names Tagaloa Mana (powerful) and Tagaloa Fa'atutupunu'u (creator). Within the Tagaloa pantheon were such deities as Tagaloa Pule (authority), Tagaloa Tetea (albino), Tagaloa Tula'i (standing), and Tagaloa Savalivali, the messenger of the gods.

Tagaloas were not worshipped, although the early literature implied that prayers were often offered up, or feast foods were dedicated to them. References to the ancient gods are made during various phases of the kava ceremony even today.

Tagaloa had no priests, and whatever attention was paid to the deity was from family heads or orator chiefs whose religious office was a part of their normal role as titled elite.

Tagaloa gods, collectively known as *atua,* were the highest of two classes of supernatural beings. Below the Tagaloa deities was a class of national, village, and family spirits referred to as *aitu.* Most *aitu* were believed to be spirits of dead ancestors and had only local significance for particular families or villages, but there was a large class of *aitu* that had national significance. Examples of the latter were Tuiatua, Sauma'eafe, Saveasiuleo, Nafanua, and Nifoloa. Some of these spirits are averred even today, and older villagers often can identify sacred places or objects that the spirits occupy.

Tuiatua is believed to have a special association with Fitiuta, although he may travel about the entire Samoan archipelago. This is the spirit of a human being who once lived in Fitiuta on a section of land known as Mutie. One old chief maintained that he always knew when the spirit was about by the sound of his staff on the village path. Returning bonito boats dedicate their catch to this spiritual being.

Sauma'eafe also was once a mortal who lived in the Manu'a island group. It is said that while still a girl, she was stolen by *aitu* and changed into a spirit. Like other *aitu,* she has the power to possess people and to speak through them.

Saveasi'uleo is a spirit who presides over Pulotu, the realm of Samoan afterlife. His daughter, Nafanua, a kind of Samoan Joan of Arc, left Pulotu in mythical times to lead her people against an oppressive political regime. During a great battle in which her forces were victorious, she wrapped coconut leaves about her body so the enemy would not discover her sex. After the battle, she made the vanquished wrap the trunks of coconut trees with palm fronds, thereby symbolically designating her ownership of the land and its products. The practice is still followed, in the form of a charm *(tapui)* used by landowners to protect their coconuts from theft.

Nifoloa, the long-toothed demon, was a disease- and death-dealing spirit. One disease, which carries the name of this *aitu,* is still much feared throughout Samoa. It is believed that once one has contracted Nifoloa, the slightest scratch will produce a serious infection, which, in most cases, leads to death. In one of the villages in Manu'a, the grave of a Nifoloa victim is carefully bordered with red flowers so that people will avoid it, for even coming near the grave of one of its victims is supposedly sufficient contact to contract the disease.

These spirits are classed under the term *folauga aitu* and are believed to be capable of travelling throughout the Samoan chain. They are purported to be able to take the form of birds, fish, reptiles, and human beings, or they can remain invisible if they choose. They possess men and women—often speaking through those they possess and affecting their behavior—a phenomenon that becomes a convenient rationalization for departures from prescribed Christian behavior.

There were also lesser *aitu* associated with only one village or one family. These often appeared to people in the form of birds, animals, or fish and were undoubtedly the basis for food tapus, which have been interpreted as totemic observances. Little remains of these ideas today, but there are villages and families in Samoa who have traditionally refrained from eating particular land or sea creatures, although they are not certain exactly why these restrictions exist.

The kind of *aitu* that are accepted in modern Samoa are the ghosts of ancestors—sometimes benevolent, sometimes mischievous, and sometimes malevolent. They are believed to be capable of appearing in recognizable human form, but, at night, they invariably wear white. There are places traditionally recognized as gathering spots for such ghosts, and few people care to dally while passing such haunts. Almost without exception, Samoans can relate eerie and often terrifying experiences they have had with these spirit beings. *Aitu* tales are so commonplace that even Europeans become affected. The following excerpt from an official Public Health Department report written in 1950 describes the *aitu* troubles encountered by U.S. Navy pharmacist's mates stationed on the island of Ofu, some seven miles distant from the village of Fitiuta.

> The dispensary in the Island of Ofu is the only building belonging to the Public Health Department which has been the recipient of ghostly visitations. The site of the building erected in 1923 was Toaga, Ofu, selected because it was convenient for Ofu islanders and also for those of the neighboring island of Olosega. The two are separated by only about 100 yards of water, and it is possible to wade across at low tide.
>
> At once the people of both islands protested, saying Toaga was well known to be the meeting place of the *aitu* (evil spirits) of the whole of the Manu'a Group. After the dispensary was built they refused to visit it.
>
> One night, about 1924 (according to the story) the pharmacist's mate on duty was called to the door by someone knocking. When he opened up, nobody was to be seen. The knocking was repeated nightly for a while. One night on opening the door, he beheld the apparition of a headless man. Next day, when he was gone on a call, his wife was harassed by unseen persons who, in broad daylight, tramped noisily through the house and moved the furniture about.
>
> Soon after, the pharmacist's mate and his wife, with two nurses, went to Ofu. They were offered a return ride that night in the longboat of a High Chief. The party set out on the four-mile journey to Toaga, leaving the nurses, who were to follow on foot next day. When the boat approached the haunted spot, a horrid sight met their eyes. On the moonlit beach a *siva* was in progress, and obscene, headless figures danced, led by the nurses they had just left at Ofu.
>
> While the veracity of this story has been denied, the fact remains that before long the dispensary was torn down and moved to Ofu village. The Medical Practitioner whose duties take him past Toaga says that even today, the old women caution him not to pass by at high noon or at night.
>
> Even the new dispensary at Ofu village is not free from contact with the other world, but now in an amiable form. Foisia, an elderly spirit with a long white beard, who inhabits a rocky islet just off the coast of Ofu, is said to pay the dispensary an occasional visit. Apparently the pharmacist's mates on duty there in recent years have not recognized him (1950:4).

According to common belief, most *aitu* cause trouble only if they do not approve of the activities in which their families are engaging or if they died in a distant village or country. The latter belief has led to some reticence on the part of the seriously ill to go to the hospital on Tutuila for treatment.

When *aitu* bring misfortune to families with whom they are displeased, it is usually in the form of an illness known as *ma'i aitu* (spirit sickness) and involves the symptoms of delirium, chills, sleepwalking, and sudden, aimless running about.

Village specialists in *aitu* medicine, known as *taulāsea,* treat these spirit maladies with various leaf and herb concoctions. Recoveries also may come about as a result of a family changing its ways or reversing a decision they believe may have precipitated the wrath of the spirit.

Numerous precautions are taken to protect against the possibility of contact with *aitu*. For example, a single house blind *(pola)* left up when all the rest are lowered is an invitation for a spirit to enter the *fale*. If two blinds on opposite sides of the house are left up, *aitu* will invariably walk through the house, and sleepers lying in their path will wake up feeling sore and tired, as if someone had walked over them during the night.

Even before the coming of the Christian missionaries, Samoans believed in an immortal soul *(agaga)* that left the body at the time of death and journeyed either to Pulotu or to Fafā. Pulotu was known as the "abode of the blessed." It was described to Charles Wilkes in 1839 as "an island to the westward," where people eat and drink without labor, and where they are "waited upon by beautiful women, who are always young" and "whose breasts never hang down" (1845:132). While Wilkes was told that Pulotu was an island to the westward, the more common belief was that it lay beneath the sea, just beyond the end of Savai'i, and was entered by way of two whirlpools—one for chiefs and one for the untitled.

Fafā was the Samoan Hades, a place of dread and punishment ruled over by *O le Fe'e* (octopus). Early literature tells us little concerning whom was assigned to this afterworld or why, and its location has been described merely as "westward of Savai'i." It is likely that, after the coming of the missionaries, Fafā was quickly conceptualized as being identical with Satan's domain. Although souls were permanently committed to these afterworlds, they were apparently free to return on occasion to their earthly village homes where, in ghostly form, they would appear to family members or intervene in the lives of surviving kin.

Mana and *tapu* seem strangely unimportant in Samoa when compared with eastern Polynesia. Samoans have always thought in terms of sacred *fono* (village councils) rather than sacred chiefs. Agricultural lands or fishing areas on the reef flat were (and still are) made *tapu* if there was danger of depleting resources when a large feast or celebration was anticipated, but these restrictions were imposed by the village council, not by an individual chief or by a deity. There were vague suggestions that paramount chiefs had more *mana* than regular chiefs and that chiefs of any degree had more than untitled persons, but *mana* was only an important consideration where royal titles such as the Tuimanu'a or Malietoa were concerned. The Tuimanu'a, for example, had to be served meals by his wife, who had comparable *mana,* or by other people who had been ceremonially rendered immune to the force of his inherent power. Since the title of Tuimanu'a no longer exists, and since most ideas of *mana* were associated with titles rather than persons, these concepts have now disappeared. In Western Samoa, special precautions against the force of *mana* inherent in royal titles such as Malietoa and Mata'afa have also become a thing of the past.

In regard to the concept of *tapu* and *mana,* Margaret Mead points out that

With the absence of any sort of primogeniture, no special sanctity of the first born, and the late accession to a title, men who would later hold high rank, lived and mingled with common men for the first twenty-five years of their lives.

Except for the *tapus* of the Tui Manua and the few *tapus* of other High Chiefs, those observances: respect for the garments, food, bed, cup name of the chiefs, which were motivated in other parts of Polynesia by the fear of the contagious sanctity of the chief, became mere etiquette. Even the sanctity of the Tui Manua was invaded by this iconoclastic conception. A man who was to be Tui Manua might be tattooed before he acceded to the title but not afterward. Children born to him before accession were treated as other children; children born to him afterward were *tama paia* (sacred children). Intrinsic sanctity of persons—not of the mere present incumbents of titles—was foreign to the Samoan feeling (1930:122).

Among the surviving indigenous beliefs is the concept of *tapui*. This idea, originally noted by George Turner during his period of mission service in Samoa (1842–1859), involves what Turner (1884) calls a class of "curses" used as a protection for property. He lists eight such "curses," which might better have been labelled "protective charms." They are the sea-pike, the white shark, the cross-stick, the ulcer, the tic-doloreux, the death, the rat, and the thunder *tapui*. Over a hundred years later, at least two of these—the sea-spike and the rat *tapui*—are still used to protect property.

In the case of the rat *tapui,* a small coconut-leaf basket filled with *vaofali* or *vaolima* weeds is hung on a coconut tree to protect plantation land from damage and theft. Violation results in rats damaging the clothing, tapa, or finemats of the guilty party. The sea-spike, or swordfish, *tapui* consists of half a coconut frond braided into a facsimile of a swordfish, which, like the basket, is hung on a tree to protect agricultural land. The charm threatens the thief with impalement by a swordfish on his next entrance into the sea. The same general concept is retained in several new *tapui* which have been developed in modern times. Among these are the boil *tapui,* the hernia *tapui,* the general sickness *tapui,* and the *tuia* (skin disease) *tapui.* Each of these charms threatens various forms of physical ailment if ownership rights to land or other forms of personal or family property are violated.

SAMOAN CHRISTIANITY

Samoans, like many people of the non-Western world, seem capable of compartmentalizing Christian and indigenous beliefs so that what appear to be contradictions in the two systems do not seem to cause any anxiety or conflict. Although nearly all modern Samoans identify themselves as Christians, there is still widespread knowledge of indigenous mythology and spirit lore. While all Christians subscribe to the scriptural belief in a Heaven and a Hell, there are few Samoans who would not recognize the word *Pulotu* or have some knowledge of traditional beliefs concerning its characteristics. When we asked an elderly Talking Chief (who had just spent several hours describing the Tagaloa pantheon) if he believed in the veracity of the Book of Genesis, he stated that he believed every word of it. When he was asked how he reconciled this belief with the story of how Tagaloa created the Samoan islands and its inhabitants, the Talking Chief replied that the story of creation as it appeared in the Bible explained the origin of the white man, but that he was absolutely convinced that Tagaloa was the creator of the Samoan people and the islands they inhabited.

While the majority of Samoans are enthusiastic supporters of the modern church, European observers have expressed some doubt as to the depth and quality of Samoan Christianity. An example is found in the statement of a missionary quoted by Felix Keesing:

> I am afraid that from the Christian viewpoint the missions have been rather a failure in Samoa. Instead of accepting Christianity and allowing it to remold their lives to its form, the Samoans have fitted them inside Samoan custom, making them a part of the native culture (1934:410).

Of course, the phenomenon of a particular culture "swallowing up" or reinterpreting a foreign theology so that it meets the needs of the society is not unique to the Samoan situation. Indeed, it probably has happened wherever Christianity (a Middle Eastern religion) has spread throughout the world.

Over the years, a number of denominational groups have tried their hand at molding religious beliefs and worship in Samoa. The Wesleyan Mission, which is known as *lotu toga* (The Tongan Church), was established by Peter Turner in 1835, approximately a year earlier than the arrival of the first resident European missionaries of the London Missionary Society. Wesleyan native teachers began working in the Manu'a Group as early as 1828, but their effect was minimal. More effective was the London Missionary Society convert, Hura, who was shipwrecked on Ta'ū Island sometime during the 1820s. With great zeal, and a portion of the Tahitian Bible he managed to salvage, he immediately set about instructing the people of Ta'ū in the new religion.

Roman Catholic Marist missionaries arrived in Samoa in 1845, but most of their influence was confined to Savai'i, Upolu, and Tutuila; the Manu'a Group has remained fiercely loyal to the London Missionary Society from the very beginning. They have tolerated the few Roman Catholic families who live among them and have permitted occasional visits to their villages by priests, but there are no Roman Catholic houses of worship in Manu'a, and there is no other evidence that the Roman church has had much success in terms of converts.

Mormon missionaries began working on Tutuila in 1888 and on Ta'ū Island in 1904, but found a mission field that was far from fertile. Elder Workman, the first Latter Day Saints missionary in Manu'a, after a period of three months, complained of strong opposition by the chiefs, even the Tuimanu'a. Meetings, he claimed, were broken up, and those in attendance were fined or otherwise punished. Mormon missionaries have been stationed in Fitiuta for several years, but their work has generally met with little success. Other denominations such as Nazarene, Seventh Day Adventist, Four-Square Gospel, and several Pentecostal churches have sent missionaries to American Samoa, but none of these have carried on any proselytizing in the Manu'a Group.

Church membership in American Samoa remains dominantly London Missionary Society, with approximately 77 percent of the population. Roman Catholics make up 13 percent; Mormons, 6 percent; Wesleyans, 3 percent; and all others,

1 percent. These figures are for American Samoa as a whole; while accurate statistics do not exist for the Manu'a situation, it can be estimated that this area contains a higher percentage of London Missionary Society members.

The church started by native teachers of the London Missionary Society in 1830 is known today as the Congregational Christian Church of Samoa. It has seven districts in Western Samoa and one in American Samoa. The church is self-governing and self-supporting. Although it is a member of the International Congregational Council and the World Council of Churches, there are no European or American church representatives in residence in Samoa. The church now sends its own missionaries to other island nations such as Niue, Kiribati, Tuvalu, Tokelau, and Papua New Guinea.

Although there is a church organization that encompasses the entire Samoan archipelago, each individual village church enjoys a great deal of autonomy. Native pastors *(faifeau)* serve and are supported by the community. While these men cannot be titled, they hold a status equal to, and sometimes greater than, chiefs and are normally in attendance whenever the village council convenes. Their views carry great weight, and their advice and leadership is highly valued.

The Fitiuta church organization consists of a group of elders, deacons, and the *Ekalesia* (ecclesiastical membership). Elders and deacons are invariably titled individuals, and such offices are important to personal and family prestige. As in many Protestant church organizations, elders are the decision-makers and supervisors of spiritual affairs, and the deacons are the keepers of the church treasury and administrators of church property.

The *Ekalesia* is the group that holds the preferred membership status in the church. These are the people who have undergone a period of instruction called the *Sailiili* and consequently observe a specific set of beliefs and code of behavior. In addition to the requirement of attending church regularly, they are forbidden to drink alcoholic beverages, attend movies, or participate in European-style social dancing. Their lives must be beyond reproach morally, and they are expected to make sizable donations to the church on a regular basis. Members of the *Ekalesia* (which include the elders and deacons) are the only people permitted to partake in Communion when it is served on the first Sunday of every month. Any violation of the behavioral code of the *Ekalesia* results in the offender being removed from membership. Reinstatement comes only after an additional period of instruction and with the permission of the entire membership.

Samoan churches are European in architectural design, with cement or limestone walls, corrugated iron roofs, and elaborate folk-art interiors involving wood inlay designs and stained-glass windows. Altars are often draped with appliqued or embroidered hangings and decorated with artificial flower arrangements and religious pictures of conservative European style. Most churches have pews, a Communion table (used mostly for collection of the church offering), a pulpit, and an altar. Ventilation is poor, and most sanctuaries are uncomfortable, as the architecture is ill-suited to the tropical climate (one of the more vital items of church-going equipment is a coconut-leaf fan). Early missionary accounts speak of construction of early churches that replicated the Samoan *fale,* but evidently, as the new religion grew in favor, the prestige of European-style churches also increased;

soon the English country church design, often with a touch of Spanish influence, became standard in every Samoan village.

SUNDAY IN SAMOA

Sunday begins early in Fitiuta—about 5 A.M.—with the ringing of the church bell. Even at this early hour, there is already activity in the village. Columns of smoke ascend from the cook houses of most household clusters of buildings; since Sabbath cooking must be completed before daybreak, a significant number of young men and women have been preparing the day's food for at least an hour. For others, the bells represent ample announcement of the first service of the day, which takes place at six o'clock. There will be sufficient time to open the large wooden trunks that hold Sunday clothing, select the proper attire, press out the wrinkles with a charcoal-heated iron, consume a piece of cold cooked taro or a cooked green banana, and still be punctual for the early church service. Attendance at this service is light—the majority of worshippers preferring the eight o'clock hour. In the thirty-to-forty-minute interval between services, the village choir congregates in the *fale* of one of its members and runs through a last-minute rehearsal of the morning choral selections; their main rehearsal takes place earlier in the week. In most of the *fales* in the village, the church-goers wait until the last minute before putting on their Sunday best so that it will not become wrinkled in the humid heat of the morning. Young women carefully dress their hair in braids and pin on their low-crowned, wide-brimmed coconut hats. Everyone carries a coconut-frond basket just the right size to hold a Bible and a hymnal. The chiefs wear white *lavalavas,* shirts and cotton coats, and solid black ties. Untitled men often leave the coat at home and occasionally sport a flowered or striped tie. Unmarried women wear a knee-length cotton frock (usually white), but married women find it proper to wear a *puletasi*—a two-tiered costume consisting of a ankle-length, white *lavalava* overlaid with a thigh-length, white cotton dress.

At approximately 7:45 A.M., the church bell rings again, and the church procession begins. Whole families emerge from their household dwellings and walk leisurely and single file along the narrow concrete pathway that cuts through the heart of the village. As the families enter the church, the members disperse, with the women filling in the right side of the sanctuary, the men the left, and the children taking seats in the middle. On the left and right sides, at the front, are special pews for the more important chiefs and their wives; directly in front of the pulpit is a section reserved for the choir and a small pump organ which is often played by the choir director, who ingeniously seems to be able to conduct and play simultaneously.

Two elderly men equipped with canes station themselves at the back of the children's section; they are there to maintain order among the youngsters prone to forget proper church decorum. Whispers or nodding heads are often responded to with a gentle, but unmistakable, rap on the top of the cranium dispensed by one of the elderly monitors.

The service begins with a hymn and a prayer followed by a responsive reading from the Samoan Bible. A hymn—more in the form of an anthem—follows this reading; this is the choir's opportunity to perform. The words are often direct translations of traditional Protestant hymns, but the melodies are frequently different. Harmonically, Samoan church music differs little from Western religious music, but the tonal quality and musical style are uniquely Polynesian. The women sing in high, nasal voices, while the men carry the lower part with full, deep tones. The female voices carry the melody, and the male voices provide a moving bass line which complements the lead voices, yet provides a contrapuntal contrast. Few Samoans read music, and hymnals do not include musical notation. Most melodies are traditional and familiar to everyone. The ability to sing in three-part harmony seems to come easily to Samoans, although the indigenous music does not feature harmony. Traditional chants of various kinds were characterized by a narrow range in melody, carefully enunciated texts, and well-coordinated unison rendition.

Samoan church music, highly influenced by European modes in its structure, differs greatly in performance in that it tends to be joyful, rhythmic, and loud. More likely than not, it resembles the vocal music used to accompany the Samoan dance, the *siva*.

The morning sermon is probably the highlight of the service. Rich in parables and Old Testament biblical history, the sermon stresses proper behavior, piety, and the wages of sin. In a society that has developed oratory as its highest art, the minister is valued for his rhetorical skill and style and for the content of his message. Sermons are normally lengthy and are concluded with a prayer. When the final hymn of the morning draws to a close and the worshippers close their hymnals, the deacons station themselves at a long table in front of the communion rail and begin reading the church roll. When each family name is called, a representative of that family comes forward and lays its morning offering on the table. The amount is observed by a deacon, recorded in a book, and announced to the congregation. In a status-oriented society such as Samoa, where generosity is praised, Sunday morning offerings are substantial.

After the service, families return home and quickly change into less-elegant attire and prepare to eat their morning meal, which was cooked well before daybreak. The *matai* of each family does not share this meal, for he and the other *matai* of the village gather in the *fale* of one of their number, eat together, and discuss things—both trivial and profound—well into the afternoon.

Sundays are for rest and relaxation. The women of the village take long strolls with neighbors, children go down to the beach and play in the surf, and elders take long naps or sit quietly carrying on lengthy conversations with friends or family members. No work is done, and the village remains quiet and lethargic.

The church bell tolls again at four o'clock, announcing the afternoon service. In form, it is much like the service held in the morning, but it tends to attract fewer worshippers, and those who appear are more informally dressed. Men arrive in shirt sleeves, and women wear simple, flowered dresses. There is usually a noticeable absence of teenage children at this service, for they have their own two hours later.

Evening is again a time for strolling and conversation, for a cool bath at the village bathing pool, and an early retirement. For most, the new work week will begin before dawn, with a journey to the plantations high on the slope and a morning of cultivation before the onset of noonday heat.

On the second Sunday in October, Samoans celebrate White Sunday—a holiday of special significance in both American and Western Samoa. On this day, the children of Samoa take center stage in church and at home, a reversal of the usual focus in this adult-centered society. Wearing new white clothes, all of the children give recitations of Bible verses and perform other roles during the morning church service. After church, families go home to eat a festive meal at which the children are served by the adults and eat first, rather than waiting for the adults to finish. Gifts are also presented to each child. Later in the day, there may be a religious play featuring the youngsters.

THE CHURCH DEDICATION

Samoans have often been accused of having a church-building obsession. An object of village pride in every community, the church is a symbol of religious commitment. It is often claimed that the completion of one church is the signal to start planning a newer and bigger one. Originally encouraged by John Wilkes to ensure proper industry among new converts, church building has become a major prestige activity. Without doubt, a church dedication is the most gala event that occurs in modern Samoa, with the possible exception of the annual government-sponsored Flag Day celebrations in American Samoa.

For Fitiuta, the church dedication at Fagasā village on Tutuila had special meaning. The Fagasā pastor was a member of a Fitiuta family, therefore, Fitiuta was expected to play a major role in the celebration. The Fagasā church was twenty-five years old and had been declared inadequate for its growing congregation. Construction had been underway on a new, much larger church for nearly a year. The date for the dedication of the new facility had been set well in advance, for elaborate plans had to be made to ensure a proper celebration. In every village in Samoa, congregations were collecting money so that a dedication donation might be made in the name of their village.

A week prior to the event, the interisland vessel began making daily trips to Western Samoa to transport the guests, and two trips were made to Manu'a. The village of Fitiuta was sending a delegation of one hundred people, which was mostly made up of a choir that would perform a specially composed anthem of commemoration. The group brought live pigs, hundreds of pounds of salt beef in kegs, and other foods; their spokesman, a High Talking Chief, carried an envelope containing Fitiuta's dedication contribution of $1,000. The transportation costs of the group amounted to an additional $800.

Three other villages also sent large choirs, each with its own original dedication song. All in all, over 2,000 guests were in attendance when the first day of the two-day dedication event dawned. The morning hours were occupied with a great kava ceremony. While chiefs of the many villages partook of the ceremonial drink and listened to speeches of welcome and speeches of eulogy for guests and church builders alike, the chiefs' wives sought the shade of Fagasā *fales,* where they sat for

People arriving for church dedication.

hours chatting with friends and relatives whom they had not seen for some time. People continued to arrive throughout the entire day, and the song contest, originally planned to begin at 2 p.m., did not get underway until nearly 4:30.

The four competing choirs, numbering nearly one hundred singers each, seated themselves on the grass of the village *malae*. Each had its own set of uniforms especially made for the occasion. Women wore print dresses, and men were attired in matching *lavalavas* and cotton shirts.

Songs were lengthy and narrative in form. They told the story of the history of the building project—who had helped raise the money, who the carpenters were, and how the new church would enhance the work of God's kingdom. After each song, the group's contribution to the expense of the new church was presented, and each donation was accompanied by a lengthy formal oration.

After all the choirs performed their special songs, the mood of the celebration changed. The choral groups now sang songs to accompany dance performances of their village *taupou* and *manaia*. Since it is generally accepted that church dedications are supposed to be joyous occasions, the guests encouraged the dancers and singers to perform one lively selection after another. Finally, a prominent Fagasā church official came forward, and the dancing stopped. He announced that Fitiuta had won the song contest. It was an honor the people of Fitiuta would long cherish and allude to in future dedication anthems.

In the evening of the first day, the women of the host village presented a *konsieti*, a classic play with music, featuring elaborate costumes, a large cast, and a plot from Roman mythology. After the play, there was group dancing and singing, and it was nearly dawn before all the Coleman lanterns were turned down, and the

Choirs gathered for church dedication.

village guests settled for the night on the sleeping mats provided by their hosts.

The actual church dedication ceremony took place at 11 A.M. of the second day when, after a long series of congratulatory speeches by *faifeau* from various villages, the Chief Justice of the Government of American Samoa led a procession to the new church and unlocked the doors. Returning to the *malae,* the church officials read the long list of contributors of money gifts, village by village, person by person. When the roll had been read, Fitiuta had won still another honor: They had made the largest total donation of any village.

The gala two-day celebration ended with a performance of the combined choirs, their volume literally vibrating the structure of the newly built church. Then it was over, and families began to leave the village on foot, by bus, and by automobile on the road that led over the mountain to Pago Pago. A $28,000 church had been dedicated in a magnificent ceremony that brought donations of $18,000 plus lots of love and good will. The Fagasā church was the newest and the grandest on the island of Tutuila, but probably not for long.

THE CONTEMPORARY CHURCH

Religious belief and practice remains essentially the same in American Samoa, with minor exceptions. A new Protestant denomination appears on the scene occasionally, but the Congregational Christian Church of Samoa is still the primary affiliation of most Samoans. One large and relatively new church visited by the authors in 1988 included such features as wall-to-wall carpeting and cushioned pews; the choir of about fifty people was obviously well rehearsed and gave a professional-quality performance, with none of the nasal tones characteristic of more traditional choral singing in Samoa.

The celebration of White Sunday has become increasingly expensive, with merchants on Tutuila stocking an array of children's white clothing—ranging in price from a few dollars to as much as $80—especially for this religious holiday. The White Sunday meal probably compares with Thanksgiving in the United States; the big food item in Samoa, however, is ice cream. One newspaper report indicated that the local producer of ice cream anticipated selling 18,000 gallons for this one day.

Church dedications are still significant events in Samoan life, occasions for travel by choirs, family members, and friends from other communities. With greater numbers of Samoans living in the United States, their church-building activities have merely enlarged the realm of travel for dedication ceremonies, and a church choir from San Francisco or Seattle may travel to Hawaii or Samoa for a series of performances, even in the absence of a major ceremonial event.

5 / The Day-to-Day World— Life Cycle, 1954

Children are born in the village dispensary with the assistance of a Samoan graduate nurse. The village of Ta'ū, some five miles away, has a small hospital with a Samoan medical practitioner in residence, so many mothers choose to walk the mountainous trail to that village and stay with relatives for several days until their labor begins. Most expectant mothers prefer the security and familiarity of their own village, however, and settle for the services of the well-trained and experienced nurse. Not so many years ago, all births took place in the household *fale* with a midwife in attendance. Mead describes the traditional procedure as follows:

> The birth takes place upon a piece of bark cloth specially prepared for the occasion. Three positions of delivery are recognized: kneeling, lying on the back, and sitting squatting on one of the logs (about two feet long and seven inches in diameter) which stand between the house posts. The last is the preferred position. The birth of the first child is always regarded as the most difficult and the birth of a girl believed to produce harder labor than the birth of a boy (1930:37).

After the mother had delivered, the midwife cut the umbilical cord and cleansed the head of the child by sucking its eyes and nose and licking its face. A child who responded to this treatment with lusty wails was pronounced strong and healthy. The newborn was then totally bathed in warm water, wrapped in white barkcloth, and laid on its own pile of tiny sleeping mats. The mother then was massaged and bathed.

When the well-being of the mother and child were assured, thoughts turned to determining the child's future by proper disposition of the umbilical cord. In this matter, modern thinking differs little from that of midwife days. To bury a piece of the cord near the oven guarantees that a boy will mature into a good cook and an industrious plantation worker. More often, the cord is buried near the church in the belief that such action will result in the child (of either sex) growing into a pious and intelligent adult. The main concern is that the cord be safeguarded lest a rat get it and cause the child to grow up dull-witted and troublesome. These ideas seem to be related to earlier, traditional notions concerning the severing of the cord. Earlier generations believed that an umbilical cord cut on a war club would ultimately produce a brave warrior, while one cut on a *siapo* board (*upeti*) would ensure that a girl would grow into an adult with ability and industry in women's activities.

Children are named by the parents soon after birth, often receiving familiar names such as *Lupe* (pigeon), *Pepe* (butterfly), *Matagi* (wind), *Galu* (wave), or such compound names as *Fasialofa* (go with love), *Sililavalesauilefalema'i* (it's better to come to the hospital), or *Asoluafuluvaluomē* (twenty-eighth day of May). Biblical names are popular, the most common being *Ioane* (John), *Paulo* (Paul), and *Iosefa* (Joseph). Sharing this popularity are names derived from events occurring at the time of the birth. The name *Sanoma*, for example, was given one male child because a ship of that name arrived in Pago Pago on his birthday. European influence is becoming apparent in the naming process, as more and more parents select names such as *Telefone* (telephone), *Kerosine* (Kerosene), and *Kalinekesi* (Kleenex). The names of ancestors are sometimes given in order to keep their memory alive, but the practice of naming a son after his father is not allowed. Once selected, names are recorded with the village pastor, the "mayor" *(pulenu'u)*, and the medical personnel at the dispensary.

The birth of a child is an occasion for a feast, particularly if the child is born into a family of high rank. First births are always celebrated, but there is an increasing tendency to celebrate all births. These feasts are accompanied by an exchange of property between families of the child's father and mother, the father's family bringing a category of gifts known as *oloa* and the mother's reciprocating with *toga*. *Toga* goods consist of baby sleeping mats, bits of cloth in which to wrap the baby, and, in families of high rank, even finemats. Food and money are the offerings of the father's people. The relatives bring their gifts, give them, and return with gifts of equal value—the parents of the child do not profit at all, and the child profits only slightly. The important thing is that an occasion of note has been celebrated with an exchange of property, formal speeches, and a generous sharing of food.

For the first four or five months, the child is fed only mother's milk and is nursed whenever it cries. The child is constantly attended to, rocked to sleep at night, and showered with love and affection. About the fourth month, solid food —in the form of mashed papaya, taro, bananas, or soft bits of fish—is introduced, but children are not completely weaned until they are approximately a year old. Even then, weaning is not traumatic and, in some cases, nursing may continue for as long as twenty-two months. The weaning experience usually involves separating the child from the mother for three or four days. During this time, the child is placed in the care of its father or removed from the household altogether and placed with a grandmother or other relative. When the child desires liquid, it is given a cup of water; when it returns to its mother, if there is still a yearning for the breast, it is sometimes given—but with the nipple smeared with lime juice.

A mother with a newborn is not expected to engage in agricultural activities for a period of four to six months; then, she resumes work with the rest of the family on their plantation land, and the child is left with a sibling or elderly member of the household. This results in irregular feeding since the mother is often unavailable to nurse the child for intervals of from six to eight hours. The problem of irregular and inadequate feeding becomes even more acute after weaning, since it is a common practice to turn the care of infants over to older siblings who are often only five or six years the baby's senior. If the older child is not attentive to the amount of nourishment the baby is getting, serious health problems can result. Malnutrition, combined with other complications (usually of a respiratory nature), takes a heavy toll of children during the early months of their second year of life.

There is a great tendency to overdress small children in dresses, bonnets, blankets, even long stockings; this promotes excessive perspiration and encourages rashes and other skin diseases. As children grow older, they are dressed in less and less clothing, and it is not unusual for healthy robust youngsters to go completely naked from the age of about four months to two years. A tiny shirt may be their only concession to modesty.

Small children are bathed daily. The child is usually held in a standing position while the mother dumps a coffee can full of water over its head and liberally lathers the child from head to toe. Finally, a cascade of fresh, cold water from the can removes the soap from the inevitably screaming child. Mothers have a unique method of removing soap and water from the baby's eyes: They place their lips against the eye socket and blow, thereby forcing water and suds out of the corner of the eye. Following the bath, the child is dried with a towel and rubbed with coconut oil.

Toilet training begins at age one. Prior to this time, the mother merely wipes up the mat after each elimination, for Samoan babies wear no diapers. When the mother decides that training should start, she merely sets the child outside the house whenever it begins to urinate or defecate. Children who fail to learn from this gentle persuasion are often spanked, because parents believe that their failures result from laziness rather than lack of knowledge or training. As most adults eliminate in the bush themselves, toilet training is mostly a matter of teaching the child to respect the inside of the house.

Most children learn to walk at about one year of age, but slow walkers are given special treatment. Mothers take them to the beach, where they are buried hip deep in the sand. The child is allowed to stand for several minutes with the support of the sand and then is violently jerked out. This is believed to make a child walk within a week or two, but if it fails, the mother takes the child out on the reef flat and swings it back and forth several times, allowing its buttocks and legs to strike the surface of the water.

Samoan tots begin to talk at about the age of eighteen months. Many parents encourage them by saying words for the youngsters to repeat, these words often being *ai* (eat), *inu* (drink), or *moe* (sleep). Such words are taught early, with the idea that it will be an aid in understanding the child's physical needs. Personal names of parents and siblings are learned early, but kinship terms generally are not mastered until late childhood.

As soon as children learn to walk, they are taught that it is bad manners to walk or stand up inside the house, because a child's head is never supposed to be higher than the head of a seated adult. It is common to see a mother push a child down time after time with the admonition, "*Nofo* " ("Sit "). Toddlers are also trained not to go near the sleeping mats of their parents, not to talk, and, above all, not to cry when guests are in the house.

Attempts at early training are often accompanied by severe punishment. Erring children are sometimes slapped on the buttocks, legs, or face or switched on the legs or buttocks with brooms made of coconut-leaf midribs, or even with leather belts. Mothers usually administer the punishment, although it is often the father who administers belt-whippings to older children. Threats that *aitu* (ghosts) "will get you" are sometimes made, but the common deterrent to improper behavior is refusing to allow children to go out and play in the moonlight when all the other children are doing so. While youngsters may be reprimanded for making too much noise or for standing in the house, little is said about the very common practice of throwing stones or bullying smaller youngsters. Parents often resort to stone throwing themselves; a crying baby may receive a shower of small pebbles accompanied by shouts of *"Soia "* ("Stop it "), *"Uma "* ("Enough "), or *"Filemū "* ("Peace ").

Until the age of three, children retire after the evening meal and sleep with their mothers. At age three, they are given a mat of their own and must roll up their mat and fold their own sheets every morning. At this age, children retire when their parents do—between nine and eleven o'clock. Parents are not rigid about their offspring's sleeping schedules, and very small children are often allowed to stay up quite late when guests are present or when the family is attending a feast or a Samoan dance.

Until the age of three or four, the care and training of Samoan children is much the same for both sexes. At this time, girls begin to assume certain responsibilities consistent with the female sex role, such as aiding in the feeding of younger children (although not providing exclusive care), running errands, and other household chores that are within their physical capacity. Boys of the same age are given much more freedom. They rarely have to concern themselves with smaller children, but they may be called upon to feed chickens, fetch fresh water, or collect coral pebbles from the beach for *fale* flooring.

By the time a child reaches age seven or eight, there are few chores to which they have not been exposed—light agricultural work, fishing or reef scavenging, cooking, or the processing of mat-making materials. A major responsibility for Fitiuta children is yard work. They pick up leaves that have fallen from the trees overnight, weed, and cut grass with bush knives. For a time, many of these duties are shared by both sexes, although boys continue to have much more free time for play than girls, because they have less responsibility for caring for younger family members.

Samoan culture is characterized by a smooth and gradual coming-of-age process through which children are given increasing responsibilities and more difficult physical tasks as they are capable of handling them. Being "too young" is never given as a reason for not allowing a child to undertake a given task. Whether it is the handling of dangerous tools, the carrying of extremely heavy loads of produce, or the maneuvering of outriggers in heavy surf, if children think they can handle the activity, parents do not object.

Children also find time to play. They play cricket, tag, marbles, and a Samoan variety of hopscotch. They swim, pelt each other with Tahitian chestnuts, fashion toy sailboats out of sardine cans and coconut leaves, and make pull-toys out of immature coconuts connected with a stick (like a barbell). Playing with dolls, however, is not a Samoan pastime. Perhaps the leisure-time activity most enjoyed is group singing and dancing. On moonlit nights (the best time for play), little clusters of children can be found on the village green *(malae)* singing and clapping in unison while one after another gets up to perform his or her version of the *siva*. When adults hold dances in connection with *malaga* entertainments, the main spectators

Children's play group, Manu'a 1954.

are always children, who stand outside the house and offer their imitations of what they observe going on inside.

Work and play patterns are, of course, greatly altered when school is in session. Children enter school later than American youngsters (at about age seven). The Fitiuta schoolhouse in the very center of the village is likewise the very center of children's lives from grades one through nine. School hours monopolize a great deal of the children's time, which might otherwise be devoted to learning and performing traditional work activities. Consequently, family patterns of labor have changed during the last generation, and adults are now required to do many more chores than was necessary before the advent of public education. Child care has been shifted more to the elderly during school hours, and now, everyone must share the petty tasks once assigned to smaller children. While most families are convinced of the value of formal schooling, there are still many who keep children home from school when they are needed for particular work projects. This attitude is rapidly passing. There is a tendency, however, to regard education as being more important for boys than for girls.

In spite of numerous Western influences in Samoan life, some traditional customs related to childhood persist. The matter of circumcision is a case in point. This operation is an important milestone in a boy's life, an ordeal in which voluntary submission proves a boy's bravery and prepares him for adult life. Women often look with disdain upon an uncircumcised lover.

At about age nine or ten, a boy makes his own decision that it is time to submit to this operation. He arranges with a friend *(soa)* to accompany him, and they seek out a native specialist *(tufuga)*. Some go to a Samoan medical practitioner, but since none resides in Fitiuta, the traditional specialist is usually patronized. The operation is relatively simple and involves a minimum of pain. A pointed stick or piece of coconut shell is inserted under the foreskin and a single longitudinal cut is made with a straight razor, bamboo knife, or a piece of glass. After this incision has been made, the boy bathes in the sea and his penis is dressed with the leaf of the *fanua mamala (Homalanthus nutans)* tree and bound with gauze bandages (formerly with white barkcloth). When the cut heals, the foreskin rolls back and the penis appears as if the foreskin has been removed; therefore, this operation is not technically circumcision. Both the boy and his *soa* undergo the operation at the same time, and, in some cases, a whole group of boys will undergo the ordeal together. The *tufuga* is given gifts of food (cooked chicken, taro, breadfruit, and *palusami*) and barkcloth for his services.

The next important milestone in a young man's life is his entrance into the society of untitled men, the *aumaga*. This event used to occur at about age fourteen or fifteen (when a young man had completed nine grades of schooling), but today it occurs somewhat later because many young people now go to Tutuila for a high school education. First, the young man must ask his *matai* to sponsor his request for membership. If the *matai* agrees, he will go with the youth to the village council. While the young man sits outside the house, his *matai* presents the assembled chiefs with a kava root in the boy's name, thereby asking the council's official sanction in support of the boy's request. When the council accepts the kava root, they are in effect giving the young man their blessing. Now, he must prepare for his actual entrance into the *aumaga*. At the next meeting of this society of untitled men, the initiate goes alone to their meeting place with a gift of food known as *momoli*. This usually consists of a six-pound tin of corned beef plus other foods such as taro, breadfruit, and *palusami* (coconut cream and taro leaves). After placing his food items in the middle of the floor, the initiate takes a seat in the back of the house and waits patiently until the matter of his induction into the group is reached on the society's agenda. Finally, a speech of welcome is delivered by a *tamato'oto'o* (a Talking Chief's son who serves as he group's orator). The initiate replies to this speech, then asks the group to share his food gift. A Talking Chief's son distributes the food, and they all eat together, thus recognizing the novice as a permanent part of the group. The new member then takes a seat at a housepost corresponding to the rank of his family head. It will be in the front of the house if his *matai* is a Talking Chief and in the ends of the house if his family head is a Chief.

For teen-aged girls, the most important associational group is the *aualuma*. When this group functioned in the traditional manner, it consisted of a group of unmarried women whose main function was to serve as a court to a ceremonial village princess, the *taupou*. They slept with her in a house called the *fale aualuma*, groomed her, served as her constant companions, and protected her virtue, for *taupou* were required to remain virgins. Membership in the *aualuma* is still a very important aspect of every girl's life, but the group no longer lives together and no

Manu'a teenager 1954.

longer serves the *taupou*. *Taupou* are now appointed to serve on ceremonial occasions and are sometimes married women with children. In some villages, the *aualuma* even includes wives of untitled men; in Fitiuta, however, it is composed of unmarried young women (the youngest being about fifteen) and widows of all ages. The group comes together only on special occasions. The village may call upon the group to entertain a *malaga* with group dancing, or they may be asked to raise money by weaving mats for some civic or church project. On such occasions, the *taupou* is their official leader.

While both the *aumaga* and the *aualuma* engage in a great deal of community service, their members also have a good time. The societies have a social function much like college fraternities and sororities.

Fellow *aumaga* members often play an important role in a young man's courtship activities. Every young man needs an intermediary *(fa'asoa)* to play a "John Alden" role for him in approaching the young woman of his choice and in arranging a rendezvous. Young women also have intermediaries, but they are less needed since young men are supposed to make the initial advances. Intermediaries for both men and women carry messages, arrange meeting places, give warning if the woman's brother is coming, settle lover's quarrels, and, in the case of a very serious relationship, propose marriage.

Since early voyagers discovered a sailor's paradise among the amorous maidens of Tahiti and Hawaii, all Polynesia has had the reputation of being a place of liberal sexual codes that even Victorian missionaries could not reverse. Margaret Mead's description of Samoan premarital sexuality as involving "free and easy experimentation" may to some extent be true, but her observation that "the concept of celibacy is absolutely meaningless to them" (1928:98) is questionable. There are prohibitions against premarital sexual activity, and some of these undoubtedly predate the coming of the missionary. Village ceremonial maidens *(taupou)* have always been required to remain virgins; when they were married, the wedding rite involved a defloration ceremony to provide public proof of their virginity. Similar restrictions are believed to have applied to other young women in families of high rank who were not *taupou*. Although against government law, a defloration ceremony was performed on a young woman of an elite family two years prior to the author's first visit to Manu'a. Moreover, the Fitiuta village council imposes heavy fines on any family in which a member gives birth to a child out of wedlock. Mothers are concerned about their daughter's sexual behavior, and there is much less freedom than has been sometimes described. If Samoa is the land of such sexual freedom, one is hard pressed to explain the necessity of the well-known *moetotolo* phenomenon. *Moetotolo* may be translated "sleep crawling," and is recognized as a form of sexual aggression that would seem to be unnecessary if sexual opportunities were as easy to come by as some observers claim. Considering that Samoans have little or no knowledge of contraceptives and that the illegitimate birth rate is not particularly high, one would be inclined to conclude that premarital sexual experimentation is probably no greater than that among American young people.

Samoan standards of beauty differ somewhat from those in the United States. A Samoan male finds a young woman attractive if she has a plump (but not fat) figure with firm, but not necessarily large, breasts; large, but not muscular legs; long, wavy hair; clear, dark eyes with long lashes; full lips; good teeth; olive skin; and graceful, well-proportioned hands.

Men marry at about age twenty-five, and women marry at about age twenty. Samoan men and women marry because they need each other economically and socially, although there is a tradition of romantic love, as may be seen in numerous myths and legends. Sina and Tigilao were romantic characters, indeed; these two, and often others, are depicted in mythology as dying for love. There appears to be a strong emotional tie between lovers and between husbands and wives, but there is much less emphasis on personal happiness as a reason for marriage than is to be found in Western cultures. While Samoan young people choose their own mates, marriage is definitely more of a family affair than a personal or individual affair. Samoans love children, and marriage is the proper institution in which to produce them. Nearly everyone marries in Samoan society sooner or later; the society is simply not set up to support unmarried men or women either socially or economically.

THE WEDDING

Samoan weddings feature an exchange of a vast amount of property *(toga* for *oloa),* and the engagement period is always a busy one for both families involved. The origin of this institution of lavish gift exchange at weddings and a number of other important occasions is not known, but various students of Polynesian culture have speculated on the function it fulfils in the social organization. One position is that it adds some spice of life to an ordinarily humdrum existence. It is, so to speak, a matter of having Christmas several times a year, with all the fun of receiving gifts and affirming the goodwill that exists between individuals and between families. Other observers see the phenomenon as being simply another economic system developed to promote the equal distribution of resources throughout the community. In a subsistence economy without entrepreneurs or markets where local products are sold, there must be a method of product distribution. Robert Maxwell sees the reported "generosity" of Samoan islanders as merely a means of dealing with surplus. Remembering that the *oloa* gifts given by the male's side of the family consist mostly of food, Maxwell's ideas concerning the exchange system seem sound. He maintains that, in Samoa's climate, "food spoiled quickly unless consumed. The food given to others was not forever gone. Sooner or later, others would have a surplus and would return in like amount. The effect was that one's neighbors acted as storage bins for food" (1970:142). Whatever the reason for gift exchange, it continues to be a vital part of the system and one that consumes much time and conversation of families preparing for a wedding.

There had been a great deal of excitement in the village since Lemalu and Lise announced they would be married. In traditional fashion, the announcement was made exactly two weeks in advance of the important day. The members of the *aumea mamae* (wedding party) were selected from among relatives and friends, and Lise's mother had been working for days on the wedding dress. The material was white satin, shipped over from the store in Pago Pago, and there was a veil of white lace. The dress was like one Lise had seen in a magazine; it was cut out from a pattern and sewn on a hand-powered Singer sewing machine. Lemalu would wear his white cotton Sunday coat, a white lavalava, a white shirt, and grey tie. He had ordered matching gray ties for the men in the wedding party, and the women in the party would all be wearing matching dresses of pastel pink and large, flat, straw hats.

The preparations of the extended families of the bride and groom were no less

Samoan bride and groom, Manu'a 1954.

elaborate than those of the immediate families. Storage trunks in a score of *fales* were opened, and the best of their cache of barkcloths, finemats, and lengths of floral print trade cloth were selected for the forthcoming event. Invitations to the wedding and wedding feast had been mailed to relatives and friends in other villages or hand-carried to nearly every family in Fitiuta. The households of the bride and groom would share the expense and labor of a great wedding feast, which would feature kegs of beef, cooked whole pigs, tinned corn beef, canned sardines and salmon, dozens of baked chickens, special traditional items such as *palusami* (cooked young taro leaves and coconut cream) and *tafolo sami,* and prestige items such as cakes with pink and green frosting and two-inch-thick peach custard pies with formidable crusts. Other families would bring food offerings as well, and, on the day preceding the wedding, columns of white smoke would rise from nearly every cook house in the village.

On the day of the wedding, the *aumea mamae* gathered in front of Lise's house. Soon, the groom joined them and, after a few last-minute adjustments of her veil, Lise came out. She and Lemalu led the wedding party in a double column off through the village. Their destination was the home of the Samoan district judge. When they reached his *fale,* everyone crowded inside and sat on the floor mats. The judge read a civil ceremony, pronounced the couple "man and wife," and gave them his blessing. From there, the wedding party went to the church where, before an assembly of family and friends, the village *faifeau* (pastor) performed a second marriage ceremony—this time a religious one.

Following a ceremony much like that performed in a Congregational church in

Bride and attendants on their way to wedding.

the United States, the wedding party, families, and friends moved to a large grassy spot in the center of the village, where a framework covered with coconut fronds had been built to shade the guests at what would be a lavish wedding feast. Two long parallel rows of mats had been laid down, and between them was a long row of leaf baskets overflowing with food. Little boys armed with coconut branches stood by to shoo the flies. At the suggestion of a Talking Chief from Lemalu's family, all the guests found a spot on the mats and sat cross-legged while a series of village chiefs gave speeches welcoming everyone and wishing the newlyweds well. After the *faifeau* gave "thanks to God," everyone began to eat from the leaf baskets before them. As usual, there was much more food than could be consumed by twice the number of guests present. Shortly after the meal began, little boys arrived with coconut-leaf baskets, and each of the guests began piling great quantities of the food into these containers. The food would be taken home so that it could be shared with those who could not attend the festivities.

As the meal proceeded, there was joking and laughter. One of the old chiefs, an uncle of Lemalu, stood up and began to dance a ludicrous dance. Everyone clapped in rhythm and sang in order to encourage him. Soon, dancers were getting up everywhere. Some of the young men ran to a nearby *fale* to get their guitars. The feast was transformed into a dance, and everyone moved into a nearby house. First members of the groom's family danced, and then they challenged the bride's family to match their efforts.

Suddenly, a great cry went up outside the house. The words "*Mua O*" were being shouted by a score or more of voices. Thirty young men dressed in bright barkcloth costumes came running down the path. It was the village *aumaga* arriving in a group to honor Lemalu, one of their own. The group formed into ten lines three deep. Their drummer positioned himself in front of the group with his percussion instrument—an empty kerosene can—and a stick. He began a steady, vigorous rhythm on the can; on his signal, the *aumaga* began their *sasa siva*. In Samoan, *siva* is the word for dance, and *sasa* means "to strike." Thus, the choreography involved the men clapping their hands together, slapping their bodies in unison, and going through a long series of coordinated dance movements—always in rhythm and always in concert. The dancers squatted down, leaped high into the air, turned slowly in a full circle with one arm outstretched, slapped their thighs, made the motion of paddling a canoe, and made a motion like that of throwing a spear. The dance went on for about five minutes and ended in a great war whoop.

It was at this point that Talking Chiefs representing both families announced the gifts that were to be given. There were presentation and thank-you speeches and much "oohing and aahing" as the gifts were produced and taken to the houses of the two families. All the gifts, with the exception of a few linens and lengths of trade cloth for lavalavas, went to the families, not to Lemalu and Lise. After the gift exchange, the young people began dancing again. This went on far into the evening, the jubilation being materially aided by several gallons of "home brew," a special contribution of the *aumaga*.

When the long day was over, the newly married couple went to Lemalu's household, where the family had prepared them a special place to sleep. Barkcloths had been hung to form a room separate from that occupied by the rest of the family. The next morning, Lise would begin her life as a housewife—working with the other women of Lemalu's household. Samoan custom does not include the concept of a honeymoon.

DOMESTIC LIFE

Although Lemalu and Lise moved into the home of the husband's family, the newly married couple is free to choose with which side of the family they will live. There is no such thing as neolocal residence, that is, establishing a home separate from either family. Where the couple will live is largely dependent upon where the husband seems to have the best chance of succeeding to a *matai* title. If the wife's family has a shortage of men, there is excellent opportunity for a young bridegroom to establish himself as a vital, contributing member of that household and therefore be a front-runner for election to a title in her family should one become vacant. If the young man, on the other hand, is the eldest son of the *matai* in his own household, he would likely bring his bride to live with his people.

Regardless of where the bride and groom choose to live, their activities within the family are much the same. They must work with other family members in the cooperative labor of the household whether it is agricultural work, household chores, child care, or fishing activities. There is less leisure time for young women than for their husbands. Respite from a thousand-and-one household tasks comes only on Sunday afternoon, when it is possible to relax and nap for a few hours between church services.

A wife's most important role is that of childbearer. Large families are always desired, for they ensure an adequate labor force for family enterprises and promise a leisurely old age for the parents. Samoans believe that the only natural state for an adult is to be married and to be a parent. Divorce is rare, but that does not mean that there are not a significant number of cases of marital discord. The lack of privacy in the Samoan household undoubtedly reduces the amount of overt conflict, and Samoans perhaps expect less of marriage than do Americans. Unhappy marriages are probably tolerated longer in Samoan culture than in American because personal happiness is not a major concern in the union in the first place. Legal divorces are rare, perhaps because they cost money, but separations are not. The chief grounds for divorce in Manu'a is adultery, and to be guilty of this indiscretion is considered worse for a woman than for a man. Cruelty and desertion are also grounds for divorce, as is laziness, particularly in the case of the wife. Children of a divorced couple tend to remain in the household where they have lived and are visited infrequently by the parent who lives elsewhere.

Every adult male looks forward to the day when he will be elected to a *matai* title, but it cannot be said that the untitled men are envious or covetous of the position of their family head. They work diligently and faithfully for the family and believe that if they are patient their efforts will someday be rewarded. When the time comes that a man's family (or his wife's) selects him for a chief's title, new responsibilities are taken on. A passage from Copp's book *Samoan Dance of Life* gives some insight into this new status:

And so I got to be a *matai*. And I can't go often now and play cricket with my boy-gang or sing love songs along the road by the moonlight. And also, when a happiness-time is in the village, I can't sing and dance any more like I used to make them laugh, but I have to sit in my place and watch the company of young men sitting there in their own place and doing everything.

And I'm sorry for this. But I'm glad too. Because now I am a real family Head, and I can sit with the other chiefs in the meeting *fale* and give my opinion too and have my share of food (1950:172–173).

*Matai*ship is the crowning achievement of middle age. Few acquire this status before their late thirties or early forties. It is a time of responsibility and service to family and village as a fully mature and capable adult, and it brings prestige and respect. The *matai's* wife also enjoys an elevation in status, and, with it, an extra measure of responsibility. She now plays a decision-making role in the Women's Committee of the village, a role the importance of which is equal to that her husband plays in the *fono*. In the household, she is a fictive "mother" to all who live under her roof and she directs domestic activities in a manner similar to the way her husband coordinates the family work in the fields and on the reef and sea. The *matai* and their wives are the pillars of Samoan society, the perpetuators of *fa'aSāmoa* (the Samoan way of life), and, all in all, Samoa's solid citizens.

OLD AGE

Old age begins about age fifty, when men are referred to as *toeaina or matuaali'i* (old man) and women as *to'omatua* or *olomatua* (old woman). Sometime within the next ten to twenty years, the word *vaivai* (weak in the body) may be added, even if this is not actually the case. Old age is invariably identified by young and old alike as "the best time of life." It is a time when one is highly respected, when demands on one's time and energy are at a minimum, when most of life's taboos have been lifted, and when one can sit back if he wishes and rely on the support of children and relatives. Most Samoans, however, believe that extreme longevity is the result of working every day.

Samoa is a pleasant place in which to grow old. The climate is mild and permits maximum social contact and societal participation. The elderly are well integrated into their society and see themselves as valuable participating members in family and village enterprises. They enjoy interacting with young people and are often found working or just visiting with groups of young fishermen on the reef or with groups of young adult women engaged in mat weaving. Even the architecture of Samoa favors the elderly. Because the traditional Samoan house is open on all sides, old people need not even leave their homes in order to greet friends and neighbors as they pass on the path, and they are able to keep reasonably well-informed of much that is going on in the village.

One of the advantages of old age is a softening of taboos and an easing of the rigid code of etiquette that governs much of Samoan social and ceremonial life. The brother-sister avoidance requirements are no longer in force. Elderly siblings of the opposite sex are free to sit together for long hours, enjoying each other's company without feeling ashamed or guilty. Moreover, in village council meetings, special deference is shown to old chiefs—even the most intemperate of remarks is tolerated. The aged feel no compunction to maintain a dignified image and, in fact, they often play the clown at dances or other social gatherings.

Samoans feel that the aged have a right to engage in any form of labor of which they think themselves capable, and there is no stigma if they decide to do nothing at all. There are, however, a number of activities that are associated with the elderly, and these tend to be sennit making, light agriculture, and reef fishing for men, and child care, mat and *siapo* production, sewing, and weeding the yard for women. Gender does not determine work activities as strongly as it does among younger people, and old men find no shame in helping their wives with domestic tasks, even baby-sitting. Traditionally, it has been the elderly who have generally been recognized as the most adept at bush medicine, massage *(fofō)*, tattooing, midwifery, and story telling. One of the most important positions in the village—that of *tu'ua* (advisor to the village council)—is always reserved for an elderly High Chief or High Talking Chief. Retirement is a concept foreign to Samoa, although some chiefs, upon reaching advanced age, will give up their *matai* title and, therefore, their influential position in the village council so that a younger family member may achieve recognition for a lifetime of faithful service to the family.

Life expectancy is much shorter in Samoa than in most countries of the Western world. The average age of death is 38.4 years, but, because of a high infant mortality rate, this figure is misleading. The number of people who reach the age of sixty-five in Samoa is 2.7 percent of the population. Seriously ill people usually refuse to go to the hospital in Pago Pago, believing that, if they should die away from home, their spirits will be troubled and cause the family harm. They prefer to remain at home, where relatives can be in constant attendance, and the local nurse or Samoan medical practitioner from Ta'ū village can make an occasional call to check on their progress and prescribe any needed medication.

When a person dies in the home, all blinds that might have been lowered to shade the patient are immediately raised, and a boy of the household is sent to toll the death on the bell in the village church. Members of the female branch of the family, the *tamasā*, immediately begin to prepare the body, in full view of anyone who chooses to watch. This usually includes a throng of curious children. The corpse is dressed in white clothing and placed on a pile of sleeping mats that have been covered with a white sheet. Relatives in the *tamasā* branch of the family position themselves around the body and watch over it until it is removed for burial. The village pastor usually remains with the family to assist in any way he can. Grief is not excessive, and there appears to be no retention of earlier practices, reported by the first missionaries, in which mourners bruised their heads with stones or cut themselves with sharp objects.

Within a short time after the announcement of death, the church choir calls a rehearsal to prepare for their ceremonial visit *(leo)* to the grieving family. Within four or five hours of the death, the choir, dressed in black, arrives at the home of the deceased and is seated within the house. A few hymns are sung, and a speech for the dead *(lauga i maliu)* is delivered by a choir member (usually a Talking Chief). This visit is made with the express purpose of consoling the family; therefore, a representative of the family must respond with a speech thanking them for their thoughtfulness. After the exchange of speeches, another hymn is sung, and the choir leaves.

As long as the body remains in the house, the women of the family will never leave it. They are forbidden to sleep; if one of them should nod off, ashes will be smeared on her forehead, which cannot be washed off until after the funeral. Throughout the long night, young men from the village come in to play guitars and sing so that relatives will find it easier to stay awake. Because corpses are not embalmed, and the climate is tropical, burials normally take place within twenty-four hours of death. In the meantime, messages must be sent to other villages, and, within a few hours, relatives and friends begin to arrive with gifts of trade cloth, *siapo,* and finemats. If the deceased is a chief, there will probably be a considerable show of wealth. This wealth, consisting mainly of finemats, will be displayed on the mosquito netting wires strung about the house. The chief's family provides one large and particularly valuable finemat *(afuelo)* that will hang just behind the body. After the funeral, this treasure will be given to the female relative who has taken care of the cleansing and dressing of the corpse.

The family head selects the gravesite somewhere on the village land of the household. In the case of a deceased family head, the site is chosen by another influential titled member of the family. The grave is dug by members of the deceased's family, aided by friends. If the dead man was titled, fellow chiefs will dig the grave and receive a special payment *(lafo)* after the funeral for their labors. The body is wrapped in the sleeping mats, sheets, and *siapo* on which it has lain in state and is carried to the gravesite by members of the village choir or members of the household. Graves are dug in two levels, and the corpse is placed in the bottom level in preparation for the funeral service.

The funeral service, much like one in a stateside Congregational church, is read by the village pastor *(faifeau)* with the family, friends, and church choir at graveside. The choir closes the service with a hymn which says, *"Tofā, Tofā"* ("goodbye, goodbye"), and the pastor and mourners throw three handfuls of sand apiece into the grave. When the mourners have left the graveside, sheets of galvanized iron are placed over the lower level of the grave that contains the corpse. The metal sheets are weighted down with heavy rocks, and sand is shovelled into the grave. The grave of a titled man will usually be marked with a rock cairn or a headstone of poured concrete, but the grave of a woman, an untitled man, or a child will be marked only with a coral slab. The grave will be supplied with flowers for a year, then forgotten.

Following the funeral, the mourners are fed and given food to take with them to their homes. Special shares of pork, chicken, fish, and taro are set aside for the *faifeau* and all other friends who assisted in the burial. Special care is taken to reimburse the donors of finemats and *siapo* by giving them food and other goods of equal value. Some finemats will be given as *lafo* to village chiefs and to the pastor for services rendered, and the rest will be stored away until there is another death in the village, and once again every family is expected to bring their gifts of sorrow and respect for the deceased.

6 / The Changing Samoan World

Until very recently, most anthropologists who have worked in Samoa have been impressed with the traditional nature of Samoan culture. While U.S. government initiated cultural change has greatly affected much of American Samoa in the last twenty-five years, Western Samoa and Manu'a remain relatively conservative. Douglas Oliver, writing on the history of Westernization in Polynesia, described Samoa as:

> presenting a radically different picture from the usual South Seas spectacle of native peoples cheerfully and unknowingly losing their identity and their heritage in a setting of successful and expanded economy established and controlled by white men (1961:220).

In 1943, Oxford and Cambridge geographers, in a handbook titled *The Pacific Islands,* singled out the Samoans as a "people with such a conservative nature that new elements (foreign goods, money, Christianity) have never been allowed to sweep the land with the devastating effects to be observed in some other Pacific island communities" (1943:608).

In a time when even the most isolated of primitive peoples are rapidly losing their cultural identity in favor of Western ways, the Samoans are an enigma, particularly when one surveys other Polynesian societies. Descriptions of the way of life of islanders in 1943 in the Northern Cook Group, an area where interisland boats call as infrequently as four times a year, include such statements as, "The old types of canoes have completely disappeared." "Houses are now made of sawn timber." "Changes in the culture of the people due to European influence have been considerable" (Geographical Handbook Series 1943:552–559). An island group farther east, the Marquesas, is described as a place "where much of the native culture . . . has disappeared" (Geographical Handbook Series 1943:271).

Even the remote and sparsely populated atolls of the Tuamotu Group have undergone sweeping changes. The traditional culture of the island of Raroia, for example, is almost completely gone. Danielsson tells us that:

> . . . changes have been profound. . . . The material culture is almost wholly Western, and the natives use European tools exclusively, dress in the European way and frequently have such luxuries as radios, bicycles and refrigerators (1956:104).

Even the untrained observer is aware that in places such as Hawaii, Tahiti, and New Zealand, the traditional native culture is to be found only in adulterated form, if at all, and then it is often maintained only as a tourist attraction.

The Samoan phenomenon of relative cultural stability therefore presents an interesting anthropological problem. Why has this island group been able to retain much of the traditional way of life during 160 years of European contact, while other Polynesians have abandoned theirs in favor of the ways of the white man?

Keesing has suggested that Samoan conservatism results from the archipelago's "smallness, isolation, and tropical climate, together with the political rivalry of the powers (Great Britain, United States, and Germany) and the elements of disunity inherent in the native polity . . ." (1934:477). A careful analysis of Samoan history, however, establishes the fact that none of these factors is completely unique to Samoa. Samoa is no smaller in land mass or in population than many other highly acculturated island groups and has probably been less isolated than most. Douglas Oliver has established that Samoa, Tahiti, and the Marquesas were particularly popular ports of call for a great many whaling ships working in the Pacific. In the year 1846, for example, seventy-two vessels called at Samoa, and many stayed an extended period of time. Samoa was discovered in the late eighteenth century, roughly about the same time that other Polynesian islands were first visited by Captain Cook and other European navigators. Samoa was merely one of many island groups missionized between the years 1814 and 1836. Traders were also extremely active in Samoa from an early date. In fact, the largest trading concern in the Pacific, the Godeffroy Company, maintained its headquarters in Western Samoa between 1857 and 1878.

The colonial experience of Samoa may have been somewhat different from that of other Polynesian societies. Samoa was the object of a long and bitter struggle for economic and political control among Germany, Great Britain, and the United States. But the continual courtship of the loyalty and political support of the people by these three powers over half a century should have resulted in as much or more change than any experienced by other island groups.

The answer to the question of why Samoa has managed to retain much of its traditional culture is believed by the authors to lie within the nature of the culture itself, particularly with regard to its attitudes and institutions relating to family, government, and the supernatural. It is also believed that in most situations where two cultures meet, cultural change will usually be the greatest in those societies in which the traditional system rewards the fewest number of people; that is, when a new, more egalitarian system presents itself, there will be less tendency on the part of the majority of people to cling to a system that rewards only a few.

In most areas where acculturation has been marked—Tahiti, New Zealand, the Cook Islands, the Marquesas, Hawaii, the Tuamotus—the cultures placed great importance on primogeniture, senior lineages, and other forms of stratification. Furthermore, the few elite who profited from these arrangements were securely supported in their positions by religious sanctions in the form of *mana* and *tapu*. While the bulk of the population may not have liked the situation in which only a select few enjoyed power and prestige, it was difficult to oppose a system that had the blessing of the supernatural.

When the white man first settled in Polynesia, it was mainly for the purpose of winning converts to Christianity. The white man's god was usually perceived as more powerful than Polynesian gods—even by people of rank—for, after all, this foreign god had provided his followers with magnificent ships, efficient weapons, strong and beautiful clothing, a myriad of attractive trinkets, and useful tools.

Because very few people profited from the traditional social system, and the gods no longer threatened the average person if they failed to support their traditional rulers or the system which put them in power, most central and eastern Polynesians turned to the ways of the white man as an avenue of achievement. Furnas suggests that in Hawaii, for example:

> The commoner was flattered, perhaps stirred, when the white *kahuna* (priest) finally got round to telling him that any native, of whatever social stratum, had a soul of which Christ was solicitous. Nothing in his pre-white culture had ever led him to consider himself important to anybody (1948:137).

According to Barnett:

> In New Zealand, the members of ranking families as a group resisted education, whereas those of lesser birth sought it and used it to lay the foundations for a new kind of leadership, one based upon the knowledge of the ways of the foreigner (1953:405).

Keesing adds that "a new standard of *mana* rose to rival that attained in forwarding the tribal purposes, namely that of accomplishment in *pakeha* knowledge and habits, and possession of *pakeha*[1] goods" (1928:58).

In Samoa, things were very different. There were chiefs, but they received their elite position not through primogeniture, but through election by their extended family. All who were reasonably wise, efficient, hard-working, and loyal to family interests were eligible. Nor was there the concept of senior lines which gave special advantage to certain branches of the family. Grattan points out that "progress from untitled to titled rank is the normal aspiration sooner or later of most adult males" (1948:14). Goldman comments that the Samoans "come close to broadening the concept of aristocracy to include the common man" (1970:262).

The appeal of this traditional system can readily be appreciated from the statement of a native informant, who pointed out that, "In our system, everyone can trace a relationship to a king or at least to a High Chief." Furthermore, it is within the range of possibility that if he "played his cards right," he could someday conceivably be elected to one of these High Chief titles, if not to one that had once been a royal title.

Another important factor to be considered regarding Samoa's conservatism is that religion was not part and parcel of the social and political system. In other words, it was possible for the society to accept another religion without affecting the status or authority of chiefs. Samoans speak of sacred *fono* rather than sacred chiefs. The *malae* in Samoa was a village green where the village council met to decide local and regional issues. The *marae* in central and eastern Polynesia, on the other hand, was a place where priests conducted religious ceremonies. What was undoubtedly the most devastating influence for change on most Polynesian cultures—the coming of Christianity—had little effect on the social structure of Samoa, since Samoan culture had less invested in religious sanctions. Samoa had always been ruled by the will of men, not by the will of the gods or by men acting for the gods. Since Samoan chiefs had never claimed divine rights, the loss of traditional deities or religious concepts did little to alter their role and status within the society.

[1]*Pakeha* is the term used by native populations of New Zealand to refer to Caucasians.

Homer Barnett has observed that "when cultures meet, the majority of those who switch their allegiances are individuals with the least opportunity for full participation in the most valued activities of their society" (1953:404). Samoan society allowed its members wider participation in social, economic, and political affairs than any other Polynesian group.

THE WINDS OF CHANGE

The point of the previous discussion was not that changes have not taken place in Samoa, but that changes have been less cataclysmic and pervasive in Samoa than in other parts of Polynesia. As a way of systematically documenting the change that has taken place since the beginning of white contact, the authors would like to suggest the following periods of Samoan-European acculturation:

1. 1830 to 1869—The period of Samoan-mission-trader equilibrium, when "the Samoan accepted those goods he wanted from the trader, and bowed to the voice of an evidently superior Deity" (Keesing 1934:476).
2. 1870 to 1899—The period of "political and judicial changes in accordance with the will of alien authorities whose word was backed by warships and prisons" (*Ibid.*).
3. 1900 to 1951—The period marked by the acquisition of American Samoa as an unincorporated territory of the United States under the control of the U.S. Navy, whose governing strategy might best be described as one of "benign neglect" or "non-intervention in native affairs." For Western Samoa, this period would include the years 1900 to 1962, a period in which this country was a German colony, a New Zealand mandated territory under the League of Nations, a trust territory under the United Nations, and, finally, an independent nation.
4. 1951 to 1977—The period in which control of American Samoa shifted from the U.S. Navy to the Department of the Interior. This was a period of politically appointed American governors, most of whom neither spoke Samoan nor understood Samoan culture, but, because of a revived interest in America's Pacific island territories by Congress, were charged with the task of molding the cultural and economic future of American Samoa along Western lines. This was a time when new ideas were developed and plans formulated—regarding education, industrial development, and tourism—by American consultants and contract personnel with generous funding from the U.S. Congress. It was also during this period that Western ideas and ways began to replace traditional ones, and the first signs of secularization, urbanization, and social disorganization began to threaten the status quo.

When Lowell Holmes returned to Samoa in 1962, after an absence from the islands of eight years, he recorded the following observations:

> Samoa had changed. The United States had tripled its appropriations. A new cluster of high school buildings (in Pago Pago) had made possible universal secondary education. Plans were underway for the establishment of an educational television circuit and for the construction of 26 elementary schools. But in spite of improved plane and ship com-

munications, tourism had increased little because the island still had but one small government-operated hotel. The Samoan government seemed mainly interested in education and tourism however, for most villages still had their antique and inadequate water systems, and no effective facilities for sewage disposal. Samoans eliminated either on the beach or in the bush. Medical facilities were roughly the same as in 1954.

Prosperity had come to American Samoa. Because of employment in the new construction program and in a tuna cannery, Samoans had more money. Beer and soft drink consumption had soared. Bush stores sold a wide variety of European tinned food. Taxi-cabs and private cars were numerous and traffic was becoming a problem. Girls in the Pago Pago Bay area and even in outlying villages had begun to wear makeup and European hair styles; some of the younger ones were daring enough to appear in capri pants. Bay area children knew how to twist as well as to *siva*, and stereo phonographs were not uncommon household possessions. Tahitian rhythms could be heard everywhere; the governor, in an attempt to "retain the best of Samoan culture," had employed a Samoan-born nightclub entertainer and dance instructor from Los Angeles, California, who taught Samoan school children Tahitian dancing and drumming, to the irritation of the Samoan chiefs (Holmes 1964:446).

Even in isolated areas such as Manu'a, changes in family structure were becoming evident. It could readily be sensed that there was a general lessening of the economic and political influence of the *matai* and greater opportunity for the individual family members to control their own affairs than had traditionally been the case. All these changes, however, were minor compared to what was in store for American Samoa.

5. 1977 to the present—This period begins with a major political change—the right of American Samoans to elect their own governors. It has also been a period of expanded governmental services, in most cases administered by Samoan governmental employees, many of whom have returned from working and being educated in Hawaii or mainland United States.

THE CHANGED FACE OF SAMOA

When we returned to the islands to do research in 1988 (our first visit since 1976), we began to observe changes even before arrival in Samoa, as most of our fellow passengers on the flight from Hawaii were Samoans. It was their clothing that first caught our attention at the Honolulu airport. Elderly people in the crowd were dressed in what has been for a long time typical attire for Samoans—men in a *lavalava* (wrap-around skirt-type garment) and shirt; women in a floral print long dress or *puletasi*, ankle-length *lavalava* with hip-length overblouse. Many young adults, children, and even a few middle-aged people, however, were wearing very contemporary American-style apparel—jeans, slacks, jogging suits, shorts, boots, Reeboks, even some high-heel shoes. Some of the young men and boys had haircuts characteristic of current fads in the United States—designs shaved into the hair or cut short with a long rattail centered in back. As we flew south for the next five hours, we had increasing curiosity about how different Samoa would be after our long absence.

Since one almost always arrives in these islands in the dark—and this trip was no exception—we knew it would be the next day before we could really begin to assess how much things had changed. We immediately noticed the new technology in the air terminal, where carousels now deliver the luggage (albeit somewhat slowly), and rental carts are available to transport things through customs and out of the terminal. There were also other improvements to the airport facilities such as an expanded check-in area and departure lounge, electronic security, a covered loading zone in front of the terminal, and a paved parking lot. En route to town by taxi, our curiosity was further piqued by glimpses of many new business developments along the way.

The next day, a new scene greeted us immediately as we left the hotel grounds: The volume of automobile traffic on the main road was tremendous. Cars were literally bumper to bumper in both directions; crossing the street posed a real challenge. The number of vehicles is increasing rapidly in spite of the limited road area and parking space. In May of 1990, *The Samoa Daily News*[2] reported that there are approximately five thousand cars in American Samoa, and traffic-counting devices were indicating ten thousand to twelve thousand cars per day driving in the bay area on Tutuila.

Adjacent to the hotel is a new convention center and another facility for the repair of nets for the fishing fleet. Before, a row of white frame houses—remnants of the colonial-type naval administration in Samoa—stood facing the bay on the way to the business area. They are now gone, and the view toward town is dominated by large, metal shipping containers stacked three high next to the dock, which has been expanded to accommodate more vessels, especially the American-owned purse seiners. These ships, equipped with very modern technology including

Tuna fishing boats in Pago Pago harbor.

[2]This is the new name of the former *Samoa News*, adopted when it began publishing five issues a week.

helicopters for spotting tuna, have expanded the fishing fleet, an important part of the Samoan economy. In 1976, the tuna canneries were supplied with fish by Korean and Chinese fisherman; the purse seiners have brought Samoans (as crew members) into this aspect of the industry.

Fagatogo, the main business center, port town, and site of the Samoan legislature, is a mixture of old and new. The same buildings were there as in 1976, facing or near the *malae* (village square), a large, open, grassy area in the center of town. There had been a few changes in proprietorship or in the variety of goods sold in stores; the government liquor store was gone, as were a couple of long-established general stores. New additions included a car dealership, a video-game parlor, a privately owned liquor store, a new restaurant called Sadie's, and a large building under construction by the bay—the future home of Tedi of Samoa. We found Tedi's current downtown store up the hill in Fagatogo and quickly suspected this might be the source of much of the change in clothing styles. This store offers a wide variety of dresses, pants, shorts, and jewelry, for example, with current stateside styles and prices.

We quickly confirmed that many Samoans are routinely wearing American-style clothes in their home territory and not just when traveling abroad. Traditional native styles are most typical of employees in tourist-related businesses such as the Rainmaker Hotel, for ceremonial occasions, and for older Samoans in general. Many young people of both sexes were wearing shorts in town, something almost unheard of even a decade ago, especially for women. The transition from the bare feet of thirty years ago to the ubiquitous rubber thong sandals so popular in 1976, has progressed to very Western-style footwear.

Fagatogo malae *and business district on Tutuila.*

The public beach at Utulei on Pago Pago Bay, Tutuila.

In the village of Utulei, just west of Fagatogo, the public beach is now a much busier place than ever before. Picnic tables and barbecue facilities are in place, and portable snack bars operate in the parking area. This is a popular site for a variety of gatherings, including political campaign events. On weekends, there were always many groups gathered to swim, sing, and eat, and the tantalizing smell of chicken cooking on grills filled the air. One does not yet see Samoans in skimpy swimsuits at this public beach—shorts or *lavalava* with the addition of a tee shirt for women is still the norm.

It soon became apparent that, in terms of visible changes, increased development has occurred largely in the bay-area villages and in the area west toward the airport. In the outlying villages toward the western end of Tutuila and in most of the eastern district, change is much less obvious, although a few larger stores have appeared. An occasional bush store (small, family-owned general store) in predominantly residential settings still characterizes many villages.

Housing is now almost entirely Western style, constructed of wood or concrete blocks, and usually rectangular in shape. An occasional family guest house retains the more open, traditional structural style, but even these are now concrete, with corrugated metal roofs. This movement away from traditional-style *fales* can be seen in all parts of the Samoan island chain—even in Western Samoa, which usually prides itself on maintaining old ways. A study by Roger Neich (1985) reveals that in a sample of 13 villages in Upolu and Savai'i with a total of 887 houses, only 22 were traditional. Five of the villages did not have a traditional *fale* at all, and Falealupo, the most isolated village of all (on the western end of Savai'i), had only 11 traditional houses out of 115. In the Manu'a islands of American Samoa, the disappearance of traditional housing is at least partly the result of hurricane damage in recent years.

Along with the changes in housing, many of the old traditions of housebuilding are gone as well. The modern European-styled houses that predominate are no longer the products of *tufuga* and their crews of apprentices. Most residences and guest houses are constructed by either family members (some of whom may have construction experience from government employment) or one of several contracting companies. Little of the ceremonialism that once marked house construction is found today, although it is commonplace to mark the completion of a house with a celebration where friends and relatives are feasted and entertained. This event is undoubtedly a survival of the festivities associated with *uma sā,* the payment of the final portion of the carpenters' fee.

Many Samoan houses now have European furniture, some of which resembles lawn or patio furniture. With the establishment of furniture stores on the island of Tutuila, a variety of styles is now available, and more homes have upholstered furniture, dining tables, and beds. People still sit on floor mats more than on chairs, however, and many continue to sleep on mats on the floor. It is even possible to find an occasional bamboo headrest, but most are used for daytime napping or lounging, and older Samoans claim they are good for watching TV and are "cooler than a pillow." Telephones (there are 7,800 telephones in service) are standard equipment in American Samoan households, and we found the telephone system in the islands

Modern European style house in Fituita.

greatly improved since our 1976 trip. Remarkably, a call to Manu'a is considered to be a local call, in spite of the distance.

There are changes regarding some of the traditional kinds of household or family personal property. Mat making continues to be an important activity for women, and women's work groups, *fale lalaga,* convene for this purpose. Such activities would more likely occur today among older women in areas such as Manu'a and Western Samoa—or in special craft programs—but mats do represent household wealth, and all Samoan homes (even European style) use plaited floor mats.

Finemats *(i'e tōga),* the most valuable articles of family property and the items most frequently exchanged on ceremonial occasions, are still produced (although more in Western Samoa than in American Samoa), but modern production is marked by many production shortcuts. While such mats formerly took months—even years—to complete, they may now be completed in a matter of days. Finemats are no longer decorated with red parakeet feathers. Now, any feathers, dyed green or blue and sewn in with a sewing machine, will do. Edges of the mats are stitched rather than finished off with braid. These mats are not as supple as those made in earlier days and are actually a great deal like regular *laufala* (floor mats), but with feathers and fringe added (Neich 1985).

Barkcloth *(siapo)* is now almost a thing of the past. Many families have quantities of these tapacloths, but little is being manufactured. Neich (1985) maintains that no barkcloth is made in Upolu and, therefore, it is doubtful if there are any Manu'an producers. Some comes from Savai'i, and Tongan tapa is now used in exchanges, but there is almost none available for the tourist trade as there once was. Tourists may have to settle for small Fijian barkcloths. While *taupou* and *manaia* formerly wore finemats and *siapo* as ceremonial garb, silk, satin, and velvet have become contemporary substitutes.

The Samoan world offers many new options for entertainment and services. Many locally owned fast-food and full-service restaurants offer varied opportunities or dining out, and several bars and nightclubs are now found in the bay area. There are restaurants serving Korean, Chinese, or Mexican food, and a new delicatessen. Matai's Pizza Fale is a popular spot for pizza. Sadie's, which is named for Sadie Thompson of W. Somerset Maugham's short story "Rain," is located on the site of the island's original hotel, the setting for that story. This gourmet establishment offers not only a taste of history, but a continental menu, Sunday brunch, and such unexpected fare as blackened catfish and green beer on St. Patrick's Day. New Year's Eve entertainment at a club or the hotel, with dinner and champagne, may cost almost $100 per couple.

Laundromats, which were nonexistent in 1976, seem to be everywhere. South Pacific Traders has a store, the size of a small-town mainland Walmart, in the village of Nu'uuli. Here, one can buy fabric, shoes, clothing, cosmetics, housewares, appliances, toys, and games, most of which could be found in a similar store in the United States. There are supermarkets stocked almost entirely with Western food items and several privately owned liquor stores. Furniture stores, whose offerings even include waterbeds, and florists are new to the Samoan scene as is a children's shop, Kids Are King, selling expensive clothing and equipment such as car seats, playpens, high chairs, and fancy cribs. One can rent tents for special occasions, rent or buy tuxedos, and there are businesses selling books, office supplies, copy machines, computers and supplies, and photographic services.

Video cassette rental is a big business as color television sets and video-cassette recorders are common household items. Even Nintendo has arrived in Samoa. The three locally available television channels provide a range of programming and personalities that would be familiar in any U.S. community. For example "Sesame Street," "Days of Our Lives," "The Cosby Show," "Nova," Larry King, Johnny Carson, and major sporting events are all available for viewing. The latest recordings of music by Samoan artists as well as current U.S. pop stars such as Willie Nelson, Madonna, LL Cool J, and others are also available. A community theater, golf tournaments, bingo games, and a wide range of civic organizations such as YWCA, Lion's and Rotary clubs, and Ladies' Hospital Auxiliary are only a few of the other activities now part of the Samoan scene.

Most Samoans are quite familiar with air travel; flying to Hawaii and the U.S. mainland is a commonplace event. Unfortunately, in 1990, only one major air carrier, Hawaiian Air Lines, served American Samoa. While the flights are in great demand, tickets are expensive, and schedules are erratic at best—more of an ideal than a reality. Samoans and Americans who must depend on this service express great concern about their plight.

Air travel between Tutuila and Manu'a in American Samoa and to Western Samoa is also available. Travel between Western Samoa and Tutuila has long been possible via interisland vessels and the Western Samoan-owned airline, Polynesian Air. As many as three locally owned American Samoan airlines have served these routes at one time in the late 1980s, but plane crashes and other difficulties have often resulted in lengthy suspensions or termination of service by one or more carriers. The people of Fitiuta and other Manu'an villages have become dependent upon air travel in recent years, since passenger service was discontinued on the interisland boat between Tutuila and Manu'a. It appears this situation may soon be rectified with the recent appropriation of funds for a new vessel, which will carry passengers as well as cargo. The new airstrip being built in Fitiuta is recognized by many as a step toward greater air safety for travelers to Ta'ū island.

The changes described are most apparent on the main island of Tutuila. The residents of the isolated Manu'a group of islands are well aware of change. They can sample it on visits and purchase new merchandise to take or ship home, but they do not have access to this lifestyle on a daily basis. There are docks on Ofu and Ta'ū islands facilitating shipment of goods, but commercial development has essentially bypassed places like Fitiuta.

The most dramatic change in Manu'an villages in recent years came about not through modernization but from the forces of nature. In January 1987, Hurricane Tusi devastated this area, destroying virtually all buildings and much of the vegetation, but remarkably, there was no loss of life. Our visit to Ta'ū island in 1988 was some eighteen months after the hurricane, and the scene still showed effects of the overwhelming destruction. The Federal Emergency Management Administration (FEMA) was providing new, concrete "hurricane" houses, but this process had been much delayed. In Ta'ū village, some families were living in shelters made from packing crates and plastic tarps while waiting their turn for a new house. Major landmarks such as the old London Missionary Society church (abandoned years ago), were almost totally gone—only the bell tower remained standing.

On the bumpy road to Fitiuta, we passed coconut trees that looked like telephone poles: The hurricane winds had wrenched off their tops. As the road descended from the mountain side and skirted the beach, we knew we were nearing Fitiuta. Then the road turned, and we entered the valley that sheltered the village.

Ta'ū village guest house after the hurricane.

Ta'ū village today. No traditional fales *and much evidence of storm damage.*

The narrow, concrete sidewalk now had a gravel road running parallel to it (an innovation of the 1970s), but the village was almost unrecognizable. Not one traditional *fale* could be seen. Although the village had been almost completely destroyed by the storm, no attempt had been made to construct traditional houses. Perhaps the villagers had given up on the old ways and now put their faith in concrete. Nothing stood but makeshift shelters and occasional cement hurricane houses, the residences of the more fortunate who had been high on the list to have a FEMA-built house. They did, however, have cook houses behind, where food was still being prepared in the traditional way—on a bed of heated stones.

The village looked strangely exposed and vulnerable, for the coconut and breadfruit trees that sheltered it to seaward were gone, allowing an unobstructed view of the broad Pacific. Before, the sea had seemed very far away. There was also an unobstructed view of the area known as Saua, the land just to the south of Fitiuta, which Samoan myths described as a Polynesian Garden of Eden; now the garden's coconut trees were without fronds or fruit. The church was only partially destroyed

FEMA hurricane house in Fitiuta.

and perhaps repairable. There were newly established bush stores and a surprisingly modern two-unit motel structure built in anticipation of the construction of a new airstrip in this village.

The village seemed to be struggling to return to normal. Young men with shoulder yokes and baskets of produce were seen coming down from the hills. Taro and bananas were available now, but it would be years before the newly planted breadfruit and coconut trees would begin to bear fruit. It was depressing to see what had once seemed to us to be the prototypical idyllic South Sea village in this condition. The direction of future development in these villages remains to be seen. It seems unlikely that Manu'a will ever experience the level of change that characterizes Tutuila, but the seeds of change are there.

ECONOMIC DEVELOPMENT

A dominant element of change in American Samoa has been economic development. What was once primarily an agricultural, subsistence-based society is now an almost entirely industrial, commercial, cash-oriented economy. Labor force participation has increased from 4,900 individuals in 1970 to approximately 11,000 in 1990, with the government and the tuna canneries employing about 70 percent of these workers. The remaining 30 percent work for the increasing numbers of retail outlets, small manufacturers, and service-related business, including tourism. Agriculture has minimal significance in most of American Samoa.

A recent statistical report (American Samoa Government, 1988) indicates over 1,800 businesses registered in the territory. Many of these are family-owned "bush stores," or " *'aiga* bus" operations, but there is also a variety of other employment options in American Samoa today.

American Samoa has a special minimum-wage structure, which is lower than the rates prevailing in the United States, and cannery wages are considered as a separate issue from other occupations. These hourly minimums have ranged from about $1.50 to $2.90, depending on the type of job; the rate for the canneries has been $2.82. Actual wages paid tend to be somewhat higher than the established rates. This special wage system is, in part, intended to provide incentive for businesses to locate operations in American Samoa and to allow employment of more people. Nevertheless, unemployment rates in recent years have been about 13 percent. While a shift to dependence on a cash economy has occurred, many households (about 58 percent) live below the U.S. poverty level.

Employment of "aliens" is an issue of some concern to the Samoan government. There is a desire to attract outside industries to the territory, but foreign investors often want to bring in a sizable workforce as well. Such an arrangement may provide a limited number of additional jobs for Samoans and remains a point of contention in negotiations between the government and potential developers. An-

The tuna canneries on Pago Pago Bay are part of American Samoa's largest private industry.

other aspect of the employment problem is that a significant number of Western Samoans are already working in American Samoa. A survey in 1985 indicated that 42.9 percent of the employed persons were from the neighboring country (ASG, 1988). Given the lower wages available in Western Samoa, it is not surprising that so many people would seek entry to, and jobs in, American Samoa.

The same rationale also can be used to explain, at least in part, the migration of American Samoans to the United States. This stream of migrants of working age out of the country often allows Western Samoans to acquire jobs that would otherwise be held by American Samoans. When the American Samoans return home, as some do, they may face unemployment or restricted access to jobs because foreigners are filling the available positions. Even though there is a policy requiring qualified American Samoans be given priority over others in hiring, problems remain.

An important factor relating to economic development is the Samoan land tenure system. Land in the Manu'a Islands continues to be owned communally by extended families and administered by the *matai*. This is true of 97 percent of the land in American Samoa as a whole, although in the last twenty-five years, increasing numbers of families are temporarily allocating sections of family land to untitled heads of constituent nuclear family units to work as they see fit. There has also been a movement toward individualization of land on Tutuila. In the past ten years, nearly 25 percent of the land registered has been to individuals. In the Tafuna plain near the airport, bush land has been cleared, occupied for a period of time, then registered as the personal holdings of the homesteader. The individuals who claim these parcels of land (rarely more than an acre) are employees of the government or private industry and have created what appears to be a kind of suburb, although without the usual attributes of a Samoan community. Such "individualized land" will be willed to the owners' offspring and will not be subject to 'āiga control (Stover 1990).

It should be noted that the government of American Samoa has not promoted land individualization. From the very beginning of its administration, the U.S. Navy established a policy of honoring the traditional Samoan land tenure system. A regulation that land cannot be sold to anyone whose ancestry is not at least 75 percent Samoan continues to be vigorously enforced. While extended leases of land to foreign entrepreneurs is permitted, the isolation of the Manu'a group has tended to rule out such arrangements there.

Most of the development and employment opportunities are found on Tutuila. In the Manu'a Islands of Ofu, Olosega, and Ta'ū, there has been an increase in labor force participation since 1970, when only 136 people were involved, to a 1980 level of 423. These jobs are almost all some type of government work, with only about 20 private-sector employees. Businesses are primarily bush stores. With their low population level and limited resources, these isolated islands seem unlikely prospects for much economic development in the near future. There is some potential for development, but solutions will be far from simple.

All land cultivated in Manu'a—less than four hundred acres—is used for subsistence agriculture. Since copra is of almost no value anymore, there is little commercial agriculture in Manu'a today. There is also little chance that any will be carried on in the foreseeable future. Banking is possible only when a clerk flies over from Pago Pago (perhaps one day a week); there are no brokers or middlemen; there is no market information, and, worst of all, there is no satisfactory transportation for moving agricultural products to what would be a very lucrative market—Tutuila. Traditional foods are very much in demand in Tutuila, but because nearly all adults have government or private-sector employment, almost no agriculture at all is being carried on. Breadfruit, bananas, and taro are imported from Western Samoa and Tonga to meet the demand. While both these countries have vessels that maintain regular schedules to Tutuila, the government of America Samoa has no such arrangement with Manu'a. When an interisland vessel does call in the Manu'a group, the freight rate is considerably higher than that charged by the foreign vessels delivering to Pago Pago (Templet Resources, Inc. 1986) This fact, plus the fact that much higher wages are earned in American Samoa than in Tonga or Western Samoa, puts would-be commercial farmers in Manu'a, which was once called the "breadbasket of American Samoa," at a competitive disadvantage.

Fishing has always been a major subsistence source in the Samoan islands, and the people of Manu'a have always had great interest and ability in acquiring food from the sea. They still are more than able to acquire sufficient seafood for their own use, but there is no commercial industry serving customers outside Manu'a. About a dozen plywood or aluminum catamarans (alia) operate out of Ofu and Ta'ū village harbors, but there are no longer any old-style outrigger bonito boats or tautai (fishing specialists) in the traditional sense. A few outrigger canoes (paopao) can be seen pulled up on beaches in most villages. These are used for family subsistence fishing. Few are visible on the island of Tutuila, however. Manu'an families pay the handful of local commercial fishermen $1.00 to $1.25 for snapper, grouper, bonito, wahoo, and mahi-mahi. In 1985, these anglers brought in about thirty-seven thousand pounds of fish (Ibid.).

As is the case with Manu'an agricultural products, Tutuila could represent a very lucrative market for Manu'an seafood, but the lack of sufficient freezer storage, ice, and dependable and reasonably priced transport represent obstacles to such a development. The government interisland vessel, which brings supplies for the schools and public works projects, charges $55 freight for a 128 cubic-foot container or 50 cents per cubic foot for cargo not in containers. The tuna canneries in Pago Pago will only pay 50 cents a pound for tuna or wahoo and require delivery to the canneries (Ibid.). Even if the economics of the enterprise could be worked out, there are real problems associated with harbor facilities in Ta'ū.

Although a harbor with a protective sea wall was constructed in Ta'ū village in 1979, the facility leaves much to be desired. A government document describes the harbor facilities as follows:

Ta'ū . . . is a boater's nightmare eight or nine months of the year. Floating docks deployed there in 1986 lasted only a matter of days before they broke apart due to constant and heavy surge. The channel entrance is narrow and shallow with breaking surf across its entire width on days with even moderate seas and/or swells. . . . The concrete wharf inside the harbor is too high to be of practical use to the fishing boats and is open at the bottom allowing small boats to be pushed underneath while docking (Templet Resources Inc. 1986:vi.2).

Ta'ū village harbor and dock with fishing catamaran (alia) *tied up.*

Transportation-related issues affect economic development in all of American Samoa. The dependence on imported goods of all kinds means that a reliable system of shipment is essential. Ships carrying freight arrive and depart the port of Pago Pago regularly, and the facilities for handling containerized freight in the port town have been expanded considerably over the past fifteen years. Surface shipping is a reliable, albeit slow, means of distribution between American Samoa and other countries, but remains problematic within the territory. Commercial air transportation is much less effective, however; any business needing rapid shipment of goods might be hampered in operating because of the lack of dependable air service to major Pacific cities.

Transportation also will be a factor affecting the development of tourism in American Samoa. Tourism is an important source of revenue in many South Pacific island economies, and Samoans are anxious to see this industry flourish in their country. They will face obstacles in making tourism a viable aspect of their economic development, however. Getting the tourists to Samoa and providing acceptable lodging will be major challenges. Airfare is expensive, and with only one major airline providing service in 1990, potential tourists and Samoan travelers alike are a captive audience. Residents have no choice, but tourists might select other locales for vacations where options are more competitive and schedules more predictable. For those who do go to American Samoa, there is adequate ground transportation available in the form of car rentals, taxis, and buses, at least on Tutuila.

The main source of lodging for visitors since the late 1960s has been the Rainmaker Hotel, a large facility centrally located on Pago Pago Bay on the island of Tutuila. The exterior of the buildings and surrounding grounds are attractive, but the general condition of the hotel has been a topic of much concern in the last few years. The deterioration between 1976, when we spent some time living in the hotel, and 1988 was significant. Tropical decay, inattention, and management problems are probable explanations for this situation. With rates comparable to better motels/hotels in midwestern U.S. cities, the average American tourist—and many from other countries—might well expect more for the price.

In early 1990, an American developer proposed a grandiose plan for a "five-star" quality resort with a hotel, four restaurants, a golf course, multiple swimming pools, and a marina to be built on the north shore of Tutuila. Any such plan will be contingent upon working out acceptable agreements with Samoan families who own the land in the area, and this represents a formidable challenge at best. If it becomes a reality, it could be a boon for tourism in American Samoa.

There is already good food available at the many restaurants on Tutuila, and at reasonable prices. At most of the establishments likely to be patronized by tourists, one finds few, if any, native dishes being served. The adventurous visitor would no doubt like to sample something characteristic of the more traditional Samoan diet—taro, breadfruit, *palusami*—and eat local fresh fruit rather than canned varieties.

The biggest assets for tourism in Samoa are the people themselves, who are attractive, pleasant, and friendly, and the sheer beauty of the islands. A high, volcanic island in the South Pacific is lush and green, with colorful and fragrant flowers growing everywhere on trees and bushes; even the people wear bright colors and flowers. Driving along the serpentine main road, which follows the shoreline on the south side of the island of Tutuila, one breathtaking vista after another appears around each bend. Contemporary houses are often painted or trimmed colorfully,

Rainmaker Hotel on Pago Pago Bay, Tutuila, American Samoa.

and yards are neatly trimmed grass or swept clean if sandy. Even laundry drying on a line may present a rainbow of color to passers-by.

Because the islands of American Samoa are small, sightseeing on the main island does not take long. Opportunities to visit Manu'a could greatly enhance tourist activities; a study to assess economic development prospects for Manu'a suggests that tourism is perhaps the most feasible option (Templet Resources, Inc. 1986). To entice more visitors to the area, provision of food service and lodging facilities, now almost negligible in these islands, will be essential, as will improved transportation, especially air service.

Promotion of scuba diving off the island of Ofu, where there is already a guest house, is a new tourist attraction. There is even discussion of developing a national park in American Samoa, most of which would be in Manu'a according to existing proposals. If and when such a park comes into existence, tourism could become a much more important factor in Samoa's economy, with the Manu'a islands playing a new and larger role.

FAMILY AND VILLAGE LIFE

In Manu'a, the increasing influence of the West has altered many of the traditional activities and cultural values of the family. Thus far, however, the *matai* system survives, in somewhat modified form, as the foundation of social, political, and economic organization. The majority of Manu'a *matai* continue to be supported by the communal farming and fishing activities of their household members, although about one-fourth of the island group's inhabitants now hold government jobs. Those who have found the *matai* system not to their liking have long since departed for Pago Pago or for the United States, where they can control their own economic and social destiny. However, even many of those who prefer living independently support the concept of the traditional system through remittances.

Such remittances from overseas relatives average about $1,900 a year per household, and some *matai* receive as much as $400 per month from these sources. This kind of support strengthens the status of the extended family—and its chief— by permitting greater participation in status-conferring activities such as donating generously to the church, engaging in extravagant gift exchanges, or purchasing prestige goods such as radios, television sets, refrigerators, or VCRs.

There are, however, changes in the ways the *matai* system works, even in such isolated areas as Manu'a. An increasing number of families are allocating sections of family land to untitled heads of constituent biological family units to work as private land, if only for a limited time. As early as 1962, 66 percent of the families of Fitiuta permitted untitled members to work "private" land. In spite of this, every *matai* in the village claimed that he received generous donations from the members of his household to promote family prestige and well being. While at one time a *matai* might have expected family members with government jobs to turn over their entire paycheck to the family head, this is a rare occurrence today. Family members might be expected to donate a generous share for the support of the *matai* and the *'aiga,* but the bulk of the income would be theirs to spend on themselves and their immediate family. There are still constant demands for donations for *fa'alavelave* (family trouble) situations, but *matai* today are finding this more and more difficult to collect.

Since every untitled man looks forward to someday being elected to a title, and since gifts to the *matai* and to the family as a whole are considered to be a form of service (an important consideration in the selection of a *matai*), there is still a great deal of income-sharing within household units. In spite of the greater emphasis now being placed on the individual in the economic and social interactions of the household, the average Samoan is still committed to the traditional system. Even among teachers and government office workers in Tutuila (the most acculturated of Samoans), it was found that more than three-fourths believed that the *matai* system is adequate for shaping the future of Samoan society.

Even though inhabitants of Tutuila are much less traditional in their economic activities and attitudes, many of them are not completely in favor of what has been happening to the Samoan life-style over the last twenty-five or thirty years. The tuna canneries, for example, have never been popular places to work. Some Samoans express great joy at being fired for inefficiency because they can then go back to their *matai*, having tried to make extra money for the family but having failed because of the factory's "unreasonable demands" on its workers. The cannery, however, has never had a shortage of workers because many of the employees are Western Samoans who have been lured to Tutuila by the higher pay scales of American Samoa.

Although Samoan social organization is one of the more tenacious and supportive aspects of Samoan culture, the system is beginning to break down in many respects, especially on Tutuila. As early as 1970, Robert Maxwell reported:

> Family heads, who previously commanded the distribution of wealth, now find themselves with a decreasing economic basis for their political authority. And they themselves are not unaware that their power is being threatened from all sides. . . . And their moral influence even within their own families, is waning, as more youngsters move out from under their scrutiny and control and establish themselves as wage earners elsewhere (1970:145).

In many of these Tutuilan villages, households include distant relatives who have moved in from the more remote areas to work in industry or for the government. Although the chief in whose household they reside is a kinsman, he often is not the *matai* to whom they owe their primary allegiance, and his control over their actions and attitudes is often less than effective. Regarding this breakdown of family authority, Alan Howard writes:

> When Samoans migrate the structure of supports for authority, including parental authority, is eroded, leaving the burden of controls on the individual. But to the extent that the individual has been trained to rely on external authority and social submission, the appropriate channeling of underlying anger may not occur. The result is an increased variability in ways of handling anger and a greater frequency of socially inappropriate outburst of hostility (1986:414).

In outlying villages like Fitiuta, village councils are able to control the behavior of the local inhabitants through a system of fines imposed upon the family head of an erring individual. In the more urban villages of Tutuila, however, councils do little of a punitive nature. Violations of law tend to become police matters rather than council matters. Pago Pago Bay-area households are extremely fluid in composition, and people come and go and rarely develop any sense of belonging or family loyalty. Delinquency in the form of property destruction, truancy, pilfering, and drunkenness has become a major problem among teenagers and young adults.

A headline in the *Samoa News* on June 20, 1989, read "American Samoa leads U.S. in Drunk Driving Arrests." The accompanying article reported that, in 1988, this territory with less than 37,000 people had 347 DUI arrests with a conviction rate of 94 percent. It also pointed out that alcohol played a role in other crimes as well. Department of Safety (police) records maintain that 100 percent of homicides were alcohol related, and alcohol was a factor in 67 percent of rapes, 72 percent of assaults, 33 percent of robberies, and approximately 68 percent of public peace disturbances. This represents a significant change in Samoan behavior, since, in 1954, we observed almost no consumption of alcohol and almost no crime.

Although being a *matai* may have its down side, it is not unusual in Samoa today for people to return to the islands from well-paying jobs in the United States for the express purpose of acquiring a *matai* title. Being titled is a source of prestige and a prerequisite to holding office in the Senate of American Samoa.

Something of the respect still accorded the *matai* system and the importance of chiefly rank in Manu'a can be seen in the following description of a *Pa'i i Faleula* (official inauguration ceremony) for new title holders to the village council of Fitiuta. In July 1989, the *Samoa News* reported,

> The new title holders were La'apui Taiealo and Sega To'o of To'oto'o (High Talking Chief) rank, and Logoai. A total of 32 *matais* of lower ranks were also admitted to the council during the ceremony. Most of them have held their respective titles for some years, but they had to wait until last Thursday to make it official at the *"Pa'i i Faleula"* ceremony. All individuals who have been granted *matai* titles of lower ranks . . . cannot be admitted without coming in the shadow of a high talking chief.
>
> The *fono* began at 8:00 a.m. and the ceremony was not over until 1:00 p.m. One of the reported reasons for such a lengthy session was the fact that every "candidate" to the council had to give a speech (his admission to the council is subject to the acceptance of his speech by the council as a whole). The feast which followed the ceremony was reported to be lavish (*Samoa* News, July 3, 1989).

In all Manu'an villages, village councils still have strong decision-making authority in ceremonial and civic matters; they still settle disputes between families and work for community welfare and prestige. In recent years, however, the role, function, and authority of the village council has generally declined in American Samoa as a whole. Village councils rarely meet because most of the *matai* hold jobs and do not have the time; when they do meet, more often than not it is for ceremonial functions rather than civic leadership.

Along with the decline in the leadership role and authority of village councils in much of American Samoa has gone a decline in the importance of the *aumaga*, the organization which was once referred to as the "strength of the village." This group of untitled young men still exists in most villages and can be mobilized when need be, but mostly they carry out ceremonial functions and rarely, if ever, engage in

Aumaga *members make up* fautasi *crew for Flag Day competitions. Note tattooing on two of the oarsmen.*

cooperative work projects such as planting a village taro patch or conducting a fish drive on the village reef. They are more likely to represent the village as a competitive dance group, as a *fautasi* rowing crew at a Flag Day celebration, or as a rugby or cricket team at an island sports competition. The nature of *aumaga* activities is reflected in the headline "Fagatogo Aumaga and Lions Club are Working Together on Youth Project" (*Samoa News,* July 6, 1989). This project involved raising funds for a Youth Center with a basketball court and a children's playground.

In Manu'an villages, where *aumaga* were vital parts of village life not too many years ago, councils are hard pressed these days to mobilize anything of this nature at all. There are so few young adult males living in Manu'a now that villages are lucky to have enough untitled young men present to wring and serve the *kava* and prepare a meal for the chiefs, let alone engage in civic work activities. If and when interisland vessels need to be unloaded these days, the labor is carried out by middle-aged or elderly chiefs.

The situation is much the same for the *aualuma,* the group of unmarried women who traditionally served as the handmaidens of the *taupou.* This group, in most American Samoan villages, exists in name only and has been merged with the Women's Committee (composed mainly of chiefs' wives) and assists in benevolent and charitable activities such as raising money for the church or for the local school.

Other changes in Samoan social behavior should be noted as well. Everything about family life has been affected by modernization, American style. Households are smaller, couples have fewer children, and a large percentage of women are employed. Robert Franco has observed that, today, many of the family responsibilities fall unevenly on young people. He states that there is great pressure on American Samoan youth, as frequently parents are working forty hours a week in the relatively strong American Samoan economy and . . . when a family crisis occurs much of the labor burden falls on students who must be pulled out of school to work preparing food, cleaning the village and guesthouses, and even working part-time to contribute to family *matai* (1985:6–7).

Most young people do, however, finish high school, and many leave the islands for the United States immediately after graduation. A large number go into the military, and recruiters from all services make frequent visits to Pago Pago. High schools in Manu'a and Tutuila look much like their counterparts in the United States, with teenage couples in latest fashions holding hands and lounging on the campus grass. A generation ago, such public displays of affection would have been considered scandalous.

Courtship behavior definitely follows American patterns, and marriage has been taking place at a later age. Weddings are still important events, with large numbers of groomsmen in formal wear and bridesmaids in expensive gowns. Wedding feasts are lavish, and costly, and repleat with gift exchanges between the families; occasionally, a wedding reception is held at the Rainmaker Hotel. These events undoubtedly strain the resources of everyone involved.

In 1954, spouses did nothing together as a couple outside the home—even when attending church, men sat on one side and women on the other. Couples did not go to other people's homes for a social evening, and marriage partners certainly did not go out to parties or to restaurants together. Men socialized with their male relatives and women with women. It is now common to observe couples—sometimes whole families—dining out. Another innovation in Samoan life is the increase in the divorce rate; in 1954, a divorced person was rare indeed.

Although many families on Tutuila have adopted more American patterns of immediate family behavior, such change has been within the traditional extended family context of kin cooperation and concern. Family remains a dominant institution in Samoan life, and one rarely escapes its influence.

The aging process has traditionally been marked by increasing authority and patterns of respect and support by younger family members. While many elders still claim that old age is the best time of life, old age in Samoa today is not untouched by the forces of change. Generally improved health care has resulted in increased life expectancy—72.8 years for men and 79.1 for women in 1986 (United Nations 1990). This is to some extent due to reduced infant mortality, but people are also actually living longer. People aged 60 and older represented 5.1 percent of the population in 1985, an increase of 1 percent just since 1974 (ASG 1988).

Older Samoans are still living within extended family households, and most care is provided within that context, although the many competing activities outside the home may compromise the special attention and services from younger family members that were so characteristic of the past. However, the aged themselves are participants in elements of the new lifestyle, especially such things as bingo games, which are very popular with this age group. They also travel to the United States, since most have family members living there. The notion of retirement has become quite familiar to Samoans, and because more and more of them have earned Social Security credits through employment, they now have monetary resources not widely available in years past. Perhaps because of access to pension programs and extended life expectancy, old age is considered to begin at 60 to 65 years rather than age 50, as perceived a generation ago.

For the aged in American Samoa, there are special U.S. government-supported programs provided through the Territorial Administration on Aging, although special concessions have been negotiated in an attempt to accommodate cultural differences. Programs include food vouchers, an employment program, and transportation assistance. The latter is especially valuable for Manu'a residents, who may travel to Tutuila by air once a month. Tutuila residents receive bus-fare assistance.

A home for the aged was opened in American Samoa in 1987. As part of *Fatu o Aiga,* a large Catholic church complex in Tafuna, it is operated by the Poor Sisters of Nazareth. In 1988, a year after opening, it had very few residents and, perhaps, represents an idea whose time has not yet come in this setting. The Sisters turned part of the facility into a preschool, which met with greater success.

When death comes to either old or young, the cultural response is quite different from what it was in 1954, when people were buried in the front yard within twenty-four hours. Burial still takes place largely on family land, although there are small cemeteries next to some village churches. Today, however, funerals may take place long after death. There are refrigeration facilities to preserve corpses until relatives can arrive from the United States. While burial was once entirely the responsibility of the families, there are now morticians available to handle service arrangements complete with hearses, imported caskets, and American funeral etiquette.

POLITICAL ORGANIZATION

Until 1977, all governors of American Samoa were appointed by the president of the United States and, with a single exception, they were all non-Samoans. Since American Samoans have been electing their own chief executive, there have been just two governors—Peter Coleman, who has been elected for three terms as a Republican, and A. P. Lutali, who served a single term as a Democrat. Such party labels are new in Samoa, but so are other political phenomena such as rallies in the park, promotional dinners at the Rainmaker Hotel, and substantial campaign spending. In the 1988 political campaign, candidates for office spent a total of $623,642, or about $46 per registered voter.

Although Samoans prefer to elect their own, they are quite content to remain within the American national sphere. They reject ideas of independence and also of consolidation with Western Samoa. Although American Samoa collects income and sales taxes and has other forms of revenue, the territory continues to receive a large portion of its annual budget (47 percent or $51,684,000 in 1987) from U.S. congressional appropriations.

The constitution of American Samoa mandates a bicameral legislature, with a Senate composed of legislators (one from each of eighteen counties) chosen from the highest traditional titleholder ranks at a general meeting of the paramount chiefs

Governor A. P. Lutali, American Samoa's chief executive from 1984–1988.

of the county's several villages. The composition of the Senate can roughly be compared to that of the House of Lords in England.

The Samoan House of Representatives consists of twenty-one legislators, elected by popular vote, with one from each legislative district. They need not be titled individuals. American Samoa also has a delegate to the House of Representatives in Washington, who has no vote, but serves as a lobbyist for Samoan interests.

The people of American Samoa have found great satisfaction in their ability to control their political future through the election of gubernatorial administrations, and voter participation is remarkable, often amounting to nearly 80 percent of registered voters. Participation of Samoans at all levels of government has also been greatly affected. In 1962–1963, when Lowell Holmes studied village and territorial political organization, he described Samoan politics as follows:

> While American Samoa has many able potential leaders the present governmental situation is depressing. The current administration [of H. Rex Lee], perhaps through suspicion, lack of confidence or lack of understanding, does not encourage Samoan leadership. . . . There is little to induce educated Samoans to return to the islands . . . due to the discrepancies in wages and other benefits between Samoans and similarly qualified Europeans . . . (1964:448).

In the 1960s and 1970s, Samoans were actually discriminated against for top governmental positions, but today there is a kind of reverse policy in which educated and qualified Samoans are given preference. The day of the American contract employee is nearly over. In November 1988, a long-standing legal precedent was broken when Lealaialoa F. Michael Kruse was sworn in as American Samoa's first Samoan Chief Justice of the High Court. In our 1988 research, we were pleased to find that several college-educated Samoans with whom we had worked in the San Francisco Bay area when we studied the migrant Samoan community had returned to their homeland and were working in key government positions.

Even the popular election of governors has not solved all of American Samoa's problems, and the territory is having its share of growing pains. Most of the criticisms of recent administrations seem directed toward "misguided spending priorities," and a complaint, often from the more Americanized of the citizens, which has to do with the elite nature of the Senate. Some believe that a legislative body selected solely on the basis of chiefly rank conflicts with participatory democracy. In response to this criticism, Governor Coleman is on record as countering, "I disagree that the *matai* system should stay out of politics. In my assessment, there is far more wisdom in the Senate than in that free-for-all in the House of Representatives" (Booth 1985:460).

THE ENVIRONMENT

Increased industrialization and modernization, coupled with rapid population growth, have produced ecological problems. Prior to the government's program to modernize American Samoa, there was little environmental deterioration, and conservation of natural resources was not an issue. The relatively small population could easily support itself on family land, with a minimum of agricultural labor, and there was no problem obtaining ample food from the sea. Since there was no way of preserving the fish, only as many fish were caught as would supply a family meal and perhaps also allow for a generous food gift to a neighbor.

Until recently, sanitation and waste disposal problems were minor. Most materials Samoans used for day-to-day living were biodegradable. Houses were made of wood and leaves, food trays were woven from coconut fronds, banana leaves served as plates, the Samoan fork was a piece of bamboo, coconut shells served as water containers, produce was carried from the bush and stored in coconut-leaf baskets, and body decorations consisted of flowers or colorful leaves. In a village like Fitiuta, there were no cars, refrigerators, or other household appliances—in fact, there was no electricity and no roads. Canned food (mostly corned beef from New Zealand) has been around for a long time, but not in such quantities that the cans caused much of a refuse problem. They did sometimes contribute to health problems, however, because empty tin cans often collected rain water and were excellent breeding places for mosquitos.

The variety of material goods now available is leading to disposal problems. More packaged and canned foods and household supplies are used in Samoan homes. For example, there is great demand for canned beer and soda pop, and, like their American counterparts, Samoan babies now wear disposable diapers, a significant issue in a small island nation with a very high birth rate. Houses are much more likely today to have American-style furniture rather than the minimal furnishings of the past, and the large number of cars in a climate conducive to rust and corrosion of metal suggests the nature of the potential trash problem facing this nation.

The American Samoan government has a garbage disposal service, but there are problems related to inadequate landfill space and negotiations of leases of communal land for such purposes from families. There are perennial complaints about trash in the stream beds and in the harbor. Periodic beautification campaigns are launched in an attempt to inspire residents to keep the island clean.

As of 1990, the government water system provides service only to part of the main island of Tutuila. Villages have a variety of catchment systems, some of which were installed when populations were much smaller; many remain untreated and unfiltered. Heavy rains often cause debris to clog the lines, interfering with supply. It is not unusual to see notices in the newspaper recommending boiling the water for health reasons.

These are not new concerns in Samoa, and the government and most citizens are aware of the need for improvement; gradually, steps are being taken to solve the existing deficiencies in water delivery systems.

Industrial development and other aspects of modernization have brought other serious environmental concerns for American Samoa. In the spring of 1990, the Samoa News (March 23) reported "A recently completed study of water quality in Pago Pago Harbor concludes that if nothing is done to curtail pollution, 'Pago Pago Bay Harbor will die.' " At an open hearing on this issue, testimony of citizens recalled the clean, clear bay water of fifty years ago in contrast to the dirty conditions present today. The tuna canneries are a major source of waste, which presents the government with the problem of protecting the environment while not antagonizing the country's largest private employer.

The many fishing boats necessary to supply tuna to the canneries also contribute to the pollution problem by illegally dumping waste oil and, sometimes, raw sewage in the harbor area. The American Samoa Environmental Protection Agency collected $50,000 in fines in 1988 for oil spills. The country is completely dependent upon imported oil and gas, and the frequent passage of oil tankers in and out of the bay sets the stage for more massive oil spills. Oil storage facilities are already creating hazards with the need for replacement of older tanks, seepage of waste into the ground near the shoreline, and the necessity for relocation of residents of nearby homes for their safety.

There is a sewage treatment plant on Tutuila, but not all of the bay area is connected to the system. On occasion, the treatment plant experiences mechanical breakdowns, which result in an overload of the system and subsequent dumping of raw sewage into the harbor. We were present on the island in June, 1988, during such an occurrence. Inadequacy of the budget was a factor in that instance.

Efforts to clean up the harbor are hampered by insufficient funds. Clean-up services are contracted out to a local company, but recently, there has not been enough money to pay for continuous service. This and other environmental issues will no doubt become more challenging for Samoans in the future as population pressures and modern development magnify the problems.

EDUCATION

In November 1964 the Crown Prince of Tonga (now King Taufa'ahau Tupou IV) addressed a congregation of some seven thousand Samoans in Pago Pago, stating,

"In ancient times the environment of Samoa and Tonga ended at the seashore of Samoa and Tonga. Today, the world is smaller. Now the whole world is our environment."

This statement would be truer for American Samoans than any third-world population in the world, for unlike any other, they have been exposed totally to the most pervasive Western educational influence ever devised in a developing terri- tory. That influence has been the educational television system established in 1964 at a cost of nearly twenty-four million dollars. When in full operation, the system brought 180 video lessons a week into classrooms in twenty-four government schools in Tutuila, Aunu'u, and Manu'a. In addition to elementary and secondary school programming, the system also was used to teach Samoan teachers (after school hours) and to educate and entertain those older than school age.

Credit (or discredit) for the establishment of the system must be given to Governor H. Rex Lee, appointed by President John F. Kennedy to serve American Samoa as chief executive from 1961 to 1967. Selected originally to direct a crash program to rectify the ills described in a *Reader's Digest* article (Hall 1961) titled "Samoa: America's Shame in the South Seas," Lee immediately set about to produce what politicians might conceive of as a properly developed and adminis- tered territorial possession. After lengthening the jet airstrip, blacktopping the main roads on the island of Tutuila, and building a hotel for tourists, Lee turned his energies to the area of education, particularly to the problem most likely to disturb a government administrator who does not speak the native language—the fact that the natives were not fluent in English. In order to upgrade the level of fluency in English in particular—and educational quality in general—the governor, on the advice of Vernon Bronson, executive consultant for the National Association of Educational Broadcasters, turned to educational television as the most economical and, hopefully, effective means of improving the local educational system. The realities of the situation were that most of the teachers were Samoans with little or no college training and with a competency in English that, in many cases, was little better than that of the children they were trying to teach.

Advice on establishing a television curriculum was sought from Superintendent Lawrence Shepoiser of the Wichita, Kansas, school system, who had experimented extensively with video education. A major hurdle at the outset was the matter of installing the broadcasting hardware. In order to cope with the problem of broadcasting a signal to twenty-four consolidated schools in all parts of the mountainous islands of Tutuila and Manu'a—the latter being sixty miles away—it was determined that a 226-foot transmitting tower must be located on the 1,603-foot summit of Mt. Alava, near Pago Pago, along with a $140,000 tramway system to transport the technicians to the lofty control room. Another problem related to the fact that very few of the villages had electricity; therefore, power lines had to be installed to make the television circuit operational. Margaret Mead dedicated a power plant on Ta'ū island in 1971, signalling the completion of the electrification program.

Special teams of educational advisors determined that the new curriculum should emphasize language arts, science, mathematics, and social science. Since the teaching of language arts (mostly oral English) was seen to be the most important aspect of the the new educational enterprise, a specialist was brought in from New Zealand to establish a unique linguistic approach to English similar to one that had been successfully used to give European immigrants to Australia a quick, but fundamental, knowledge of the language.

Emphasis on television instruction did not mean that the Samoan classroom teachers would be eliminated. Teachers, however, were given no role in the planning, decision making, appraising, or reviewing of the program, nor were community leaders or parents consulted. Classroom teachers supposedly functioned as aids to television instruction and as catalysts to learning. More often than not, they saw themselves as classroom monitors or baby-sitters rather than educators, and they felt threatened by the new approach. Television presentations accounted for about 25 to 30 percent of the child's educational experience. Each televised lesson lasted about twenty minutes. The television was then turned off, and the Samoan teachers took over, administering supplementary exercises, or drills, all developed at the broadcasting center by contract American educators. Ideally, the Samoan teachers were supposed to provide feedback to the broadcasters by evaluating the effectiveness of the lessons for children whose culture and behavior they understood. Because the teachers were able to speak Samoan, some of the less-ethnocentric American educators believed that they could clarify concepts which students were having difficulty comprehending when presented only in English. However, it was generally felt that too frequent use of Samoan in classrooms was a bad thing.

There was, however, a genuine interest in encouraging children to learn about their cultural heritage. Courses such as Polynesian history, Samoan language arts, Living in the South Pacific, Samoan language and culture, Samoan writing, Samoan reading, and Living in Samoa were important aspects of the educational experience.

Adult education programming was also a part of the program. Because families did not have television sets in the late 1960s and early 1970s, schools were left open in the evenings so that families could take advantage of three hours of evening broadcast. These evening programs consisted of industrial films and travelogs, commercial programs (situation comedies and westerns preferred), and National Educational Television programs. Locally produced shows for adults included English language instruction, public health education, and agricultural information, as well as Samoan and world news broadcasts.

During the early to mid 1970s, the television-centered educational system was reported to be accomplishing marvelous things for the territory's ten thousand school children. Daily attendance averages were said to be 94 percent, and the high-school graduation rate was 90 percent. Budget cuts by Congress during the 1970s, however, were threatening what many considered the "bold experiment." By 1979, station KVZK was still broadcasting 565 hours a week of educational television, but these were reruns of locally produced shows (some as old as six to ten years) and some mainland imports such as "Sesame Street" and "The Electric Company." Television no longer provided the core of instruction in the Samoan system. Instructional programs were limited to only three elementary level subjects—oral English (with English sound drills), social studies, and language arts. The classroom television set was functioning more as a supplement or an enriching source. Instead of the original three hours of extracurricular programming targeted for adults, American Samoa now was providing 174 hours a week of U.S. network programming on three channels. Almost every Samoan household had its own television set, and prime-time programming was significantly influencing Samoan attitudes, values, and lifestyles.

Critics of the educational television experiment (Schramm, Nelson, and Betham 1981) contend that educational television, if properly used, can improve a school system, but it cannot produce a miracle, which is what Governor H. Rex Lee sought. Too little time was devoted to planning, program production, consultation with classroom teachers, evaluation, and consultation with parents and community leaders in the effort to turn the Samoan school system around overnight.

Actually, remarkable strides were made in a few short years. By the end of the 1970s, the territory had twenty-six modern consolidated elementary schools, compared to fifty-one poorly equipped schools in 1961. Universal high-school education had become a reality—there were three high schools on Tutuila and one in Manu'a group in the village of Ta'ū. More and more high-school graduates were going on to college on the mainland (many on football scholarships), and a community college on Tutuila had an enrollment of more than one thousand students.

The American Samoa public school system today services approximately 14,200 students and comprises ninety early childhood education centers (preschools for three- four-year-olds) located in villages, nineteen consolidated elementary schools, five high schools, a vocational-technical school, a center for special education, and the American Samoa Community College. There are also nine parochial schools, plus a Montessori preschool on Tutuila operated by the Poor Sisters of Nazareth. These church-sponsored institutions enroll approximately 2,000 Samoan students at tuition rates that average about $100 per month. Education in the territory is compulsory through the twelfth grade or until the age of eighteen.

Modern consolidated elementary school buildings.

The past thirty-seven years have witnessed an extraordinary growth in education throughout the islands. In 1954, when Lowell Holmes first worked in the villages of Fitiuta and Ta'ū, almost no one had more than an elementary-school education. The local schools only went through the eighth grade. A tally of 933 Manu'a people age 15 and older conducted in 1980, however, revealed that 187 (26 percent) graduated from high school, 20 (2 percent) graduated from college, and 5 (.05 percent) attended graduate school.

While educational policy was once made by American contract employees hired by the Department of the Interior, Samoan administrators in the Department of Education today completely control the direction and content of Samoan education. Although Samoan administrators set policy, the system continues to emphasize "education for export." The department sees as its mission to "prepare each individual for the personally satisfying and socially useful life wherever he chooses to live. As long as a majority of young Samoans migrate to the United States to search for the type of job they want, local schools should help prepare emigrants to compete for overseas jobs" (*Samoa News,* September 9, 1988).

It is particularly interesting that the goal of modern Samoan education is also "to help each person reach his fullest potential as a unique individual." It is interesting because this goal appears to be directed toward fulfilling individual needs rather than communal needs such as service to family (*tautua*) and to the village—values that have always been preeminent in traditional Samoan society.

The emphasis on what some have labelled "education for export" would appear to be appropriate, considering the realities of modern emigration trends. A study of 645 high school students carried out by the Economic Development and Planning Office in 1987 revealed that only 9 percent planned on staying in American Samoa after graduating from high school or community college. Approximately half of this sample anticipated emigration "in order to earn a higher salary or to find a job that is interesting," while another 33 percent planned to leave to pursue additional education. When asked what kinds of jobs they wanted after completing their education, not a single one was interested in farming or fishing, the age-old occupations of Samoa. For females, the top career choices were secretary, travel agent, bank officer, and accountant. Males preferred careers as mechanics, TV/radio technicians, electricians, carpenters, welders, or police officers (*Samoa News,* September 9, 1988).

The high-school population of American Samoa today is surprisingly heterogeneous. Only 56 percent consider Samoan to be their first language, while 36 percent claim English as their first language. In spite of this, school officials complain that 88 to 90 percent of public school students are having difficulty with their school work because of limited knowledge of English. Dr. Salu Reid, of the Department of Education, contends that conversing in English is not the problem—reading and understanding the language is. She estimates that 70 percent of high school students do not know how to read English.

The high-school student body is also nationally quite diverse. While American Samoa is the birthplace of 56 percent of students, 19 percent were born in Western Samoa, 14 percent on the mainland, and 6 percent in Hawaii.

For those who choose to further their education in the territory, there is the

American Samoa Community College where 30 to 40 percent of high school graduates enroll annually. The two-year college, which charges only $2.00 per credit hour tuition, has a broad curriculum offering Associate of Arts and Associate of Science degrees. The student body, numbering approximately one thousand, majors primarily in business subjects (including computer science), nursing and health sciences, and administration of justice.

One of the more practical courses is one which teaches the making of traditional Samoan artifacts. These classes are taught by senior citizens who instruct students in the making of floor and sleeping mats, *siapo* (tapa cloth), finemats, baskets, and hats. They also maintain a demonstration garden which grows pandanus (used in mat-making), paper mulberry (for tapa), and Samoan tapa dye plants. For those who choose to remain in Samoa, this education could prove to be very profitable, for there is great demand by tourists for traditional artifacts, but very little is available for purchase.

While station KVZK-TV was once the mainstay of Samoan education, it is no longer under Department of Education control, but is connected to the Office of Public Information. There is still some educational broadcasting, but the station's main function is transmitting commercial television, which arrived via satellite for the first time in March, 1987. Prior to that time, programming from all major networks arrived in the form of tapes flown in from the United States.

SAMOAN HEALTH

The U.S. Navy maintained a hospital in the Pago Pago Bay area and operated a nurse training program during their administration. They trained Samoan medical practitioners to staff outlying dispensaries, although in some cases, pharmacist's mates were assigned this duty. During her research sojourn in Ta'ū village in 1925–1926, Margaret Mead resided with the family of Chief Pharmacist's Mate Edward R. Holt. Under the Department of the Interior administration in 1968, the deteriorating and spatially inadequate Navy hospital was replaced by the Lyndon B. Johnson Tropical Medical Center in the village of Faga'alu, just outside the Pago Pago Bay area. Initially, it was staffed by U.S. Public Health physicians and provided comprehensive medical care for little or no cost. Currently, the fee for inpatient care is only $7.50 a day for resident Samoans. The present staff—no longer confined to Public Health doctors—includes surgeons, gynecologists, pediatricians, family practice generalists, and a psychiatrist and is capable of handling all but the most serious medical problems. Heart and eye surgery, chemotherapy, and radiation therapy cases are sent by air, at government expense, to Tripler General Hospital in Honolulu. In 1987, the government of American Samoa spent nearly $2 million on airfare and hospital costs at Tripler, although they have a comprehensive rate agreement of $480 per day per patient. Resident Samoans have the option of being treated in other hospitals in Honolulu, but are required to pay charges in excess of Tripler's rates.

The islands of the Manu'a group are served by four dispensaries—in the villages of Fitiuta, Ta'ū, Ofu, and Olosega. These are staffed by licensed practical nurses and, occasionally, registered nurses; medical doctors make periodic trips to the island group to staff clinics. Patients whose ailments are beyond the capabilities of the attendant nurses are sent by air to the hospital in Tutuila. The Samoan legislature is currently contemplating providing Manu'a with a resident medical doctor. In 1954, Ta'ū village had a resident Samoan medical practitioner, who, although not a medical doctor, had considerable medical training and experience. He even performed surgery.

Although American Samoa is blessed with medical resources as good as most rural communities in the United States, there is one medical problem that has caused considerable consternation for both medical personnel and the highly acculturated Samoans: the tendency for tradition-minded Samoans to turn first to bush medicine specialists. The following letter from a member of the Johnson Tropical Medical Center staff, published in the *Samoa News* on November 17, 1988, describes the problem:

> The most disturbing preventable problem has been the use in children of local Samoan bush medicine. By this I mean the plant and herbal medicines given by taulesea or fofō. In the past year, we saw at least six children die after being given "Samoan medicine" by mouth from a fofō. The picture was not a pretty one. The children initially had mild cases of the "flu." They were then given "Samoan medicine" and soon developed seizures, kidney failure and increased acid in the blood. Despite intensive care at the hospital, these children died within three days. . . . Many of the medicines given by a fofō are probably safe for children, but some are poisons and will quickly kill a child. In the first half of 1988, more children died in American Samoa from being given "Samoan medicine" than died from any other cause.

The conflict between the new and the old in Samoa is of considerable consequence with regard to Samoan health in a number of ways. As Samoa has moved toward modernization, the ramifications have been both positive and negative. During the thirty-seven years we have been interested in the Samoan population, there has been a decline in the death rate from infectious diseases, an increase in the death rate due to degenerative diseases, and a rise in average blood-pressure rates. While modern Samoans generally have improved nutrition, greater control over infectious diseases, and have eliminated parasites to a great extent, modernization has not been accompanied by increased growth rates in their children, in average stature, or in an earlier onset of puberty (Baker and Hanna 1986). There have also been a number of unexpected developments.

Most third-world people, when moving in the direction of modernization, experience a drop in fertility, a consequence usually associated with increased education and better employment opportunities for women. This, however, has not been true for American Samoa (*Ibid.*), where the conservative nature of the traditional family (*'āiga*) has not only encouraged large families, but has provided the child care which makes them possible. The most impressive positive corollary with modernization has been the drastic reduction of infant mortality. When Margaret Mead worked in Ta'ū and Fitiuta in 1925–1926, the death rate for babies under one year of age was 240 per 1000. By 1954, the infant mortality rate had dropped to 80 per thousand and in 1987, the figure was 10.4 (ASG 1988).

Another development is related to the effects of the modified diet that has accompanied modernization in Samoa. The diet today very likely will include not only many of the traditional foods listed below, but such imports as pizza, french fries, hamburgers, dairy products and eggs, sugar-coated cereals, and alcoholic beverages—particularly beer—in great quantities.

While weight increases are commonplace for most third-world people undergoing such dietetic modification, the Samoans seem to have surpassed everyone else in the world in their propensity to achieve massive weight gains. This has been the result of not only a changed diet, but a reduction in the average daily energy expenditure. Although these weight gains also result in a decreased work capacity, this excessive weight does not appear to be associated with cardiovascular-related mortality the way it does among African-Americans and whites (Baker and Hanna 1986). In Samoa, the problem of obesity would appear to be inevitable and irreversible, however, considering the Samoan association of corpulence with high social status and with the importance of food and feasting socially and ceremonially.

Although obesity seems an inevitable problem in modern Samoa, researchers have found that modernization has not resulted in a serious rise in cholesterol and triglyceride levels. Samoan levels in all parts of Samoa, even among Samoans living in Hawaii, are well below levels characteristic of mainland United States, in spite of the fact that Samoans are today often eating a typical American diet, have high levels of body fat, and have a relatively low physical fitness index (Ibid.). Health professionals in American Samoa are attempting to increase awareness of health risk factors through campaigns such as the Nutricise program, which involves an antismoking campaign, nutrition education, and an exercise agenda including a walking program known as Ola Malosi. Women have also been alerted to the fact that low-cost mammograms are available for those who plan to be in Hawaii—the nearest source for this procedure. In spite of modernization-generated problems, life expectancy has increased from thirty-eight in 1954 to about seventy-three for men and seventy-nine for women today.

Traditional Foods*	Western Foods
Taro	Bread
Breadfruit	Rice
Banana	Flour
Coconut	Sugar
Fish	Butter
Shellfish	Milk and cream
Poultry	Tinned meat and fish
Greens	Fresh beef and pork
Papayas	Mutton
Mangoes, limes, lemons	Canned fruits
Pork	Cocoa
	Lard
	Beverages (soda and fruit drinks)
	Alcoholic drinks
	Vegetable oil

*Adapted from Hanna, Pelletier, and Brown 1986:295.

Populations undergoing modernization invariably experience high levels of emotional stress, and American Samoa is no exception. Both life history data and studies of hormone excretion (carried out during the late 1970s by Pennsylvania State University researchers) document the presence of extreme stress for Samoan islanders living in modern urban areas such as Pago Pago and Honolulu. Some of the aggressive behavior sometimes associated with immigrants in Hawaii or California may be directly related to this problem. Stress undoubtedly also has played a role in the rise in blood-pressure levels, although such factors as obesity and increased salt intake cannot be discounted. It is interesting to note, however, that mean blood pressure is lowest in Western Samoa, which is generally much more traditional than American Samoa, followed by Manu'a, outlying villages on Tutuila, and the Pago Pago Bay area, and highest among Samoans living in Hawaii (Baker and Hanna, 1986).

SAMOAN MIGRATION TO THE UNITED STATES

One of the more important realities of modern Samoan life is that Samoans are leaving the islands in large numbers to take up residence in urban centers in Hawaii and the west coast of mainland United States. It is estimated that nearly fifty thousand Samoans now live within the states of Hawaii, California, Oregon, and Washington. The greatest concentration of immigrants in mainland America is to be found in California, primarily in the Los Angeles, San Diego, and San Francisco Bay areas. It has been reported that those in the community of Oxnard are largely from Manu'a—Olosega and the village of Fitiuta (Macpherson, et al; 1978:29). It would also be safe to assume that there are some Samoans residing in all fifty states. Independence, Missouri, for example, has a Samoan population of approximately three hundred.

Until 1951, there was little in the way of migration from American Samoa to the United States, although the territory was acquired by the U.S. Navy as early as 1900, and there never have been immigration restrictions on these island people. In 1951, when control of the territory was transferred from the Navy to the Department of the Interior, the men who had served in the Fita Fita Guard, a local naval auxiliary unit, were permitted to transfer to the regular Navy. These men, and their families, were assigned to a variety of bases in Hawaii, California, Washington, even New York.

The departure of the Navy left American Samoa with serious economic problems. Gone was the $282,000 annual civilian payroll. Economic conditions were largely responsible for the emigration of more than 1,500 Samoans to the United States during 1952. From that beginning, emigration has increased over the years to a point that many villages in American Samoa now have almost no young people between the ages of twenty and thirty-five.

With the coming of greater prosperity, more Western ideas, better transportation, and better education, young people seemed more inclined to leave the islands in search of better job opportunities and advanced education. Some insight into the Samoan migration mentality may be obtained from the following passage from the book *Sons for the Return Home* by Samoan novelist Albert Wendt:

Navy recruiters in Pago Pago, American Samoa. Young Samoans find the armed forces very attractive as a career.

The promise of the future and their dreams of lucrative jobs, money, houses, cars, a good education for their children, calmed their fears, gave meaning to their journey into what they all believed would be only a temporary exile from which they would return unharmed, unchanged, rich (1973:216).

The migration pattern has generally been that young people, mostly men, have come to the United States looking for well-paying jobs, which will enable them to obtain material possessions beyond their reach in Samoa. There is also a desire to obtain education for themselves or their children and, for some, a desire to escape what they consider to be an oppressive traditional social system involving heavy obligations to *matai*. Some, no doubt, leave out of a sense of adventure and curiosity. Large numbers of young men, and a few young women, join the armed services after high-school graduation, and Army, Navy and Air Force recruiters are frequent visitors to Pago Pago.

After adjusting to the new environment, often with the help of relatives already established stateside in mainland communities, migrants send for wives or other relatives to join them. Since living costs are much higher in the United States, and most Samoans cannot command high wages because of a lack of technical skills, it is often necessary to have several members of each household employed. Many families have teenagers working part time and contributing their earnings to the support of the household; heads of some households often are forced to hold more than one job. The need to have someone at home during the day to tend small children and to maintain the home for its working members often prompts Samoan couples to send for their parents or other elderly relatives. More often than not, these visits are anticipated to be brief—just until the financial situation improves—but in many cases, the move becomes more or less permanent

The authors conducted a study of thirty-five Samoan households in the San Francisco Bay area. We found that the Samoan community in the San Francisco Bay area is widely dispersed, although there is a concentration of Samoans near Daly City and in South San Francisco. There are no such things as Samoan ghettos, although Samoans, who tend to be poor, often settle in areas populated by underprivileged minorities. In many cases, they were found in public housing projects along with African-Americans, Puerto Ricans, and Mexican-Americans. There are also large numbers of middle income Samoans who own their own homes and live in middle-class neighborhoods. Samoans are not particularly conspicuous as a minority, and most residents of San Francisco are amazed when told that several thousand of these South Sea people live among them.

Samoan families in San Francisco are relatively homogeneous in composition. Family heads and their wives tend to be young to middle aged. There is a high percentage of children, and, in many cases, these include nieces, nephews, grandchildren, and other collateral relatives. There are a few old people, the majority of which are women. Families vary in size from six to fourteen individuals, with the average being about eight people per family. Although some homes are located in less-than-desirable neighborhoods, all the homes we visited were clean, in reasonable repair, and most had adequate furniture. Many were cramped, considering the number of family members housed. Most families appeared to be maintaining a very modest lifestyle, but there was no real neediness apparent.

The biggest problem for most households was the disruptive effect of American urban culture on the teenagers and young adults. Intergenerational conflicts are common, and adolescents seem to have an extraordinary capacity for getting into trouble with the law. In the new urban setting, these young people are not subject to the traditional controls of family and village discipline operative in Samoa and are often, as one author put it, "lost in their freedom." Evidence of this is found in a series of articles in the *Samoa News* in 1989 which described the problems of crime, drug addiction, and gang organization in Seattle. These articles reported that an organization of Samoan chiefs, The Samoan National Chief's Council, believed that the delinquency problems of their young people could be eliminated by a reassertion of traditional Samoan family and community values.

In general, however, the Samoan immigrant population would appear to be adapting surprisingly well to modern urban life in America. Joan Ablon concludes from her experience researching the Samoan population of San Francisco that "Samoans by and large have adjusted with relative ease to an environment that in total perspective could hardly be more different from that of their native islands. Few are returning, although many say that they will 'retire' to Samoa" (1971:386).

Samoan immigrants are not without their serious problems, however. The 1980 census data for the state of Washington revealed that Samoan-Americans had the lowest per capita income and the lowest family incomes of any ethnic group in the state except for Vietnamese. While the average family income in the state was $21,696, the Samoan figure was $13,500, and 50 percent of Samoan adults were unemployed. In the Seattle area, 27 percent of Samoan high-school students dropped out during the 1986–1987 school year compared with 13 percent for all other students. While the dropout rate has been declining over the past few years, it is still exceeded only by the dropout rate for Native Americans.

Samoan immigrants have two important support systems—the extended family and the church. In many ways, the stateside Samoan extended family is more supportive than its counterpart in the islands. These families, which can include scores of individuals, are regularly called upon to help family members financially, provide care for ailing relatives, or find jobs for new arrivals from the islands. In terms of family cohesion, it has been said that stateside Samoan families are more Samoan than those in Pago Pago. No Samoan immigrants ever face the prospect of not having a roof over their heads or going without a meal. There are no homeless Samoans. When Samoans encounter difficulties, they immediately turn to the extended family for help. Thus, the adaptive strategy of kin reliance—as opposed to the American predilection toward self-reliance or peer reliance—means that there is not only a tendency to turn first to family for help, but that such action is a matter of pride. When discussing the needs of their elderly or infirm, Samoans vehemently maintain that the family takes care of its own and that they have no need for government aid, nursing homes, or other kinds of welfare assistance. Samoan families may even oppose efforts of human service agencies to aid their elderly because such assistance might be interpreted by other Samoans as a failure on the part of the family members to meet their filial obligations.

Samoan churches, of which there are close to two dozen in the San Francisco Bay area, are well attended by both young and old. While Samoan churches are basically evangelical in orientation and do little in the way of deliberate social action, they do bring people together and facilitate mutual aid. Ishikawa notes that in San Diego the church serves as an information exchange agency. He writes, "Samoans 'know of' other Samoans and hear of arrivals and returns to Samoa, illness and health, of births and deaths, of weddings and funerals and of achievements and hard times" (1978:36).

Of prime importance for Samoan immigrants, however, is the fellowship and ethnic identity the church provides. Sermons are in Samoan, hymns are performed in traditional musical style, and every service is followed by a feast. Joan Ablon describes this typical social event in Bay Area Samoan churches as follows:

> A significant component of the Sunday routine of almost all Samoan church groups is the mid-day or afternoon fellowship meal, to which those who attend contribute food. While some families choose to return to their homes to eat, most stay for this sumptuous affair. Traditional Samoan foods are served: chicken, pork, ham, fish, taro, bananas, salt corned beef, salad, potato salad, a specialized dish called "chop suey" made with Chinese long rice, and other foods, supplemented by rich desserts (1971:88).

Immigrant Samoans maintain close contact with their families in the islands. Many stateside individuals send home remittances on a regular basis for the support of their *matai* and family enterprises. Phone calls are made frequently to inquire after the welfare of relatives, and Samoans are constantly flying back and forth for extended visits. On such occasions, excess baggage is the norm because islanders are asked to bring traditional island foods and handcrafts, and stateside relatives are asked to bring small appliances, electronic equipment, and no end of modern luxuries which can be obtained at a much lower cost in the United States than in American Samoa.

A number of Samoan-Americans return to American Samoa, particularly those who went to the mainland for educational purposes. Now that the government of American Samoa is more in Samoan hands, with its own elected governor, more and more upper-echelon positions in the island government are opening up for Samoans with stateside college educations and work experience. These people also have high prestige among their fellow countrymen and are without question agents of change. A few of those who have returned have done so to accept family titles and are contributing a new dimension to the philosophy and operation of the *matai* system.

Postscript / Samoan Character and the Academic World: The Mead/Freeman Controversy

On January 31, 1983, the *New York Times* carried a front-page article, the headline of which read, "New Samoa Book Challenges Margaret Mead's Conclusions." The book that precipitated this somewhat unexpected turn of events was *Margaret Mead and Samoa: The Making and Unmaking of an Anthropological Myth* by Derek Freeman, an emeritus professor of anthropology at Australian National University in Canberra. This work, which some claim set off the most heated controversy in sociocultural anthropology in one hundred years, is described by its author as a "refutation of Mead's misleading account" of Samoan culture and personality as presented in her 1928 ethnography, *Coming of Age in Samoa.*

The *New York Times* article was of special interest to me because, in 1954, I had conducted a year-long methodological restudy of the Mead data under attack. I had lived in Ta'ū village, where Mead had worked twenty-nine years earlier, and had used many of her informants in a systematic and detailed evaluation of every observation and interpretation she had made about the lifestyle of the people in that Samoan village. A methodological restudy, incidentally, involves a second anthropologist going into the field with the *express purpose* of testing the reliability and validity of the findings of a former investigator. This restudy is made in order to establish what kinds of errors of data collection or interpretation might have been made by certain kinds of people, in certain kinds of field research situations, researching certain kinds of problems. For example, Margaret Mead was a twenty-three-year-old woman investigating a male-dominated society that venerates age. She was a student of Franz Boas and, therefore, went equipped with a particular theoretical frame of reference. She was also on her first field trip—at a time when research methods were crude. My task in this methodological restudy was not only to analyze how my findings might be different from hers (if that would be the case), but I would also attempt to speculate on how differences in the status of the investigators (for example, sex, age, family situation, education) and other personal factors might affect the collection and interpretation of data.

My critique of Margaret Mead's study was presented in my doctoral dissertation, *The Restudy of Manu'an Culture: A Problem in Methodology,* which by 1983 had been collecting dust on a Northwestern University library shelf for some twenty-seven years. I was therefore eager to obtain a copy of Freeman's new evaluation of Mead's work from its publisher, Harvard University Press. In reading the book this is what I found.

In *Margaret Mead and Samoa: The Making and Unmaking of an Anthropological Myth* (1983), Derek Freeman argues that Mead perpetuated a hoax comparable in consequence to that of Piltdown Man when, in 1928, she described Samoa as a paradise where competition, sexual inhibition, and guilt were virtually absent. Refusing to believe that adolescents in all societies inevitably experience emotional crises—storm and stress—because of biological changes associated with puberty (as hypothesized in *Adolescence* in 1904 by psychologist G. Stanley Hall), Mead set out to discover a society where the passage to adulthood was smooth and without trauma. She described such a society in *Coming of Age in Samoa*. In delineating this "negative instance" (which challenged Hall's theory of universal adolescent rebellion and strife), Margaret Mead had in effect established that nurture (culture) is more critical than nature (biology) in accounting for adolescent maturation behavior in the human species. Derek Freeman, on the other hand, rejects the idea that human behavior is largely shaped by culture and believes that Mead and her mentor, Franz Boas (commonly called the "Father of American Anthropology"), were guilty of *totally* ignoring the influence of biological heredity. He believes that Mead's "negative instance" results entirely from faulty data collection and that Mead's Samoan findings have led anthropology, psychology, and education down the primrose path of pseudoscience. Freeman's book, therefore, is an attempt to set the record straight through his own, more accurate, observations of Samoa and Samoans—although his observations of Samoan behavior were in another village, on another island, in another country, and fourteen years later.

Freeman's main theoretical approach in this evaluation of Mead's work derives from the German philosopher of science, Karl Popper, who maintains that science should be deductive, not inductive, and that progress in scientific research should consist essentially of attempts to refute established theories. Thus, Derek Freeman is out to destroy the credibility of what he interprets as the "absolute cultural determinism" to be found in the work of Margaret Mead as well as in much of the work of Boas and his other students. This claim is, of course, spurious, as any student of American anthropological theory knows. For example, in Melville J. Herskovits' biography of Franz Boas, we find the statement that, because of his "rounded view of the problem Boas could perceive so clearly the fallacy of the eugenicist theory, which held the destiny of men to be determined by biological endowment, with little regard for the learned, cultural determinants of behavior." By the same token, he "refused to accept the counter-dogma that man is born with a completely blank slate, on which can be written whatever is willed. He saw both innate endowment and learning—or, as it was called popularly, heredity and environment—as significant factors in the making of the mature individual" (1953:28). Herskovits also points out that "numerous examples can be found, in reports on the various studies he conducted, of how skillfully Boas was able to weave cultural and biological factors into a single fabric" (*Ibid.*).

Marvin Harris concurs: "American anthropology has always been concerned with the relationships between nature (in the guise of habitat and genic programming) and culture (in the guise of traditions encoded in the brain, not in the genes). Neither Boas nor his students ever denied that *Homo sapiens* has a species-specific nature" (1983:26). In his book, *The Rise of Anthropological Theory,* Harris writes, "Boas systematically rejected almost every conceivable form of cultural determinism" (1968:283).

EVALUATION OF THE MEAD DATA

My restudy experience in Ta'ū village in 1954 led me to conclude that Margaret Mead often overgeneralized; that, in many cases, we interpreted data differently; and that, because of her age and sex, some avenues of investigation apparently were closed to her—particularly those having to do with the more formal aspects of village political organization and ceremonial life. However, her overall characterization of the nature and dynamics of the culture were, in my judgment, quite valid and her contention that it was easier to come of age in Samoa than in America in 1925–1926 was undoubtedly correct. In spite of the greater possibilities for error in a pioneer study, Mead's age (only 23), her sex (in a male-dominated society), and her inexperience, I believe the reliability and validity of the Ta'ū village research is remarkably high.

I look upon an ethnographic account as a kind of map to be used in finding one's way about in a culture—in comprehending and anticipating behavior. Mead's account never left me lost or bewildered in my interactions with Samoan islanders, but I also felt that if one were to come to a decision about the comparative difficulties of coming of age in Samoa and the United States, it would be necessary to know something about what life was like for adolescents in America in 1925–1926. Joseph Folsom's book, *The Family,* published in 1934, but researched about the time Mead was writing *Coming of Age in Samoa,* provided that information. Folsom describes the social environment in which children came of age at that time as follows:

> Children are disciplined and trained with the ideal of absolute obedience to parents. Corporal punishment is used, ideally in cold blood. . . . All sexual behavior on the part of children is prevented by all means at the parents' disposal. . . . For the sake of prevention it has been usual to cultivate in the child, especially the girl, an attitude of horror or disgust toward all aspects of sex. . . . Premarital intercourse is immoral though not abhorrent. . . . Violations are supposedly prevented by the supervision of the girl's parents. . . . Illegitimate children are socially stigmatized. . . . The chief stigma falls upon the unmarried mother, because she has broken an important sex taboo (1934:10–25).

In Willystine Goodsell's book, *Problems of the Family,* the author comments concerning the 1928 family environment in America as follows:

> That the home is not successfully meeting either the demands of society or the deepest needs of its members is evidenced by the prevalence of juvenile delinquency and crime,

by outbursts of suicidal mania among youth, by the establishment and spread of child guidance clinics, juvenile courts and the probation system. Unsuccessful functioning of the family is further revealed by the alarming growth of mental and nervous diseases, culminating in nervous breakdowns. . . . The conditions of modern life in our huge urban centers are so complex that both the child and his parents find difficulty in adjusting to them. . . . At present, both adults and children in our large cities live under conditions of hurry, noise, competition and nervous tension (1928:420).

While Freeman contends that Mead was absolutely wrong about nearly everything (partly, he maintains, because the teenage girls she used as informants consistently lied to her), I found discrepancies mainly in such areas as the degree of sexual freedom Samoan young people enjoy, the competitive nature of the society, the aggressiveness of Samoan behavior, and the degree of genuine affection and commitment between lovers and spouses.

I saw Samoan culture as considerably more competitive than Mead, although I never considered it as inflexible or aggressive as Freeman does. I observed a great preoccupation with status, power, and prestige among men of rank and, on more than one occasion, was present at fierce verbal duels between Talking Chiefs trying to enhance their own prestige and, incidentally, that of their village. The best fisherman, housebuilder, dancer, weaver, or orator was often pointed out to me, but no one respected the man or woman who was immodest and self-serving. I also cannot agree that Samoans are characteristically an aggressive, violent people with quarrelsome personalities and a long history of conflict. It was my impression, derived from five field trips to Manu'a over a period of thirty-four years, that Samoans go to extremes to avoid strife and to arrive at peaceful compromises. Village council decisions always have to be unanimous, and council meetings often drag on for days while the assembled chiefs make adjustments and concessions until everyone is satisfied with the collective decision. Breaches of sanctioned behavior require elaborate ceremonies of apology, called *ifoga,* during which persons, families, even entire villages must publicly humble themselves, with mats over their bowed heads, until forgiven by the offended party. Even murder and manslaughter would be dealt with in this way if the territorial government authorities would permit it.

I also found that Samoan culture was not as simple as Margaret Mead claimed, nor was Ta'ū village the paradise she would have us believe. She often romanticized, overgeneralized, and, on some occasions, took literary license in her descriptions of Samoan lifeways. For example, her very dramatic chapter, "A Day in Samoa," crowds typical activities (some of which occur only at particular times of the year) into a typical day and thereby presents a village scene that was much more vibrant, bustling, and picturesque than I ever encountered in any twenty-four hour period. Mead's chapter is good prose, but is it good anthropology? Note, for example, the more realistic description of a Samoan village written by P. H. Cook:

Any visitor who has lived in a Samoan village must have been impressed by the monotony and simplicity of the life. While the young men and women go about their activities, in themselves not very exciting, the *matai,* who retire from work at the age of about thirty to thirty-five, sit around on the floor of their *fales,* or native houses, talking, smoking, drinking the ceremonial kava, sleeping, eating, and so far as one can judge, often just sitting (1941–1942:302).

I also did not agree with Mead on the degree of sexual freedom supposedly enjoyed by her informants, but I believe her characterization comes closer to the truth than that of Freeman. Samoans have a very natural and healthy attitude toward sex. Judging by the number of illegitimate children in Ta'ū village when I was there and by the fact that divorce frequently involved claims of adultery, I would conclude that, while Samoans are far from promiscuous, they are not the puritanical prudes Freeman paints them to be. However, I must admit that it was difficult to investigate anything of a sexual nature, primarily because of pressure from the London Missionary Society church. Even today, older Samoans seem more distressed over Mead's claims that they are sexually active than Freeman's claims that they are aggressive with strong passions, even psychopathological tendencies. I would assume, however, that Mead was better able to identify with, and therefore establish rapport with, adolescents and young adults on issues of sexuality than either I (at age 29—married with a wife and child) or Freeman, ten years my senior.

Freeman maintains that Mead imposed her own liberated ideas of sexuality onto the Samoans and that her teenage informants consistently lied to her about these matters solely out of mischief. He has recently made contact with one of Mead's informants, Fa'apua'a Fa'amu, who lived in Fitiuta while Mead was working in Ta'ū village. Freeman believes this informant when she says that she consistently lied to Mead (while also identifying her as a good friend), but Freeman does not seem to consider the possibility that she may be lying to him. The possibility of Mead's informants being successful at such long-term deception is simply not credible considering the fact that Mead was an extremely intelligent, well-trained Ph.D. who constantly cross-checked her data with many informants. Anyone who has studied her field notes in the Library of Congress, as I have, must be impressed with her savvy and sophistication.

I must also disagree with Mead's statements that all love affairs are casual and fleeting, and no one plays for very heavy emotional stakes. Custom dictates that displays of affection between spouses and between lovers not take place in public. However, expressions of love and affection were often observed in the families of my informants, and many of these same people spoke of feelings for their wives or husbands which involved much more emotional depth than mere compatibility or economic convenience. It is also true that the folklore of Manu'a contains many examples of fidelity and expressions of deep emotional attachment between spouses and between lovers. Mead's statement that romantic love does not exist overlooks those cases of unrequited love involving a husband, wife, or sweetheart that have ended in suicide. These were rare but they did exist.

Although I differed with Margaret Mead on many interpretations, the most important fact that emerged from my methodological restudy of her Samoan research is that, without doubt, Samoan adolescents have a less difficult time negotiating the transition from childhood to adulthood than American adolescents. This, I believe, can be explained by the following sociocultural factors:

1. The structure of the Samoan household is such that there are several adults who may discipline or respond to the needs of the children in the residence unit. This

means that there is a diffusion of both authority and affection, rendering individual parent-child relationships less intense and stressful.

2. There is very little age segregation in Samoan households; therefore, there is greater communication across generations.

3. Samoan children are more familiar with the facts of life—sex, childbirth, death, and family responsibility—than American children, and this knowledge better prepares them for adult experiences, roles, and obligations.

4. There is no dichotomy between a child's world and an adult's world. Coming of age in Samoa is a matter of assuming family tasks and obligations whenever the child considers itself physically and mentally able. Full responsibility for caring for siblings is given to children as early as age five or six, and many adolescents function as adults in agricultural, fishing, or domestic activities long before their American counterparts.

5. Flexible residence patterns permit Samoan youth to switch to the household of a relative when parent-child strains develop. One informant consulted on this issue maintained that, when he was growing up, he moved from household to household to avoid onerous work activities.

6. Life is simpler in Samoa than in the United States, and there are fewer decision-making dilemmas. Samoa in 1954 (and undoubtedly in 1925–1926) offered fewer career choices, fewer lifestyle alternatives, and fewer conflicting moral and ethical codes. In Margaret Mead's Samoa, the majority of young people grew up knowing that they would spend their lives as subsistence farmers or farmer's wives; most men were assured that if they worked hard for their family and their village, they would someday acquire a chief's title and be responsible for a village household unit. In Fitiuta and Ta'ū in 1925 (and in 1954), there was but one sanctioned religious denomination—London Missionary Society—and church membership and attendance were compulsory.

7. There is a well-established idea of what is acceptable behavior and what is not. It is a simple formula and applies to everyone. If one oversteps the acceptable behavior limits, punishment is expected and accepted. History records that when the first Samoan was about to be hanged for a capital offense in Western Samoa, he thanked the authorities for punishing him for the serious crime of which he was guilty.

8. Samoan society has a very healthy, natural attitude toward sexuality, which was not present in the culture of the United States in 1925–1926. While village *taupou* (ceremonial maidens) were required to remain virgins until their marriage to a man of rank, sex was, for most young people, casual and without traumatic consequences. While Mead does not mention that any of her adolescent informants became pregnant, it must be realized that she was only in residence in Ta'ū for five months and that most of her girls were very young and probably not yet sexually active. Ta'ū island villages in 1954 were not without their out-of-wedlock pregnancies, however. While families were embarrassed by such situations, retribution was short lived, and the babies were not the recipients of any permanent social stigma whatsoever.

CRITIQUE OF THE FREEMAN REFUTATION

My objections to Derek Freeman's picture of Samoa are much more substantial than to the picture presented by Margaret Mead. Basically, I question Freeman's objectivity and believe he is guilty of an age-old temptation in science, which was recognized as early as 1787 by Thomas Jefferson—no slouch of a scientist himself. In a letter to his friend Charles Thomson, Jefferson wrote, "The moment a person forms a theory, his imagination sees, in every object, only the traits which favor that theory" (Martin 1952:33).

Not only does Freeman ignore counterevidence, he also ignores time and space and assumes that it is legitimate to assess data obtained by Mead in Manu'a in 1925–1926 in terms of the data he collected in Western Samoa in the 1940s, 1960s, and 1980s.

Time Differences   Freeman plays down the fact that Mead did her study of Ta'ū village in the Manu'a Island group of American Samoa fourteen years before he arrived as a teacher (not as an anthropologist) in Western Samoa and that he did not return to Samoa with the express purpose of refuting Mead's study until forty-three years after her visit. Minimizing this time gap, he arbitrarily states that "there is . . . no reason to suppose that Samoan society and behavior changed in any fundamental way during the fourteen years between 1926, the year of the completion of Mead's inquiries, and 1940, when I began my own observation of Samoan behavior" (1983:120).

However, Freeman did not visit Ta'ū village, the site of Mead's research, until 1968. Having established to his satisfaction that there had been few changes in Samoan culture during this long period of time, Freeman went on to state that he would "draw on evidence of my own research in the 1940s, the years 1965 to 1968, and 1981" (1983:120). I might add that he would draw upon historical sources, some of which go back as far as the early eighteenth century, to prove his points. My own analysis of Samoan cultural change, as published in *Ta'ū, Stability and Change in a Samoan Village* (1958), indicates, however, that while there was relative stability in the culture from 1850 to 1925 and from 1925 to 1954, change definitely did take place, particularly in the twentieth century. There is absolutely no basis for Freeman's dealing with Samoa as though it existed in a totally static condition despite its long history of contact with explorers, whalers, missionaries, colonial officials and bureaucrats, entrepreneurs, anthropologists, and, more recently, educators with Western-style curricula and television networks.

Place Differences   It also must be kept in mind that Sa'anapu (where Freeman observed Samoan culture) is not Ta'ū village (where Mead did her study). They are different villages, on different islands, in different countries, and there are great historical and political differences between the island of Upolu in Western Samoa and Ta'ū island in the isolated Manu'a Group of American Samoa. Western Samoa has experienced a long and often oppressive history of colonialism under Germany and New Zealand, while the Manu'a Group and American Samoa in general have been spared this. The U.S. Navy administration (1900–1951) exerted little influence outside the Pago Pago Bay area on the island of Tutuila, and the Department of the Interior, which took over from the Navy, has been an ethnocentric—but still benevolent—force in the political history of the territory. While Sa'anapu is on the opposite side of Upolu from Apia, it has daily bus communication with that port town, with all of its banks, supermarkets, department stores, theaters, bookstores, and nightclubs. Cash cropping has always been more important in Western Samoa than in American Samoa, and today, the economies of the two Samoas are vastly different. In 1954, there was only a handful of government employees on Ta'ū island (mostly teachers) and almost no cash cropping outside of copra, which brought in very little income. Nearly everyone was engaged in subsistence agriculture, even the few bush store owners. As recently as the late 1970s, the island had no dock, and interisland vessels called only about once a month The village council handled all matters of social control, and the government of American Samoa had little impact on either the system of justice or the political functioning of the village. *Matai* were largely in control of both family economic matters and the behavior of its members. Disputes were settled in an orderly manner, and I never observed any overt aggression between village members. On five separate research trips to Manu'a, I have never witnessed a single physical assault or serious argument that threatened to get out of hand. However, urban centers such as Apia in Western Samoa and Pago Pago in American Samoa have a very different character. As early as 1962, there were delinquency problems in the Pago Pago Bay area involving drunkenness, burglary, assaults, and rapes. Young people who migrate to urban areas such as Pago Pago and Apia are no longer under the close supervision and control of their *matai* and often behave in very nontraditional ways. It is difficult, indeed, to make a blanket statement that all villages in Samoa are the same and that all behavior within the two Samoas is comparable. I have studied several villages during my thirty-seven-year contact with Samoa, and I find each unique in numerous social, ceremonial, economic, and political respects.

Freeman's Subjective Use of Literature   A serious scientist considers all the literature relating to his or her research problem. One does not select data that is supportive and ignore that which is not. Freeman violates this principle repeatedly. For example, he cites Ronald Rose's book, *South Seas Magic* (1959), to document his claims concerning inherent aggressive tendencies of Samoans. Rose stated that Samoans are not without their mental disorders and stresses and suggests that they have compulsive mannerisms such as *fitifiti* (drumming on a mat)(1959:219), which Freeman interprets as "a form of redirected aggression." When Rose's writings can be used to corroborate or advance Freeman's position, he is quoted; however, where Rose's statements concerning Samoan sexual behavior run contrary to Freeman's claims, and fall in line with Mead's observations, his work is ignored. For example, while Freeman insists that Samoans are puritanical and sexually inhibited, Rose writes that "sexual adventures begin at an early age. Although virginity is prized, it is insisted on only with the taupo. . . . If a girl hasn't had a succession of lovers by the time she is seventeen or eighteen, she feels she is "on the shelf" and becomes the laughing stock among her companions (1959:61).

With regard to the matter that Freeman believes was Mead's spurious example of a "negative instance"—a culture where coming of age is relatively less stressful—Rose writes (but understandably is not quoted by Freeman) as follows:

> Mental disturbances, stresses and conflicts occur at puberty but, as might be expected, these are not quite as common as in our society where taboos associated with sex abound" (*Ibid.*:164).

One can question the objectivity of a scientist who describes Samoans as "an unusually bellicose people" (1983:157) and attempts to substantiate the claim with citations from the eighteenth century, but fails to quote the favorable impressions of the very first European to come in contact with Samoan islanders from the village of Ta'ū, the very village Mead studied. In 1722, Commodore Jacob Roggeveen anchored his vessel off the village of Ta'ū and allowed a number of the islanders to come aboard. After a two-hour visit, the Commodore wrote in his log:

> They appeared to be a good people, lively in their manner of conversing, gentle in their deportment towards each other, and in their manners nothing was perceived of the savage. . . . It must be acknowledged that this was the nation the most civilized and honest of any that we had seen among the Islands of the South Sea. They were charmed with our arrival amongst them, and received us as divinities. And when they saw us preparing to depart, they testified much regret (Burney 1816:576).

Rather than quote Roggeveen, Freeman chooses to discuss, as an example of Samoan bellicosity, the La Perouse expedition's visitation at Tutuila in 1787 that ended in tragedy. It is true that Samoans in the village of A'asu attacked a shore party, killing several crew members, but what Freeman fails to mention is that the attack occurred only after crew members punished a Samoan for pilfering by hanging him by his thumbs from the top of the longboat mast.

Freeman also describes what he claims was a dangerous, life-threatening confrontation between a throng of islanders and Samoa's first European missionary, John Williams, upon his arrival in 1830. However, Freeman conveniently fails to quote Williams's own account of his initial meeting with his potential flock. He recorded:

> Many hundred also of the natives crowded round us, by all of whom we were treated with the greatest possible respect, and these rent the air with their affectionate salutations, exclaiming "*O le alofi i le ali'i,* Great is our affection for you English Chiefs" (1839:302).

It also should be noted that the eminent writer, Robert Louis Stevenson, who lived among Samoans the last four years of his life, recorded in his chronicle of Samoan events, *A Footnote to History,* that Samoans were "easy, merry, and pleasure loving; the gayest, though by no means the most capable or the most beautiful of Polynesians" (1892:148) and that their religious sentiment toward conflict was "peace at any price" (*Ibid.*:147).

Observers contemporary with Mead in Samoa also record descriptions of Samoan character that do not square with Freeman's allegations or his citations from early literature. For example, William Green, the principal of the government school in American Samoa in the 1920s writes:

Personal combats and fist fights are rather rare today. I believe there has been no murder case in American Samoa since our flag was raised in 1900. Natives will suffer indignities for a long time before resorting to a fight but they remain good fighters. Boxing contests are held occasionally. . . . Respect for elders and magistrates has, I suppose, tended to discourage frequent combats. Life is easy, and one's habitual tendencies and desires are seldom blocked (1924:134).

PSYCHOMETRIC ANALYSIS OF SAMOAN CHARACTER

Considering the great disparity between Margaret Mead's and Derek Freeman's assessment of Samoan behavior, it would seem appropriate at this point to turn to the rich literature describing psychological studies as a guide in our quest for consensus concerning Samoan character. More than a dozen researchers have attempted to construct a psychological profile of Samoan islanders using a broad spectrum of methods—folklore and literature analysis, projective, verbal, and nonverbal testing, observation and interview, controlled laboratory observation, personality inventory, value schedule analysis, and ethnosemantics. The methodology and findings of the major researchers of Samoan character follow.

Margaret Mead   This analysis of Samoan culture and personality may be cultural anthropology's seminal psychological, problem-oriented study. The investigation of thirty adolescent girls in Ta'ū village, American Samoa, involved no psychological testing, although intelligence tests—color naming, rote memory for digits, word opposites—were administered. Mead primarily employed participant observation and interview (including life history) methodology and arrived at the following conclusions regarding Samoan adolescent personality. Her subjects, she maintained, displayed (a) a lack of deep feeling or involvement toward relatives and peers, (b) a liberal attitude toward sex and education, (c) a lack of conflicting attitudes regarding ideology, political doctrine, and morality, and (d) a lack of emphasis on individuality. Mead found the adolescent Samoan female relatively free from emotional conflict, tension, or rebellion. They were situationally rather than individually oriented, apathetic, passive, and submissive to the aggression of others; they were unwilling to invest heavily in interpersonal relationships and generally casual in their attitudes toward life.

E. Paul Torrance and R. T. Johnson   This study, carried out by educational psychologists in 1962, focused on creativity and original thinking and tested the hypothesis that original thinking is associated with cultural discontinuities in education and sex role independence. Using three verbal and three nonverbal tests, they compared one thousand Western Samoa school children with samples from Australia, Germany, India, and the United States. All of the children showed continuous growth from the first through the sixth grade, but Samoan subjects ranked the lowest in original, creative thought at all levels. The investigators concluded that the following Samoan values were responsible for the Samoan performance: (a) emphasis on remembering well, (b) unquestioning acceptance of the authority hierarchy, (c) emphasis on submission to authority, and (d) doing nothing until told to. The investigators thought that it might be possible to increase Samoan creativity, but at the risk of producing personality conflicts and making coming of age in Samoa a somewhat more traumatic experience.

Louise Gardner This research, carried out in Western Samoa in 1965, used a modified version of the Kluckhohn Value Schedule plus a projective picture test of Louise Gardner's own design in order to assess common values held by Western Samoan children and adults and how values change as children mature. A study of thirty children and thirty adults revealed that (a) Samoans are present or future oriented, (b) they feel secure with societal members but apprehensive about outsiders, (c) they are oriented toward familial goals and well being rather than individual satisfactions, and (d) they lean toward accomplishing societal goals rather than spontaneously expressing impulses and desires.

Jarrell W. Garsee This study, carried out by a missionary turned social scientist, tested observational generalizations about the nature of Samoan values using Gordon's Survey of Interpersonal Values, with particular attention to Conformity, Recognition, Independence, and Benevolence. Comparisons with American norms revealed that Americans and Samoans of both sexes value leadership, but Samoans were prone to acceptance of group-oriented values emphasizing benevolence to others, but reject individual actions that set the individual apart from the social context. Benevolence, defined as "being generous and sharing with others," was cited as a dominant characteristic of Samoan personality, and they surpass Americans in this characteristic by scores that are nearly 25 percent higher.

Lowell D. Holmes and Leland Blazer In 1962, Holmes tested sixty-eight Samoan adolescents in American Samoa using the California Test of Personality, The Edwards Personal Preference Schedule, and the Rogers Test of Personality Adjustment. Aided in the analysis by a graduate student, Leland Blazer, Holmes found that the young people had strong tendencies toward (a) Deference—doing what is expected and accepting others' leadership, (b) Order—enjoying organization, (c) Abasement—being timid in the presence of superiors, and (d) Endurance—keeping at a job until finished. On the other hand, subjects scored low in (a) Autonomy—being independent of others in decision making, (b) Dominance—directing the actions of others, (c) Exhibition—being the center of attention, and (d) Achievement—doing one's best to be successful.

Eleanor Ruth Gerber This study, conducted in American Samoa in 1972–1973, was an examination of the cultural patterning of emotions in Samoa. With the help of her informants, Gerber selected forty-four key terms having to do with salient emotions. She then asked informants to group them into clusters of terms similar in meaning. She also made a content analysis of informants' descriptions of emotions, particularly those dealing with interrelationships of two sets of emotions—hostile feelings and feelings toward social superiors. Gerber also made informal observations of social interactions in important relationships such as those between parents and children, between siblings, and between friends. On the basis of her research, Gerber reasons that Margaret Mead erred in her view of Samoan character being "gentle and submissive" by focusing almost entirely on certain emotions that reinforce the Samoan values of mutual assistance and hierarchy. It is Gerber's conclusion that "in the Samoan case, intense anger toward social superiors is culturally impermissable, but individuals are partially unsuccessful in channeling this anger into more acceptable low-level expressions of the same basic affect. This is the source of subsequent personal and interpersonal disruption" (1985:15).

William Vinacke   This psychologist and "armchair" analyst of Samoan personality consulted Mead's publications resulting from her 1925–1926 research, Cook's Samoan Rorschach study, Copp's novel *Samoan Dance of Life,* Samoan proverbs and folktales, and a number of biased and questionable missionary accounts to construct his profile of Samoan character. His conclusions, often highly subjective and ethnocentric, are that Samoan character is a "remarkably tempered organization" with "little evidence of deep hostility, strong aggressiveness, fearfulness, or anxiety in relations with other persons." He credits three cultural features with the shaping of Samoan character. They are (a) mild pressures and demands imposed upon individuals during development, (b) influences operating at one stage of development usually being mitigated at another, and (c) a relatively strong guarantee that needs will be satisfied.

Robert J. Maxwell   This study of Samoan males was carried out in Vaitogi, American Samoa, using the theories of Hans Eysenck concerning extroversion-introversion. While Maxwell acknowledges major methodological problems—the use of tests of dubious validity and the lack of controlled conditions—the investigaton concluded that Samoans are, on the whole, an extroverted population with a modal personality that is strong-tempered, rendering males to be prone to engage in fighting and to be sexually active. Their extroversion, however, he believes decreases with age.

Lowell D. Holmes and Gary Tallman   The influence of cultural change on Samoan personality was the subject of research by Holmes and Tallman in 1974. A total of seventy-eight high-school students in American Samoa were tested with the Edwards Personal Preference Schedule and the California Test of Personality. Comparisons were made with scores obtained on these same tests (but with a different sample) in 1962. Since the period between 1962 and 1974 had been one of great change—economically, politically, and educationally—the researchers were interested in whether there would be a concomitant movement in test scores toward American norms as the island became more Americanized culturally. The result was that in 1974, Abasement—being timid in the presence of superiors—remained the highest score, as it had been in 1962, and Aggression—getting angry and disagreeing with others—remained a weak trait, as it had been in 1962. In general, 1974 test scores showed an increase in most variables in the direction of American norms—a clear indication that a change in cultural environment had been associated with a change in personality characteristics.

D. T. P. Keene   This study of child development and personality formation characterizes Samoans as aggressive and directly relates that aspect of Samoan character to child-rearing practices. The investigator believes that expressions of aggression go unregulated by family rules, but heavily punished nevertheless. Following corporal punishment, for which Keene maintains no explanation is given, Samoan parents often produce displays of affection to show that the child is loved in spite of the punishment. This, according to Keene, is a source of continuing frustration. The fact that aggressive feelings must be sublimated serves to intensify hostile emotions created by the child-rearing practices. Keene also suggests that sharing is a continuing source of frustration to Samoans. He suggests that there are many times when an individual is forced by custom to give up things he may want for himself or his family. This suggestion, however, would seem to be somewhat ethnocentric, but is a common response to communal ownership of property by those raised in a society that places an extremely high value of the rights of private ownership of property.

P. H. Cook   Cook's research of Samoan personality in 1941 represents the first use of projective testing in Polynesia. Rorschach protocols were administered to a sample of fifty young men, ages sixteen to twenty-seven, who were students at the Mission High School in Upolu, Western Samoa. Cook's stated purpose in the research was to examine various cultural factors that might affect the validity of cross-cultural interpretation of the Rorschach instrument. Culture-related problems did indeed appear, particularly in the interpretation of S (white space), C (color), and F (form) responses. If Samoans were to be judged by European norms, their responses to these three categories would have to be regarded as "abnormal." However, it must be taken into consideration that Samoa has different color preferences and associations. White is associated with superiority, purity, and goodness. Because Samoa is an extremely formal society stressing elaborate protocol and careful attention to ceremonial detail, it is not unusual that the form responses would be emphasized. Cook's somewhat ethnocentric conclusion regarding what the Rorschach responses do tell about Samoan personality is that "there is obviously a primitive, childish streak in the adult Samoan, evident in his happy-go-lucky, improvident attitudes, his enjoyment of simple pastimes, his delight in impressive ceremonial that almost have a make-believe character, his suggestability and general emotional shallowness" (1941–1942 2:304).

PROFESSIONAL REACTIONS

While it is possible that some of the psychometric instruments used in these several studies may lack cross-cultural validity, it is believed that, taken as a group, these profiles of Samoan personality present a relatively consistent picture of Samoan behavior, and tend to square with the ethnographic observations of most Samoa specialists. The majority, however, appear to be at odds with Derek Freeman's somewhat extreme characterization of Samoan character as being aggressive, competitive, and puritanical.

It is questionable whether any anthropology book to date has created such a media circus or produced such a media hero as *Margaret Mead and Samoa, The Making and Unmaking of an Anthropological Myth*. It is also doubtful whether any academic press ever mounted such a campaign of Madison Avenue hype to market a book as did Harvard University Press. The early reviews of the book and feature articles about the controversy were primarily penned by journalists and tended to be highly supportive of Freeman's critique, but once the anthropologists began evaluating the Freeman book, the tide took a definite turn. George Marcus of Rice University called the book a "work of great mischief," the mischief being that Freeman was attempting to reestablish "the importance of biological factors in explanations of human behavior" (1983:2). Colin Turnbull contended that the "myth" in Freeman's title was of Freeman's own making, since the nature/nurture issue was not what Mead set out to investigate at all. He concludes his review by stating, "Given his own dubious methodology, I doubt if Freeman's book is worth very much either as anthropology or biology" (1983:34). Laura Nader of the University of California, Berkeley, referred to Freeman's nit-picking efforts to discredit Mead as "historical tracking," and she noted that *Margaret Mead and Samoa* "is not a systematic restudy. Instead, Freeman uses history, early reports of Western missionaries and travelers, government and court records, plus his and other people's observations to refute Mead" (1983:2). Marvin Harris observed in his review that Freeman "seems obsessed with the notion that to discredit Mead's Samoan material is to discredit any social scientist who holds that 'nurture' is a more important determinant of the differences and similarities in human social life than nature" (1983:26). David Schneider of the University of Chicago began his review in *Natural History* with: "This is a bad book. It is also a dull book," (1983:4) maintaining that it falls short of even the loosest standards of scholarship. "This is a commercial enterprise," he wrote, "not a contribution to knowledge" (*Ibid.*:6).

It is only fair to point out that Derek Freeman had, and continues to have, a cadre of anthropological supporters, mostly in Europe and Australia, and the Samoans are mixed in their support of Mead or Freeman. The most recent chapter in the Mead/Freeman debate is the soon-to-be-published book *American Samoa: The Studied Pearl/Le Penina Fefulia'a* by Papu Joseph Siofele. When interviewed for an article in the American Samoa newspaper, *Samoa News* (April 28, 1989), Siofele stated that Freeman's book was an "intentional attack on Mead and an erroneous portrayal of Samoan culture to support his own personal theories. He is presenting a negative account of Mead and Samoa in order to make a name for himself." Claiming that Samoans avoid violence, love nature, and, in the recent past, had an easygoing attitude toward sex, Siofele concludes that "Margaret Mead's version of Samoan life was much closer to the truth than Freeman's."

Like most American anthropologists, and a few scholarly Samoans, we believe the Freeman book has done a disservice to Samoans and to the memory of Margaret Mead. *Margaret Mead and Samoa* is not an objective analysis of Mead's work in Manu'a, but an admitted refutation aimed at discrediting not only Margaret Mead, but Franz Boas and American cultural anthropology in general. Anthropology has often been referred to as a "soft science" throughout much of this rhubarb over Samoa and nature/nurture. It is little wonder, since Freeman's diatribe, published by a supposedly scholarly press, has been accepted by the media, by a select group of anthropologists, and by a number of distinguished ethologists and sociobiologists as legitimate anthropology. Margaret Mead would have loved to have debated the issues with Derek Freeman, but unfortunately, the book was not published while she was alive. It would have been great sport and good for the science of anthropology. As a friend wrote immediately after the publication of Freeman's book, "Whatever else she was, Margaret was a feisty old gal and would have put up a spirited defense which would quickly have turned into a snotty offense." We would have put our money on the plump little lady with the no-nonsense attitude and the compulsion to "get on with it."

Bibliography

Ablon, Joan. 1971. "Retention of cultural values and differential urban adaptation: Samoans and American Indians in a west coast city." *Social Forces* 49:385–393.

Ala'ilima, Fay. 1961. A *Samoan family*. Wellington, New Zealand: Islands Education Division of the Department of Education.

American Samoa Government. 1988. *American Samoa statistical digest, 1988*. Pago Pago.

Baker, Paul T. and Hanna, Joel. 1986. "Perspectives on health and behavior of Samoans." In *The changing Samoans,* eds. P. Baker, J. Hanna, and T. Baker. New York: Oxford University Press. pp. 419–434.

Barnett, Homer. 1953. *Innovation: The basis of cultural change*. New York: McGraw-Hill, Inc.

Bindon, James R. 1986. "Dietary and social choices in American Samoa." *The World and I.* 1(5) May:174–185.

Blazer, Leland K. 1968. *Samoan character as revealed by three tests of personality*. Master's thesis, Wichita State University.

Booth, Robert. 1985. "The two Samoas, still coming of age." *National Geographic* 168(4) October:452–473.

Buck, Peter. 1931. "Samoan chieftainship." Hearings before the commission appointed by the president of the United States in accordance with public resolution no. 89, 70th Congress, Washington, DC, pp. 70–73.

———. 1965. "Polynesian oratory." In *Ancient Hawaiian civilization,* eds. E. S. Craighill Handy, et al. Rutland and Tokyo: Charles E. Tuttle Co., Inc.

Burney, James. 1816. *A chronological history of the voyages and discoveries in the South Seas or Pacific Ocean*. London: Luke Hansard and Sons.

Churchill, William. n.d., *Fa'alupega; Manu'a*. Unpublished manuscript.

Cook, P.H. 1941–1942. "Mental structure and the psychological field: Some Samoan observations." *Character and Personality* 10:296–308.

———. 1942. "The application of the Rorschach test to a Samoan group." *Rorschach Research Exchange* 6:51–60.

Copp, John D. 1950. *The Samoan dance of life*. Boston: Beacon Press.

Craig, Robert D., and King, Frank P. eds. 1981. *Historical dictionary of Oceania*. Westport, CT: Greenwood Press.

Danielsson, Bengt. 1956. *Work and life on Raroia*. London: George Allen and Unwin Ltd.

Department of Education, Government of American Samoa. 1973. *Think children! Annual report, fiscal year 1973*. Pago Pago.

Filoiali'i, La'auli and Knowles, Lyle. 1981. "A note on White Sunday: A day of honour for Samoan children." *Oceania* 51(3):211–213.

Folsom, Joseph K. 1934. *The family: Its sociology and psychiatry*. New York: J. Wiley and Sons.

Franco, Robert. 1985. *Socialization and Samoan international movement*. Honolulu: University of Hawaii, Department of Anthropology.

Freeman, Derek. 1983. *Margaret Mead and Samoa: The making and unmaking of an anthropological myth*. Cambridge, MA: Harvard University Press.

Furnas, J. C. 1948. *Anatomy of paradise*. New York: William Sloane Associates.

Gardner, Louise C. 1965. *Gautavai: A study of Samoan values*. Master's thesis, University of Hawaii.

Garsee, Jarrell W. 1965. *A study of Samoan interpersonal values*. Master's thesis, University of Oklahoma.

———. 1967. "Samoan interpersonal values." *Journal of Social Psychology* 72:45–60.

Geographical Handbook Series. 1943. *The Pacific islands* Vol. II: Eastern Pacific. Oxford and Cambridge: Oxford and Cambridge University Presses.

Gerber, Eleanor Ruth. 1975. *The cultural patterning of emotions in Samoa*. Ph.D. dissertation, University of California, San Diego.

———. 1985. "Rage and obligation: Samoan emotion in conflict." In *Person, self and experience: Exploring Pacific ethnopsychologies*. eds. G. White and J. Kirkpatrick. Berkeley: University of California Press. pp. 121–167.

Gilson, R. P. 1970. *Samoa 1830 to 1900: The politics of a multi-cultural community*. Melbourne: Oxford University Press.

Goldman, Irving. 1970. *Ancient Polynesian society*. Chicago: University of Chicago Press.

Goodsell, Willystine. 1928. *Problems of the family*. New York: Century Company.

Government of American Samoa. Public Health Department. 1950. *History of naval medical activities in Samoa*. Pago Pago: Government of American Samoa. pp. 1–4.

Grattan, F. J. H. 1948. *An introduction to Samoan custom*. Apia: Samoa Printing and Publishing Company.

Gray, J. A. C. 1960. *Amerika Samoa*. Annapolis, MD: United States Naval Institute.

Green, Roger. 1966. "Linguistic subgrouping within Polynesia." *Journal of the Polynesian Society* 75:6–38.

Green, William M. 1924. "Social traits of Samoans." *Journal of Applied Sociology* 9:129–135.

Hall, Clarence. 1961. "Samoa: America's shame in the South Seas." *Reader's Digest* July. pp. 111–116.

Hall, G. Stanley. 1904. *Adolescence: Its psychology and its relations to physiology, anthropology, sociology, sex, crime, religion and education*. New York: D. Appleton and Company.

Hanna, Joel M.; Pelletier, David L.; and Brown, Vanessa J. 1986. "The diet and nutrition of contemporary Samoans." In *The changing Samoans*, eds. P. Baker, J. Hanna, and T. Baker. New York: Oxford University Press. pp. 275–296.

Harris, Marvin. 1968. *The rise of anthropological theory*. New York: Thomas Y. Crowell Company.

———. 1983. "The sleep-crawling question." *Psychology Today* May:24–27.

Hartman, Michael. 1980. "Census experiences in the Pacific 1976–1979." *Sartryck ur Statistisk Tidskrift* 4:307–316.

Herskovits, Melville J. 1953. *Franz Boas*. New York: Charles Scribner's Sons.

Heyerdahl, Thor. 1950. *Kon-Tiki*. Chicago: Rand McNally.

Holmes, Ellen Rhoads and Holmes, Lowell D. 1987. "Western Polynesia'a first home for the aged: Are concept and culture compatible?" *Journal of Cross Cultural Gerontology* 2(4):359–375.

———. 1989. "Return to the Samoan Isles." *The World and I* 4(6) June:624–635.

Holmes, Lowell D. 1957. *The restudy of Manu'an culture: A problem in methodology.* Ph.D. dissertation, Northwestern University.

——— 1958. *Ta'ū: Stability and change in a Samoan village.* Reprint No. 7, Wellington, New Zealand: Polynesian Society.

———. 1961. "The Samoan kava ceremony: Its form and function." *Science of Man* 1(2):46–51.

———. 1964. "Fieldwork report: Leadership and decision-making in American Samoa." *Current Anthropology* (5):446–449.

———. 1965. "Decision making in a Samoan village." *Anthropologica* 7(2):229–238.

———. 1967a. *The story of Samoa.* New York: McCormick-Mather.

———. 1967b. "The function of kava in modern Samoan culture." In *Ethnopharmacologic search for psychoactive drugs,* ed. D. H. Efron. Washington, D.C.: Department of Health, Education and Welfare. pp. 107–118.

———. 1967c. "The modern Samoan family." *University studies,* Wichita State University. 71:1–10.

———. 1969. "Samoan oratory." *Journal of American Folklore* 82:342–355.

———. 1971. "Samoa: custom versus productivity." In *Land tenure in the Pacific,* ed. Ron Crocombe, pp. 91–105. Melbourne: Oxford University Press.

———. 1972. "The role and status of the aged in a changing Samoa." In *Aging and Modernization,* eds. D. Cowgill and L. Holmes. New York: Appleton-Century-Crofts, pp. 73–89.

———.1974. *Samoan village.* New York: Holt, Rinehart and Winston.

———.1978. "Aging and modernization: The Samoan aged of San Francisco." In *New neighbors: Islanders in adaptation,* eds. C. Macpherson, B. Shore, and R. Franco. Santa Cruz, CA: Center for South Pacific Studies, pp. 205–213.

———. 1979. "The kava complex in Oceania." The New Pacific. 4(5):30–33.

———. 1980a. "Cults, cargo and Christianity: Samoan responses to Western religion." *Missiology: An International Review* 8(4):471–487.

———. 1980b. "Factors contributing to the cultural stability of Samoa." *Anthropological Quarterly* 53(3):188–197.

———. 1982. "The aged Samoan migrant in San Francisco: Needs and barriers to service delivery." In *Conference proceedings, international conference on cross cultural sensitivity to the needs of Asian and Pacific elderly,* eds. G. Nelson and Nguyen Dang Liem. Honolulu: University of Hawaii.

———. 1984. *Samoan Islands bibliography.* Wichita, KS: Poly Concepts Publishing Company.

———. 1987. *Quest for the real Samoa: The Mead/Freeman controversy and beyond.* South Hadley, MA: Bergin and Garvey.

———. 1989. "Return to Ta'ū." *The World and I* 4(7) July:656–667.

Holmes, Lowell D. and Holmes, Ellen Rhoads. 1986. "The Samoan Islands and their people." *The World and I* 1(5) May: 160–173.

Holmes, Lowell D. and Rhoads, Ellen C. 1983. "Aging and change in modern Samoa." In *Growing old in different societies.* ed. Jay Sokolovsky. pp. 119–129. Belmont, CA: Wadsworth.

Holmes, Lowell D.; Tallman, Gary; and Jantz, Vernon. 1978. "Samoan personality." *Journal of Psychological Anthropology* 1:453–472.

Howard, Alan. 1986. "Samoan coping behavior." In *The changing Samoans,* eds. P. Baker, J. Hanna, and T. Baker. pp. 394–418. New York: Oxford University Press.

Howells, W.W. 1933. "Anthropometry and blood types in Fiji and the Solomon Islands." *Anthropological Papers of the American Museum of Natural History* 33:279–3 9.

———. 1967. *Mankind in the making.* Rev. ed. Garden City: Doubleday & Company, Inc.

Ishikawa, W. 1978. *The elder Samoan.* San Diego, CA: Campanile Press.

Janes, Craig. 1984. *Migration and hypertension: An ethnography of disease risk in an urban Samoan community.* Ph.D. dissertation, University of California, San Francisco and Berkeley.

Johnson, R.T. 1962. *Observations of Western Samoan culture and education.* Unpublished manuscript. Minneapolis: University of Minnesota, Bureau of Educational Research.

Keene, D. T. P. 1978. *Houses without walls: Samoan social control.* Ph.D. dissertation, University of Hawaii, Honolulu.

Keesing, Felix. 1928. *The changing Maori.* New Plymouth, New Zealand: Thomas Avery.

———. 1934. *Modern Samoa.* London: Allen & Unwin, Ltd., and New York: Institute of Pacific Relations.

Keesing, Felix and Keesing, Marie. 1956. *Elite communication in Samoa.* Palo Alto, CA: Stanford University Press.

London Missionary Society Press. 1946. *O le Tusi Fa'alupega o Samoa.* Malua, Western Samoa.

Macpherson, C.; Shore, B.; and Franco, R.; eds. 1978. *New neighbors: Islanders in adaptation.* Santa Cruz, CA: Center for South Pacific Studies.

Marcus, George, 1983. "One man's Mead." *New York Times Book Review* March 27, 1983:2–3, 22–23.

Martin, Edwin T. 1952. *Thomas Jefferson: Scientist.* New York: Henry Schuman.

Maxwell, Robert. 1970. "The changing status of elders in a Polynesian society." *Aging and Human Development* 1 (2, May):137–146.

Mead, Margaret. 1928a. *Coming of age in Samoa.* New York: William Morrow and Company, Inc.

———. 1928b. "The role of the individual in Samoan culture." *Journal of the Royal Anthropological Institute* 58:481–495.

———. 1930. *Social organization of Manu'a.* Honolulu: Bishop Museum Bulletin No. 76.

———. 1969. *Social organization of Manu'a.* 2nd ed. with revised conclusions chapter. Honolulu: Bishop Museum Bulletin No. 76.

———. 1972. *Blackberry winter.* New York: William Morrow.

———. 1977. *Letters from the field* 1925–75. New York: Harper and Row.

Milner, George B. 1966. *Samoan dictionary.* New York: Oxford University Press.

Nader, Laura. 1983. "A historic friction in the field of anthropology." *Los Angeles Times Book Review* April 10, 1983:2.

Neich, Roger. 1985. *Material culture of Western Samoa: Persistence and change.* National Museum of New Zealand Bulletin No. 23. Wellington: National Museum of New Zealand.

New York Times. 1983. "New Samoa book challenges Margaret Mead's conclusions." January 31: 1983:1.

Oliver, Douglas. 1961. *The Pacific Islands.* Rev. ed. Garden City: Doubleday & Company, Inc.

———. 1989. *The Pacific Islands.* 3rd edition. Honolulu: University of Hawaii Press.

O'Meara, J. Tim. 1990. *Samoan planters: Tradition and economic development in Polynesia.* Fort Worth: Holt, Rinehart and Winston.

Pawley, Andrew. 1981. "Austronesian languages." In *Historical dictionary of Oceania,* eds. Robert D. Craig and Frank P. King. pp. 19–21. Westport, CT: Greenwood Press.

Pitt, David. 1970. *Tradition and economic progress in Samoa.* New York: Oxford University Press.

Popper, Karl. 1959. *The logic of scientific discovery.* New York: Basic Books.

Rhoads, Ellen C. 1981. *Aging and modernization in three Samoan communities.* Ph.D. dissertation, University of Kansas.

———. 1984. "Re-evaluation of the aging and modernization theory: The Samoan evidence." *Gerontologist* 24:243–250.

Rhoads, Ellen C. and Holmes, Lowell D. 1981. "Mapuifagalele, Western Samoan's home for the aged—A cultural enigma." *International Journal of Aging and Human Development* 13(1): 30–42.

Rose, Ronald. 1959. *South Seas magic.* London: Hale.

Rouse, Irving. 1986. *Migrations in prehistory.* New Haven: Yale University Press.

Rowe, Newton A. 1930. *Samoa under the sailing gods.* New York: Putnam.

Schneider, David. 1983. "The coming of a sage to Samoa." *Natural History* 92(6):4–10.

Schramm, W.; Nelson, L. M.; and Betham, M. T. 1981. *Bold experiment: The story of educational television in American Samoa.* Stanford, CA: Stanford University Press.

Stevenson, Robert Louis. 1892. *Vailima papers and A footnote to history.* New York: Charles Scribner's Sons.

Stoltz, Jack H. 1967. "Educational TV in a Pacific paradise." *California Teachers Association Journal* October:18–22.

Stover, Mary Liana. 1990. *Individualization of land in American Samoa.* Ph.D. dissertation, University of Hawaii.

Tallman, Gary, 1977. *Change and Persistence in Samoan Personality.* 1962–1974. Master's thesis, Wichita Staate University.

Templet Resources, Inc. 1986. *Manu'a economic development and environment management plan.* Pago Pago: Office of Economic Development and Planning.

Terrell, John. 1986. *Prehistory in the Pacific islands.* New York: Cambridge University Press.

Theroux, Joseph. 1983. *Black coconuts, Brown magic.* Garden City, NY: Dial Press.

————. 1987. "Freeman controversy continues." *Pacific Islands Monthly* 58(6):49.

Torrance, E. Paul. 1962. "Cultural discontinuities and the development of originality of thinking." *Exceptional Children* September:2–13.

Trussell, Tait. 1968. "Trouble in paradise." *Nation's Business* 56 (July):82–87.

Turnbull, Colin. 1983. "Trouble in paradise." *New Republic* 188(12):32–34.

Turner, George. 1861. *Nineteen years in Polynesia*. London: Snow.

————.1884. *Samoa a hundred years ago and long before*. London: Macmillan and International Ltd.

United Nations. 1990. 1988 *demographic yearbook*. 40th Edition. New York: United Nations.

Vinacke, William E. 1968. *Samoan personality*. Typescript. Wichita State University Library.

Wendt, Albert. 1973. *Sons for the return home*. Auckland: Longman Paul.

Wilkes, Charles. 1845. *Narrative of the United States exploring expedition during the years 1838–1842*. Philadelphia: Lea & Blanchard.

Williams, John. 1832. *South Seas journals*. London Missionary Society Records (on microfilm) at Ablah Library. Wichita State University.

————. 1839. *A narrative of missionary enterprises in the South Seas*. London: Snow.

Williamson, Robert W. 1924. *The social and political systems of central Polynesia*. Cambridge: Cambridge University Press.

Willis, Lauli'i. 1889. *The story of Lauli'i*. San Francisco: Jos. Winterham.

Worsley, Peter. 1957. *The trumpet shall sound*. London: Macgibbon & Kee, Ltd.

Wright, Louis B. and Fry, Mary. 1936. *Puritans in the South Seas*. New York: Henry Holt.

Recommended Reading

Caton, Hiram. 1990. *The Samoa reader. Anthropologists take stock*. Lanham, MD: University Press of America. Survey of the range of opinions on the Mead/Freeman controversy.

Gilson, R. P. 1970. *Samoa 1830–1900: The politics of a multi-cultural community*. Melbourne: Oxford University Press. Ethnography and history integrated into a single study of the Samoan islands as influenced by the struggle for power of Great Britain, Germany, and the United States.

Grattan, F. J. H. 1948. *An introduction to Samoan culture*. Apia: Samoa Printing and Publishing Company. Ceremonial life and social structure in Samoan society.

Gray, J. A. C. 1960. *Amerika Samoa*. Annapolis, MD: United States Naval Institute. Excellent history of white contact in the Samoan islands, particularly the role played by the U.S. Navy in American Samoa.

Holmes, Lowell D. 1958. *Ta'ū, stability and change in a Samoan village*. Wellington, New Zealand: Polynesian Society (Reprint No. 7). Study of cultural dynamics in Manu'an culture from 1836 to 1954.

———. 1987. *Quest for the real Samoa: The Mead/Freeman controversy and beyond*. South Hadley: Bergin and Garvey. Evaluation of the Mead and Freeman data based on methodological restudy.

Mead, Margaret. 1969. *Social organization of Manu'a*. 2nd ed. Honolulu: Bernice P. Bishop Museum Bulletin 76. Monograph dealing with the formalistic aspects of Manu'an social and political organization.

———. 1971. *Coming of age in Samoa*. (paper). New York: William Morrow. Classic psychological study of adolescent girls in Ta'ū village, American Samoa.

Index